Florence Warden

Strictly incog

Being a record of a passage through Bohemia

Florence Warden

Strictly incog
Being a record of a passage through Bohemia

ISBN/EAN: 9783337204518

Printed in Europe, USA, Canada, Australia, Japan

Cover: Foto ©Andreas Hilbeck / pixelio.de

More available books at **www.hansebooks.com**

STRICTLY INCOG:

BEING THE RECORD OF A PASSAGE THROUGH BOHEMIA.

STRICTLY INCOG:

BEING THE RECORD OF

A PASSAGE THROUGH BOHEMIA.

BY

FLORENCE WARDEN,

·AUTHOR OF

"THOSE WESTERTON GIRLS!" "A SHOCK TO SOCIETY,"
"THE HOUSE ON THE MARSH," ETC.

IN ONE VOLUME.

LONDON:
F. V. WHITE & CO.,
14, BEDFORD STREET, STRAND, W.C.
1896.

PRINTED BY
KELLY AND CO. LIMITED, 182, 183 AND 184, HIGH HOLBORN, W.C.,
AND KINGSTON-ON-THAMES.

CONTENTS.

STRICTLY INCOG:

BEING THE RECORD OF A PASSAGE THROUGH BOHEMIA.

STRICTLY INCOG:

BEING THE RECORD OF A PASSAGE THROUGH BOHEMIA.

— ◆ —

CHAPTER I.

" To love too much has been the only art I used."
—BYRON.

IF poor Lady May had not had such large hands and feet, such a sallow complexion, and such awkward, angular movements ; if she had not "told her love" by sighs and sentimental looks and ingenuous laments of the woes of the world, her affection might have been requited, and everything would have fallen out differently. But she would follow her cousin about with love-lorn eyes, would sit in the chairs he had sat in, would be discovered kissing the copy of *The Sporting and Dramatic* which he had just laid down, or secreting in her dress the stump of his cigar.

So she ended by not only making herself ridiculous, but him also. And Victred Speke could suffer that no better than any other young fellow of four-and-twenty.

It was unfortunate for the silly, sentimental, yet generous-hearted girl, that she had no better guardian than her brother ; for Eugene, Lord Malpas, was as unfit for that as he was for most of his other duties.

Succeeding to his father's title at two-and-twenty, he had managed, in the seven following years, to distinguish himself by his shining incapacity, to ruin his health by dissipation, and to impoverish his estate. When at length he found it absolutely needful to retrench, he came to "bury himself" for the winter

I

at Maleigh Abbey, a beautiful, historical house in
Lancashire, the modest size of which enabled him to
curtail the expenses of his establishment.

It was from one of the windows of the Abbey that
Lady May, one raw November morning, watched her
cousin Victred with disconsolate eyes. He was walking down the drive with Eugene and another cousin.
All three were carrying guns.

"They won't be back till luncheon-time!" she
murmured in a melancholy voice.

The two other ladies in the room exchanged
glances of scarcely suppressed amusement. One of
them, Lady May's so-called governess, a little prim,
insignificant thing who had prudently postponed her
own dismissal by becoming her pupil's slave, dis-
creetly left the room after this involuntary self-be-
trayal. But the second lady, being of much more
assured social position, was bolder. She came to the
window, put her hands on the girl's stooping
shoulders, and looked out at the three young men
with a little laugh.

"It is a great shame for your brother to carry off
both your admirers, isn't it?" she said.

"My admirers!" said Lady May mockingly.
"They are not my admirers, Lady Rushcliffe. You
know that."

"Indeed, I know that Tracy is quite devoted to
you. In face of treatment, too, which is, permit me
to say, scarcely courteous."

"Tracy!"

The amount of scorn which the girl put into this
exclamation would not have been out of place if the
disdained admirer had been a convicted felon.

"Don't be ungrateful, my dear. But I mustn't
scold you. You are only seventeen. At seven-and-
twenty you will know better."

"I shall not know better than to despise Tracy
Fitzalan. He is mean. He does Eugene's dirty work."

"Hush, hush, my dear! Who tells you these
things?"

"Oh, I find them out for myself."

At that moment the unappreciated Tracy, having reached a bend in the drive which was the last point visible from the house, stopped and turned to wave a farewell to the ladies at the window. His two companions followed his example.

"What splendid fellows those two Irish lads are!" exclaimed Lady Rushcliffe.

"Tracy has champagne-bottle shoulders," demurred Lady May. "Besides, he has such a pasty complexion."

"Of course, his figure is not so good as Victred's, which is phenomenal. But Tracy's is a more manageable height, and he has a well-bred look."

"Doesn't Victred look well-bred?"

"Oh, yes, yes, I am not maligning your hero. He is a magnificent young giant. I was only suggesting that you look down rather too scornfully upon the devoted one, in favour of the one who, well—who isn't devoted."

"Tracy is devoted for the reason that Eugene is kind—because I have money of my own."

"And a very good reason too. It never does to look too curiously into the quality of a man's devotion; be satisfied if the quantity is sufficient. Girls begin life expecting too much, without considering duly what they have to give in exchange for the romantic affection they think themselves entitled to. Now you have no romantic affection to give Tracy Fitzalan: yet you take his attentions, without gratitude, as a right."

"I shouldn't," answered the girl wistfully, "if only——"

"If only Victred would show a little more *empressement?* But why should he? There is only one life besides your brother's between him and the title."

Lady May, with a little colour rising in her sallow cheeks, moved restlessly, and began to play with the tassel of the blind. She still stood at the window; while her companion, settling herself comfortably in

a low chair, drew a rush work-basket to her side, and
began to play with the skeins of silk in it.

"You look at everything in such a dry, hard way,"
said the girl presently. "I know I am plain, and—
and gawky and awkward and not attractive. And it
makes me nearly crazy to think that the attention I
get is all paid just because I am an earl's daughter,
and shall have money. For all the time I know that
I am not merely a title and a bank-book. I have
deep feelings—I could go through anything—sufferings, tortures, *anything*, I tell you, for any one I really,
really cared for."

The awkward, gawky girl had turned towards her
companion. Even the latter's total lack of sympathy
could not keep in check poor blundering Lady May's
passionate desire to unbosom herself to some creature
who was at least intelligent enough to understand.
But her stammering confession was like the dashing
of waves against a rock. Pretty slim Lady Rushcliffe, with her tailor-built figure and artistic hair and
complexion, just raised her eyebrows and gently
shook her head.

"My dear May, you really must not talk like a
penny novelette. As for the sufferings, the tortures,
and the deep feelings, I quite believe you, for you
betray your unfortunate capacities whenever you
glance in your cousin's direction."

Her hearer began to sob. Lady Rushcliffe went
on inexorably, in the belief that "a little honest plain
speaking" would do the girl good.

"This is all very unpleasant to hear, I know, but
this knowledge has to come sooner or later. Deep
feelings in an heiress are unlooked for and out of
place. Women with money are simply looked upon
by men without as the title-deeds to their own estates.
It is the same with rich men. No girl ever marries
one of them for love."

There was a pause, during which the girl dried her
eyes. Lady Rushcliffe, in pleasant, incisive tones,
then continued her discourse:

" Now, if you were to marry Tracy, your money would get him into Parliament, where he would soon make himself heard of. And his gratitude to you would make him the most adoring of husbands; while——"

"Why don't *you* marry him then, Lady Rushcliffe, and earn all his adoration and gratitude yourself?"

This retort was apt enough to make it hard for Lady Rushcliffe to repress a smile.

"We widows don't want husbands, my dear," she said.

"And I don't want any husband but the ʹman I love," cried Lady May, staring with great melancholy hazel eyes out into the shrubbery. "If I can't have him, I won't have any. But if I can have him I won't ask for devotion or adoration, or even for love, but I'll just be content if he'll let me worship him as I do now. He may marry me for my money, and treat me as he likes—I don't care. It is the one great wish of my heart, and I shall go on wishing and wishing till it comes true."

"And if it doesn't come true?" asked Lady Rushcliffe, watching the girl, amused and interested by her overwhelming earnestness.

"Oh, it will, it will some day. If you wish a thing strongly enough, they say it always comes, and I wish this with my very, very soul."

"My dear," said Lady Rushcliffe, who had had enough "earnestness" for one morning, and who had mislaid her French novel, "then I hope for your sake that it may never be fulfilled. For no man in the world could fulfil such a wish without turning out a bitter disappointment."

Stifling a yawn, she got up and walked to the door, leaving Lady May to waste the rest of the morning in watching at the window for her idol's return.

When Victred did come back, about an hour before luncheon, it was with Tracy, and with Lord Malpas's gun ; but without Lord Malpas. The two young men were laughing heartily over a little adventure they had had.

In an obscure corner of the village, off the one street, they had found posted on a wall a small bill in which, in fiery and fairly grammatical language, the inhabitants were called upon to meet and discuss "the tyranny of the land-robbers, whose slaves they were," and the best means of rendering "the soil they trod on as free as the air they breathed." Lord Malpas had not only indulged in ardent language, but had threatened to shoot a stranger whom he found in the neighbourhood of the placard, and whom he chose to consider suspicious-looking. Whereupon Victred and Tracy had coaxed him to yield up his gun, on the plea that he had better consult his steward ; and had themselves hastened home to put the weapon out of the Earl's reach.

"By-the-by, who was the fellow?" asked Victred, when they had got back into the drive, away from Lord Malpas and his fury. "And if is it not indiscreet, who is the 'she' I heard you ask after as soon as Eugene's back was turned?"

Tracy Fitzalan, who was very fair, with the pale, pinky-white skin of an unhealthy girl, flushed and looked rather self-conscious. He laughed, however, lightly enough.

"Oh, he's an old vagabond I met once on the boat going over to Dublin. At least I don't know why I should say an old vagabond, for I didn't have more than ten minutes' talk with him. It's a way we've got in the Green Isle of thinking one another rogues —I suppose because each knows in his heart that he himself is one."

"And 'she?'"

"Oh, he's got a daughter, a pretty little thing, but not more than a child."

It was all Victred could obtain in the way of information on the matter, but he felt sure it was not all the story. He had noted the glances exchanged by Tracy and the stranger ; he had seen the cheeks of the former flush and his eyes sparkle with excitement at the meeting ; and he knew that the encounter, if an accidental one, was of deep interest on both sides.

"I say," continued Tracy, slackening his pace a little, "I'll be glad if you won't mention to the Earl that I've met that Socialist fellow before."

"Oh, a Socialist, is he ? "

"Something of that sort I fancy. Socialist or Fenian, or a little of each, perhaps."

" All right."

" You see, my dear fellow, the Earl is rabid about that sort of cattle. And he might misunderstand my motives. My position isn't assured, like yours, you see."

" Well, mind you don't sail too near the wind, that's all. You're a clever fellow, Tracy; but upon my word I don't feel quite sure you're not a bit of a rogue."

Tracy showed his teeth in a rather unprepossessing smile. But he affected to take his cousin's words as a joke. He could not afford to quarrel with Victred : it was as the *protégé* of the latter that he had first become known to the Earl, and he had not yet exhausted Victred's usefulness.

Lord Malpas was unmarried, and his health was uncertain. If he died childless, the title, together with the estates in England and Ireland, would go to his uncle, the Honourable Atherton Speke, whose only son Victred was. The Honourable Atherton had married an Irish lady, and settled down on his nephew's estate in Tipperary, where Victred was born. This Irish lady's maiden name had been Fitzalan, and Tracy was her brother's son. Tracy, therefore, was cousin to Victred, but there was no relationship between the former and the Earl.

Trading on a certain good-natured weakness in Victred's character, Tracy had conceived the briliant plan of establishing his own fortunes by marriage with Lady May. If Victred could be turned from an unwilling and passive rival into an active ally, he felt that he might make sure of success. There was nothing to fear but a certain crotchetiness on Victred's part, which might cause him to raise some absurdly squeamish objections on the score of Tracy's moral character. But then promises were cheap, and one could promise to reform.

So reasoned Tracy as, walking beside his cousin and glancing at his face, he perceived that the " good-natured giant," as he was popularly called, was already relenting after his last somewhat harsh words. Tracy thought this a good opportunity, so he took it. To his surprise, Victred's answer was a flat refusal to support his pretensions.

" Isn't that rather the attitude of the dog in the manger ? " asked Tracy, after a little pause. " You don't want to marry Lady May yourself, but you don't want her to marry any one else."

" Nonsense, Tracy, stuff and nonsense. I don't want her to marry *you*."

" Why ? "

" Well, I take an interest in May, and—well, you see, you're rather too much of a—a ' masher,' I believe they call it, to make a good husband."

" Perhaps you are too much of an—an ' anchorite,' I believe they call it, to be a good judge ! "

" Well, anyhow, I'm not going to help you with May."

With these words, closing the conversation in the sledge-hammer fashion popular with very big men, when they have once made up their slow-moving minds, Victred threw away the end of his cigar as he went up the steps to the house.

Tracy followed slowly. He was in a frenzy of resentment against his cousin, in whose manner he had fancied he noted a shade of contempt. This was a delusion ; for the easy-going Victred, though he himself avoided all women with what looked like a surprising touch of austerity, was tolerant to excess of the conduct of his friends. Hence Tracy's surprise at the snub he had received.

"If I only dared! If I only dared!" thought he, as he watched his cousin disappear into the house, and gloated over a certain piece of knowledge he had lately acquired, which, if he had ventured to cast it in Victred's teeth, would have turned the tables on him and quashed his airs of superiority. But reflection —and even in the height of his passion Tracy had head enough to reflect—said that Victred's chances of becoming Earl of Malpas were good, and the "pickings" to be got as the Earl's dearest friend were too valuable to be thrown away for the sake of a repartee. Besides, there were other ways, if one were not too scrupulous, of settling the account.

So he prudently turned in the opposite direction from his cousin, in order that his feelings might calm down before they met again; and as Victred went to the study he himself opened the door of the morning-room.

Unhappily, his entrance gave umbrage to Lady May, who, having conquered her impulse to go and meet Victred, had been hoping that he would come straight in and speak to her. With the horrible frankness of "sweet seventeen," she scowled when Tracy entered instead, and looked down immediately upon the needle-work with which she was pretending to be busy. But the young Irishman could not accept a rebuff from a woman. He seated himself, with a manner half deferential, half affectionate, at a little distance in front of her, and heaved a gentle sigh. But deference and affection from the wrong man brought no balm for the wounds made by the right one.

"What is the matter with you?" asked Lady May sharply, after a repetition of the sigh.

"Chiefly—you."

Her eyes flashed at him a glance of rebuke for his impertinence; but before she could follow it up by a spoken repulse, he had drawn, nay, almost crawled nearer by a tentative inch, and, with his head bent down on one side, as if trying to scoop up a stray ray of kindliness from her eyes, he was humbly pleading that he had not meant to offend her, that he had spoken without thinking, that he would try not to transgress again.

"Remember that I am an Irishman : when I feel, I must speak ; when I am hurt, I must cry out. You have hurt me, you are always hurting me. You don't care what I suffer."

"Suffer ? What nonsense ! "

Although Lady May was shrewd enough not to believe him, she was woman enough to listen to him without displeasure. There was even a curious sort of painful enjoyment to be derived from imagining what she would have felt if it had been Victred who was speaking.

"Suffering is never nonsense—to the sufferer."

"I don't believe men can suffer ; at least, not as we women can," said Lady May sentimentally.

"Then you cannot realise the feelings of a man who sees the only girl who ever touched his heart out of his reach."

Tracy was presuming upon the confidence her brother placed in him, Lady May thought. She was not a brilliant girl, but she had been educated to understand the position her rank and money gave her, and the sentimental passion she entertained for her cousin cleared her view of other men.

"Can you be in love, then, without having your heart touched ? "

"How ? What do you mean ? "

"Well, they say you are always in love, you know."

"Who says so ? Victred, I suppose ? "

"I think I have heard you say so yourself. And Eugene, he——"

"Oh, no, you listen to neither me nor Eugene. It is Victred who has been prejudicing you against me, for his own purposes, of course."

"What purposes? You know that he hates women."

Both were getting much excited, and were speaking low and rapidly. Tracy forgot his prudence and something more.

" I know that he hates *ladies*. He does not hate all women, though."

He would have recalled these words the next moment, but it was too late. He met her glance and saw that she understood, that she was burning with indignation. She drew back her chair, rose from it, and, holding the back of it while her fingers twisted the cord by which a little cushion hung suspended, said breathlessly :

" You are not in the smoking-room, Mr. Fitzalan. You forget to whom you are speaking."

She ought to have left him then, maintaining the dignity she had had the spirit to assert. But her curiosity, her passionate interest were too strong. She lingered, giving him time enough to say, with the pretty brogue which grew strong when he was excited :

" I dhon't forget. I'm speaking to a charming girl who's whasting her affection on a man who only hates ladies because he gives his affection to women of a very different class."

" I don't believe it—I don't believe it. And—and even if it were true, it is much more discreditable in you to tell me of it than in him to—in him to——"

" Of course. He may steal the horse ; I mustn't look over the hedge. But what would ye do if it was proved to be true ? "

" I would never speak to him again," said Lady May passionately. " And I will never speak to you again for telling me such things," she added, as she dashed out of the room.

Tracy remained standing where she had left him, pulling his moustache in some agitation.

" She won't dare to tell him, I should think," he meditated. " It isn't as if they were engaged, or as if

he were fond of her. But she is such a mad thing
that I shouldn't care to lay odds on her holding her
tongue. So we must have proofs, proofs."

Tracey went up to his room, and sat down to write
a note to one of his friends, directing it to a well-
known "social" club.

"DEAR ROD,
        "If Glynn Dorien is still in the land of the
living, just find her out—I don't suppose it will be
difficult, and give her the enclosed. You need not
say who it came from.
                            "Thine ever,
                                "T. F."

Then he wrote the enclosure, and put it into an
envelope directed simply to "Mademoiselle Glynn
Dorien."

"She'll take the 'Mademoiselle' for an abusive
epithet, I expect," he said to himself, with a laugh,
as he looked over the handwriting, which he had
slightly disguised by making it very large and round.
This was what he had written:

"V. S. has a violent lady admirer, and has thoughts
of marrying her. If Glynn Dorien's statements about
V. S. are true, why doesn't she pluck up spirit and
come after him? It could hardly fail to be worth her
while. He is staying at his cousin's place, Maleigh
Abbey, Lancashire."

"Now," he reflected, as he sealed up the enclosure,
"I think she's pretty sure to come up. But the Earl's
name will scare her, and she will hang about the
village, not daring to come to the house. She will
probably imbibe freely, she will certainly be seen and
heard. It will get to my Lady Simpleton's ears.
There will be a scandal, and I may have to make myself scarce for a time. But she will have been disgusted with her fancy; and after a while the faithful

Tracy comes back, and pleads forgiveness on the score of solicitude for her welfare. And, of course, I shall profess to have believed Glynn's story. Well, it's a stiffish risk—but I'm in for it now. I think I'll just take my letter over to the post-office myself."

He ran downstairs and out of the house at a quick pace, for it was getting near luncheon-time.

As he passed the study door he heard the voice of the Earl declaiming to Victred in angry tones against the right of public speaking; and vowing that if there were any attempt made at a meeting on his estate, he would himself disperse it with a horse-whip.

Tracy frowned with annoyance.

"What does that fool Dennis want, coming here with his speeches? I must let him know that if he compromises me he shall swing for it. If it wasn't for his daughter, I've half a mind to cut the cad altogether."

With these reflections he reached the outer gate of the grounds, which had once been one of the entrances to the monastery. It was broken about the top, and unrestored; and the ivy hung about it in a picturesque, but fatally close embrace.

CHAPTER II.

" My valour's fled too, with mine honesty ;
For since I would be knave, I must be coward."
—BEAUMONT AND FLETCHER.

IT was in November, a dull day on which all things were grey or brown. The valley in which the Abbey stood was steeped in heavy mists; and the waters of the Ribble, which washed the old stones of the ruins at a short distance from the house, were turbid and leaden in colour.

The house itself had been the Abbot's lodgings, and had been restored and added to so judiciously, that the old walls had not lost their antiquarian interest when the interior became a comfortable

modern dwelling.   Like a little withered kernel in an
enormous husk, the inhabited portion, the new abbey,
pœped up from among the massive and far-extending
remains of the old.   There were lawns and trim gar-
dens now in the cloisters and scriptorium; what had
once been the floor of the church was a smooth stretch
of grass.   Two massive gateways, one far away from
the present habitation, showed what the extent of the
monks' domain had been.

It was on the outer side of the more ruinous of
these gateways that Tracy, hurrying out with his
letter, met the stranger whom Lord Malpas had fallen
foul of that morning.

"Hallo!" cried Tracy, in a tone which betrayed
the fact that he was ill-pleased at this second meeting.

The stranger said nothing, but nodded, and beamed
at him out of a pair of blue, Irish eyes; those eyes
peeped out above a voluminous woollen comforter
which masked the lower part of his face as effectually
as a round, brown felt hat, some sizes too large for
his head, concealed the upper part.   He wore a long
frieze overcoat, which came down almost to his huge
boots, and a pair of enormous woollen gloves.   All his
garments, indeed, seemed to have been the property
of a very big man, whereas he himself was only of
middle height, and though sturdily built, of no abnormal rotundity.   What little there was to be seen of
his face was decidedly prepossessing.   The short,
broad nose, the drawn-down upper lip, the lines about
the eyes and the twinkle in them, all betrayed humour,
genial, spontaneous, irrepressible, and a shrewdness
almost equally attractive.   He continued to look
amiably but keenly at Tracy, while that young man,
with anxious glances all round him, opened the conversation.

"What did you come here for?" he asked
hurriedly, in a low voice.   "You can't do any good
in this part of the world, and you can do one precious
bit of harm, you can compromise *me*."

"No, no," answered the other, in a round, rich, mellow voice, which he had modulated for this serious occasion, until it was hardly more than a whisper; "believe me, sir, I'm too old a hand to do any such mischief. The country hereabouts wants working. There's some very pretty material lying about ready to hand, but it wants the master to shape it to use. And then, with the added attraction of a possible sight of you, the temptation to come this way was too much for me. So here I am, inflammatory doctrines and all, and I'm going to tickle 'em up this afternoon at a place they call the Nab, about three miles from here."

"Is she with you?" asked Tracy, with a slight involuntary change of expression and a self-conscious droop of the eye.

Tracy was not a good actor, and his careless tone did not deceive the other man.

"No, I'm saving her up for a big thing I've got on next week. Don't do to make her too cheap. She's at——"

Tracy flushed slightly, and became eagerly interested. But the observant stranger pulled himself up.

"Where do you say she is?" asked the young man, attentively re-reading the direction on the letter in his hand.

"Look here, my bhoy," said the other, dropping from the tone of extreme respectfulness which he had been using to one of genial and affectionate confidence, and at the same time assuming a strong Irish brogue. "I can't stand chattering here with you now, in full view of yer swell friends who might be coming out from the house. I don't want to compromise you, ye know. But I'll be holding forth at the Nab at half-past five, when the factories close. And if yer'll be there at a ruined (he pronounced it 'roound') cottage there is by the top of the hill, we'll have a quiet chat together."

The young man hesitated, having a not unjust

suspicion that his genial friend meant mischief by
this suggestion. The latter went on after a slight
pause :

" It's just possible me dhaughter may be up there."

Tracy took the bait with open mouth, though conscious that there was a hook with it. Remarking, as
casually as he could, that he would try to be there
about five, he made the excuse that he must catch the
post to get rid of his companion.

" Good-bye, Dennis," he said. " We must have a
talk certainly, and if we can't manage it to-day, it
must be as soon as possible. But for goodness' sake,
my dear fellow, be careful what you are about up
here. You know my sympathies are with you ; but
if the Earl were once to suspect that, it would be all
up with me, and my influence wouldn't be worth a
rap."

" All right, my dear bhoy, I quite understand. Remember, discretion is the breath of me life. If I hadn't
known how to hold me tongue, half me friends would
have been in jail before this."

He uttered these words with innocent buoyancy ;
but perhaps the change of colour which they produced in Tracy's face was not a phenomenon wholly
unexpected by the older man. They parted with
just a nod on either side—hasty and furtive from
Tracy, amused and mischievous from Dennis. The
latter walked straight off in the direction of the Nab,
with just one glance at the retreating figure of the
other.

" It's a pity that good horse Democracy has to be
contented with such shabby grooms," said he to himself, as he pushed back his roomy hat a little, and
cast a glance around him, which took in every feature
of the misty valley : the patched-up old church on
the right, with its grave-yard belted by trees, which,
in this sheltered situation, had not yet lost all their
leaves ; the grey jagged points of the ruined Abbey
on the left ; the railway viaduct beyond ; the ugly
chimney of a cotton factory up the river a mile away,

These objects, shut in by wooded hills, which had now assumed a wintry bareness, formed a picture of sharp contrasts, in which the apparent restfulness of the old days and the obvious turmoil of the new were typified side by side. Dennis M'Rena had imagination, and was not insensible to these things. But he was still more alive to the human interest of the picture, and while his gaze wandered, his thoughts remained steady.

"That young man thinks he's to be jockey, and to win the race on my beast," he reflected, "while I intend him only to sweep out the stable. He is looking about for a vocation, and fancies that of saviour of his country will do. And we—the hard workers—whom he looks down upon, are the pitch he hopes to touch without being defiled. But I mean to steep him in it up to the eyes."

And he disappeared into the mists which were thickening in the valley, while he hummed very softly to himself, "The Wearing of the Green."

Tracy Fitzalan, who was by this time returning at a run from the village post-office, saw with great satisfaction that his questionable acquaintance had taken himself off. Though not hampered by any lofty ideals of conduct, Tracy was conscious that the part of Facing-Both-Ways was not held in high esteem, and he was nettled by a sense that Dennis M'Rena saw further into his motives than was desirable. He returned to the house cursing the injustice of fate, which had forced him into shady social by-paths in search of the notoriety which was the craving of his soul; while his cousin Victred, without half his brains or his energy, sauntered through life, muddling away chance after chance of fortune and distinction.

They were sitting down to luncheon at the Abbey when Tracy came in. The Earl, who had not recovered from the morning's adventure, was relating his wrongs to the ladies, not from the moderate point of view of a latter-day nineteenth century Conservative, but in old High Tory style. Unable to find

2

words strong enough to describe the infamy of the
wretches who dared to address his tenants without his
permission, he declared his intention of finding out
the authors of the outrage, and horse-whipping them
with his own noble hand.

"I am certain," he continued, "that that fellow we
saw loafing about had something to do with it. He
was just the type of ruffian that swarms about
Kilmore. But if they think they are going to play
the 'no-rent' game here under my very nose, I'll
give them a lesson in the rights of landlords which
it will take yards of sticking-plaster to make them
forget."

The Earl, who was a florid, broad-shouldered young
man of "horsey" dress and appearance, with a heavy
jaw and a low forehead, glanced, frowning, at Victred,
who had shown him little sympathy. The Earl disliked Victred, for the simple reason that he saw, in
this healthy and handsome young man, a successor to
the position which his own shattered health no longer
permitted him to enjoy. Moreover, Victred said whatever he liked, without discretion or diplomacy, and
had extremely unorthodox notions about absenteeism.
Interpreting Lord Malpas's glance as a challenge,
Victred now said:

"You can't prevent them talking, you know."

"Can't I! By Jove, but I will," said his cousin, on
whom the presence of ladies never imposed any
severe check.

"Well, then, one of these days you will be shot.
It's much better to let them work off the steam in
talk. Then they'll be sure to quarrel and let you
alone, which is safer; because you're not popular."

Now the truth of this last proposition did not make
it the less unpleasant to hear. Victred had much
better have left it unuttered, but Eugene had tried
his patience that morning, and Tracy's eternal pander-
ing to the little-great man set his teeth on edge.

Seeing that Lord Malpas was too much overwhelmed by this insolence to express his wrath, ex-

cept by ejaculations and broken phrases, Tracy, with an air of warm and honest partisanship, broke in :

" Really, Victred, I'd be thankful to know how you can make that out—that Lord Malpas isn't as popular as any man in the kingdom ; with everybody, that is, whose opinion is worth having."

" And whose fault is it that there are so many whose opinion isn't worth having ? Factory-hands, grinding away all day, to make up the mill-rents that keep us."

"Us ! Keep us !" interrupted the Earl, husky with anger. " Not quite so fast, my dear cousin. Remember, I'm not dead yet, I may——"

" Oh, hush, boys, hush," cried Lady Rushcliffe, sailing imperiously towards the table, whence she had retreated to a window at the first sound of a quarrel. " What is the use of these exceedingly unpleasant discussions ? Mr. Speke, I am surprised at your want of tact, and at your ignorance. Nobody can be the guest of Lord Malpas without knowing that he is popularity itself."

Victred bowed, with a deference which his glance betrayed not to be quite genuine. But Lady May, seeing everybody against her hero, must needs come blundering to the rescue.

" I think Victred is quite right," she said, from her place at the table, which she had kept from the beginning of the discussion, holding an eager watch on the disputants. " The factory hands do lead horrible lives. I have often thought so. And you ought to be glad that they can talk and discuss things, Eugene. It is more honourable for you to have for tenants angry men than submissive sheep."

They were all rather taken by surprise. Lady May's adoration of her cousin had hitherto found vent rather in sentiment and sighs than in open partisanship. Victred was delighted with this spirited alliance. Encouraged by it, he forgot his recent submission to Lady Rushcliffe.

" Look what your agent, Captain Sanderson, has

2*

done for you at Kilmore. There is a revolver pointing
at him from every hedge."

"Why? Because he insists on these people paying
their rents. But perhaps," and the Earl laughed
hysterically, "you think them right in refusing to pay
rent?"

"If not exactly right, excusable. Rent is like
taxes—we all get out of paying if we can."

Lady May's little governess turned pale, and put
her hands to her ears.

"When the lazy beggars could pay quite well if
they chose to work?"

"How can we accuse them of laziness, we who
never did a day's work in our lives?"

"Yes, that's true; I've often thought about that,
too!" cried Lady May in an ecstasy of delighted
acquiescence.

But the discussion broke off short at this point,
Lord Malpas launching out into mere invective against
Victred, his tenants and all who were not exactly of
his way of thinking. Tracy gave him tacit support,
while Victred offered tacit but stubborn opposition.
In a very disagreeable atmosphere of general irri-
tation, luncheon was eaten and the party broke up.
To Lady May's delight her cousin followed her, as
she left the house, in macintosh and goloshes, on her
way to the home farm.

She had not far to go, for the sheds and barns were
built into the very walls of the ruin. Within what
had once been the refectory, the shippen was built;
and a score of hens searched and scratched the ground
of the monks' kitchen.

"Let me help you, May," said Victred.

And he opened the gate and held her egg-basket,
while she lifted her skirt above the mud and stepped
gingerly into the farmyard.

"Thank you," said she, with the shy look of one
overwhelmed with gratitude.

This frank adoration was absurd certainly, but on
the other hand it might be considered touching.

Victred thought the blush which suffused her sallow face made it for the moment rather pretty.

"You spoke up gallantly at luncheon, May, I didn't think you had it in you," said he.

The girl trembled with delight at his praise.

"I—I often think about those things—poor people, and the lives they lead, and why we should have so much when they have nothing," she said simply. "But I shouldn't have had the courage to speak to-day if—if you hadn't spoken first."

She betrayed her strong feeling, consciously, but ingenuously, in every word, in every look. Generally Victred neglected, avoided her. How could she best show her gratitude for the honour of his approbation? Tracy's insinuations, which had cut her to the heart, were all forgotten.

Though he knew her infatuation was unspeakably foolish, it made him feel rather ashamed of himself. Because she was more innocent than he, he took it for granted that she was much better; and felt therefore chivalrously humble in her presence, when for once the absence of spectators of her open worship relieved the situation of its awkwardness to himself. He felt nearer at this moment than ever before to liking this plain little girl very much. As for her, his praise intoxicated her; she looked up shyly, as into the face of a god.

And what did she see? A man of four-and-twenty, six feet four inches in height, and only just arrived at the full development of a perfectly proportioned person. As for his face, it passed for handsome, in consideration of the beauties of his figure. His hair and moustache were just fair enough not to be dark, his grey-blue eyes were kindly in expression. But his mouth—Ah! the tell-tale mouth!—betrayed the weakness of the man who cannot conquer circumstances, but is conquered by them. An attractive countenance, easy to read. On the whole, women in general would have found extenuating circumstances for Lady May's infatuation.

"I'm afraid we both made ourselves very offensive to Eugene, though. He never absolutely thirsts for my society. Now, I expect he'll absolutely thirst for my departure."

"Oh!"

The exclamation was a wail of dismay.

"You know he hates me."

"Yes. I always think that is such a strong point in your favour."

"You're getting quite cutting, May. I shall be afraid of opening my mouth before you."

There was a pause. Lady May put her hand into her basket and threw a handful of food to the clamorous chickens.

"No, you won't," she said in a low voice. "The idea of your ever being afraid of *me*!"

"There's nothing astonishing about it. When I come back from my wanderings——"

'What wanderings? You're not going away, *are* you?" with a little twitter of the voice upon the last word but one.

"Yes, if I can mange it. I want to go to North America or Africa, and—and hunt. I would have gone long before now if my father had let me."

"But why, but why? Why can't you settle down? Hardly anybody I know has such prospects as you, Victred. You will be Earl of Malpas in a few years."

"I should be very sorry to think so. My father is not an old man, thank God! and is pretty sure to out-live me. And Eugene will marry. He is only nine-and-twenty. As for settling down, if I were ever a rich man, I should use my money to travel with, that's all."

Lady May looked at him with a heart-broken expression. For the first time it dawned upon her that her hero was not really the happy man she had always thought him. If only she could comfort him!

"If you go to Africa you will marry a black woman,

I suppose," she said, trying to be flippant; an attempt which sat ill upon her natural seriousness.

To her horror this poor pleasantry was received by her cousin with a cold contraction of the lips and a marked change of expression.

"Yes, or do something equally discreditable, no doubt," he said shortly.

And, moving a few steps away, he caught sight of one of the farm-boys harnessing a horse to the farm-bailiff's gig.

More because he wished to drop the conversation with May than because he wanted to know, he asked the boy who was going to use the gig.

"Mr. Fitzalan, sir," said the boy.

Victred, with an excuse to his cousin, sprang over the wall into the stableyard, and came face to face with Tracy, who looked annoyed at the encounter.

"Hallo! where are you off to in this stealthy manner?" asked Victred.

"Stealthy manner? Nonsense. I'm only going for a drive to pass away the time till dinner."

"Take me. I want to pass away the time till dinner."

As he guessed where Tracy was going, Victred was not surprised that his cousin tried hard to put him off. But Victred could be obstinate when he liked; and Tracy, not without sulkiness, had to give way.

"What does it matter?" said Victred, as he got up in the gig and drew his share of the rug over his knees; "I know where you're going, and it is all the same to me why you're going. If you like to run with the Socialist hare and hunt with the Tory hounds, it is your affair, not mine."

"What do you mean?" asked Tracy, in a great state of perturbation; "I'm going to the meeting out of mere curiosity."

"All right. And I suppose you write inflammatory articles in a Socialist paper 'out of mere curiosity' too?"

Tracy did not start violently, because that is too risky a proceeding when you are driving a light vehicle along a bad road; but the ever-ready pink flush rose to his face.

"So you have begun 'shadowing' me for a suspect?" he said shortly.

"Rubbish! But in a paper called *The Red Flag*, I read an article signed 'Patriot' which was stuffed full of expressions you are always using, and I only want to warn you not to be so careless, for I found the paper kicking about your room."

"By Jove! Did you though?"

"Yes. And if I were you I'd give up—er—that sort of thing. It's bad form, Tracy, d——d bad form."

"You won't—h'm—you won't—er—split?"

"Need you ask?"

"Of course not, of course not. You understand that every man has a right to his own political opinions?"

"Oh, yes," said Victred drily.

And thenceforth he became monosyllabic till the meeting-place was reached.

A ruined stone cottage high up on the side of the hill, a few yards from a patch of leafless trees—that was the place of meeting. But the two young men, who had left the gig at a dirty little inn at the foot of the hill, to avoid the bad roads, found no one there. They were, indeed, a full hour before the appointed time; so Victred left Tracy, who was chafing with impatience, and took a walk over the now desolate hills, slimy and damp with mist, and blackened by the smoke of the not far distant factories.

When he returned, troops of stunted men and youths, varied by an occasional group of rough girls with shawls round their heads, were streaming to the place of meeting. The cottage itself held not a tenth part of the gathering, which filled the space between the broken walls and the copse beyond. Tracy, trying to conceal himself in what had once been a cow-house, was discovered by his cousin in a state of frantic indignation at Dennis's treatment.

"As if he couldn't be here to speak to me before all this rabble collected!" he exclaimed, peeping out over the rickety boards.

Victred could hardly restrain a malicious laugh. It was evident to him that Dennis was at least a match for his cousin in cunning, and had no intention of helping him to pull the chestnuts out of the fire without burning his fingers. When the Socialist orator arrived, and he took his stand on the remaining portion of the ruined and roofless upper floor of the cottage, it seemed to Victred that he cast a satisfied glance in the direction of poor Tracy, who, impatient and dejected, peeped up angrily at him over the heads of the listening factory-hands, whose rough shrewd faces soon lighted up with excitement under the influence of Dennis's oratory.

Victred was struck more by the manner than by the matter of the address, which covered much familiar ground in the way of diatribes against existing institutions, social inequalities and the like, and included a scathing personal attack on Lord Malpas, holding up his intellect to ridicule, and his vices to execration. Seeing that Tracy was growing hot with discomfort, and that he kept throwing uneasy glances towards a particular person among the crowd, Victred, who was openly enjoying the fun, followed the direction of his cousin's eyes, and saw wedged into the mass of factory hands, a head which he recognised as that of an underling about the estate whom he very much disliked, and whom the Earl employed as a sort of spy upon the actions of his steward, farm bailiff, and other officials.

The name by which this fellow was known was Jerry Coggin, and he was a particularly well chosen man for his post, being too stolid to be inventive, and too unambititious to be open to bribery. He had a fixed dislike to Victred, who had not scrupled to show his contempt for Coggin and his office. Before the speech of Dennis came to an end old Jerry had taken himself off, leaving Tracy in a fever of uneasiness, lest the Earl should hear through him of his own presence at the meeting.

"And shall we," wound up the speaker, amidst excited stamping of feet and ejaculations of approval, "continue to call such creatures as this Malpas—profligate, drunken, greedy, brainless—our masters, our superiors? Shall you and your sons and daughters go toiling at your looms as you have toiled, ill-fed, ill-clothed, working from morning till night under the smoke-pall which hangs over this corner of our land, while he, and successors like him, consume the fruit of your labours in dissolute luxury, shut up from the sound of the cry of your starving little ones? No! The people, the mighty people, have declared that this wrong must cease, that the idler must perish, and the worker come by his own. Rouse up, unite yourselves, as others have done. Remember, what these masters of yours try to make you forget, that you are men, rejoicing in all the strength of the manhood they themselves have weakened and degraded. Form yourselves into secret leagues until you and all the rest of the workers of our land can unite into one resistless wave, which, rolling steadily onward with the tide of advancing knowledge, shall overwhelm the feeble survivor of the tyrants that sucked your blood, and make England truly what she is now falsely called—The Land of the Free!"

Tumultuous applause followed, in which were drowned the voices of a few middle-aged hearers, whom the orator's mixed metaphors and genial manner did not greatly move.

Dennis M'Rena, tucking his bunchy umbrella under his arm, hurried down from his rickety rostrum, and approached Tracy with a good-humoured smile. Victred kept within hearing, expecting some more fun from the encounter. To his surprise Tracy expressed none of the annoyance he had so freely indulged in before M'Rena's arrival. He congratulated him, in a low voice, but fervently, upon his speech.

"Jack couldn't have done better," he added; at which Dennis shook his head.

"By the way," said he, "you haven't sent in those articles you promised for the paper?"

Tracy stammered and seemed to draw back a little.

"Well, to tell you the truth," said he at last, "I—I —I'm so busy just now, that I'm afraid I don't see my way to doing any more—er—in fact—just at present, you know, just for the present."

Dennis's eyes twinkled shrewdly. "Wants to get out of it!" thought he. But what he said, in a sad, gently remonstrant voice, was:

"Ah, I know somebody who will nearly break her heart to hear this!"

Tracy, who had his back to Victred, began to grow fidgety.

"Yes," continued Dennis musingly, "when I left my little girl this morning, she said to me, in a voice I can't forget: 'Father, don't you trouble about the articles. You can't write them, but Mr. Fitzalan can. And he's a gentleman, father, and he's promised: and a gentleman always keeps his word!'"

Tracy's hand was playing with his moustache: Victred could see that his fingers were trembling.

"Where did you leave her then?" he asked at last, in a tone of assumed carelessness, which Victred knew him well enough to see that his manner belied.

M'Rena's eyes twinkled with unspeakable cunning.

"At a cottage where I'm staying at Clough, the other side of Accrington," he answered, pretending to enter some notes in his pocket-book. "Our landlady has gone to Manchester for the night, and I shan't be back till to-morrow; so the little one has to keep house. Otherwise I should have brought her with me."

Victred noted a sudden increase in the excitement under which Tracy was labouring. He made a few remarks about the meeting, scarcely heeding the

answers, and then left Dennis with a very abrupt
farewell. Turning from him sharply, he started on
finding his cousin almost close to his elbow.

"Ready to come home?" asked Victred. "We
will be late for dinner as it is, I'm afraid."

"Oh, I'll get you back in time, never fear," said
Tracy, as they set off running down the hill to the
inn where they had left the gig.

He kept his word. Driving at as rapid a pace as
was consistent with safety along the muddy roads,
the course of which was not always well defined in
the darkness, it was within a few minutes of eight
o'clock that Tracy drew up at the old gateway of the
Abbey.

"You get down," said he, "and I'll take the gig
round to the farm by the other way."

"Oh, I'll go with you," said Victred, not moving
from his seat.

"But if the boy shouldn't be there, I'll have to un-
harness the horse myself, and I can't do it in half a
minute."

"You can do it in half the time if I'm there to help
you," said Victred.

"What's the use of making us both late?"

"The one can share the blame with the other."

By this time Tracy was evidently furious, while
Victred, who was lighting a fresh cigar, remained
curiously stolid and imperturbable.

"Well, I tell ye, I've got to go a little farther—into
the village!" blurted out Tracy, unconsciously raising
his voice somewhat.

"All right. You can run into the village on foot,
while I take the gig round to the farm."

"But I'm going farther than the village; and I tell
ye straight out that I dhon't want yer company."

"It comes to this then: I must tell you straight out
I'm going to give it you. I'm not going to leave this
trap till you do."

The dogged obstinacy of his tone said more than
his words did.

"I tell you," said Tracy, with a vicious glance at Victred's broad shoulders, "I'm going to pay a call where two are company and three are none."

"I'll wait outside."

"What do ye mean by interfering with me in this way?"

Victred turned towards him. It was too dark to see, but the hot, angry breath of the other came full on his face.

"You're going to see that tub-thumper's daughter."

"Well, her father himself gave me her address. If your ears were so wide open, you must have heard that."

Victred nodded.

"I did. She's hardly more than a child, you said?"

"Oh, that's only a way of speaking. She's sixteen or seventeen, if she's a day."

"A good ripe old age. As for the father, I think he's a knave."

"It's no business of yours."

"I don't know about that. I think it's my business to save a fellow who is my own kin from the risk of acting like a blackguard."

"You dare say that to me!"

"Awfully sorry, old man. But I've said it, and there's an end of it. Are you going to the farm?"

With a sharp cut of the whip across the horse's ears for answer, Tracy turned the gig round, and drove back to the farm. As the boy was there waiting for their return, the two young men were able to proceed straight back to the house. They walked silently, the one in front of the other; and it was not until they were under the lamps of the cosy hall that Tracy turned suddenly to his cousin. There was a smile on his face, which was little more than a distorted movement of the muscles.

"I never forget a good 'turn,'" he said as he laid his hand on the banister-rail. "Be quite sure I'll pay you back this one some day."

CHAPTER III.

" ' Know ye the stranger woman?'   ' Let her be!'"
—TENNYSON.

THE few days which followed that of the agitator's meeting at the Nab were uncomfortably spent by everybody at Maleigh Abbey except Lady Rushcliffe, who in the general discomfiture found her opportunity.

Emmeline Rushcliffe was the pretty, clever, intriguing widow of a prominent physician who, having received a baronetcy through the advocacy of powerful friends, had frustrated his wife's ambitious designs by retiring from practice, and spending the remainder of his life abroad. He died when she was thirty-four, leaving her an ample fortune; the greater part of which, however, she was to forfeit in the event of her marrying again. She felt, therefore, that she could not indulge in the luxury of an amiable and handsome, but penniless husband, and schemed her way into those houses where she could meet men who could afford to dispense with fortune in a wife. Such a man was Lord Malpas.

So well did Lady Rushcliffe play her cards, so tactfully did she await her opportunity, that nobody at the Abbey guessed that the object of the graceful, accomplished lady, who played the piano and the harp so charmingly, and sang French songs with refinement, yet without loss of *chic,* was to become Countess of Malpas.

It was at this point that Victred Speke had arrived at the Abbey, summoned by the Earl on business on behalf of his father. For the Honourable Atherton Speke, being a man of particularly strict, even strait-laced morals, would hold no personal communication with the nephew, whose heir he was.

Then Lady Rushcliffe, who, in spite of her stoicism,

was rather susceptible, fell a little in love with the young Irish giant, and decided that she would prefer the chance of a title with him, to the certainty of it with the present possessor. But Victred was proof against her subtlest approaches: he simply appeared never to notice them. It was with a feeling of vindictiveness, therefore, much stronger than her transient liking, that she transferred her hopes and designs back to his cousin, whose dislike to Victred she lost no chance of increasing.

The agitator's meeting was a grand occasion for Tracy, who, having seen Jerry Coggin among the audience, lost no time in getting the ear of the Earl before him, represented himself as having been present in the character of informer, and contrived to throw on Victred suspicion of the motives which had moved himself. This was easy, as Victred never disguised his tolerance towards discontented tenants, both in Ireland and England, and was both too lazy and too independent to offer any excuse for his presence at the meeting. "He was there: and it was great fun." That was all he said about it; and this came to be construed into an admission compared to which rank Fenianism was as light to darkness.

So that at last he was goaded out of his usual stolidity into a mood of fiery recklessness, in which he was bound to say or do something extremely foolish. The three men were all smoking together one night, when Tracy saw a cloud of ominous sullenness grow darker each moment on the face of his cousin; Eugene was taunting the latter with his tastes, which he said were those of a "slumming curate." Tracy wisely made cigarettes and smoked them, holding aloof as much as he could.

"I think it's as well in these times," said Victred at last, in a gruff but exceedingly low voice, "to put one's self now and then in the place of the people in the slums. One finds out what they think of us."

"I don't care a pin what they think of me," said Eugene, who, as usual at this period of the evening was rather unsteady of speech and gait. "There's a fellow called Red Jack who goes about tellin' 'em to shoot me. And they're very welcome to try, as far as I'm concerned." There was a pause, during which either Victred's silence, or some slight movement on his part, irritated Eugene afresh. Taking a couple of zig-zag steps, he leaned across the back of a chair, and stared at him with an aggressive expression. "I daresay you agree with me there, at all events."

Victred uttered no word. But Lord Malpas chose to interrupt his silence as acquiescence, and his anger blazed up into fury.

"But if Red Jack shoots me, it will do you no good; so you need not set him to fire except for your own amusement. I'm going to marry—yes, marry, do you hear! And neither you nor your old crank of a father shall step into my shoes."

"I think it's the very best thing you can do, to marry, if you can find a girl who knows little enough about you to have you," said Victred quietly.

"Emmeline's not a girl, and she knows all about me," snarled the Earl.

"Lady Rushcliffe!"

The announcement came so suddenly upon Victred that he almost whistled. Tracy was quite as much amazed as he. Victred incautiously went on, in a by no means complimentary tone:

"You don't mean to say that you are going to marry *that* woman!"

Certainly it was not the way in which one would have the news of one's approaching marriage received. The Earl, losing command of himself, struck his cousin across the face.

All three men were on their feet in a moment. Tracy, holding the Earl back, Victred with his fist raised to return the blow. Luckily, Eugene was no more master of his own feet at that moment than of his temper; the fringe of the Persian hearth-rug caught his foot, and he fell on the floor, dragging Tracy with him. Victred, therefore, got a moment for reflection; and, finding his anger suddenly give place to an irresistible temptation to laugh, as he watched Eugene's sprawling efforts to regain his footing, and Tracy's discomfiture as Lord Malpas clutched his head in an undiscriminatingly pugnacious manner, he took himself off before the affair had time to become more of a brawl than it had already been.

It was Tracy who, in the course of the following day, took credit for establishing a *modus vivendi* between the cousins. Victred would have left the Abbey, but that he was there as his father's representative to enable the Earl to transact certain business connected with his Lancashire property, for which the consent of his heir was necessary. But the peace was of a hollow kind. Eugene had told Lady Rushcliffe, now openly understood to be his bride-elect, enough of the quarrel to make her Victred's bitter enemy. So that Victred had now no friend at the Abbey but the devoted May; for Tracy, though he did his best to make his cousin forget the threat he had used on their return from the agitator's meeting, had by no means forgiven Victred's interference with his project.

Lady May, with a young girl's sharp-sighted inquisitiveness, detected the slight estrangement between them, gave Tracy the blame, and revenged herself upon him by avoiding his society as much as possible.

It was about a week after the quarrel when, as the ladies assembled at the sound of the luncheon gong, they heard an altercation going on at the front door between one of the men-servants and an importunate stranger. Lady Rushcliffe, who was now beginning to get in the thin edge of her authority at the Abbey, sent Croly, the butler, to see what was the matter. The only members of the party who had not yet appeared in the dining-room were the Earl and Victred, who had been busy together in the study throughout the morning.

When Croly returned, his manner was rather stiff.

3

" It was a person, your ladyship, a stranger, making
a disturbance," he said.   " I sent her away."

There was a slight movement of curiosity among
the ladies, and Tracy looked significantly at Lady
May.

" Who did she want to see ? " asked she.

But the discreet Croly busied himself by cutting
bread at the sideboard, and affected not to hear.

Impulsive May, with a flush of anger in her cheeks,
slipped out of the room, and, opening the front door,
ran down the pretty flight of terrace steps into the
grounds. By the time Tracy, the only person who
guessed her intention, had sauntered out as far as the
steps, she. was already returning. She blushed on
meeting his inquiring eyes, but gave him a look of
such contemptuous defiance as only a very young
girl dares to use.

" Well," said he, " where have you been, out on this
foggy day without your hat ? "

" Nowhere," she answered haughtily. " At least,"
she added, seeing the flicker of a smile on his face,
" I went to see who it was they were driving away so
harshly."

" And you satisfied yourself ? "

" Quite. It was an overdressed person, who certainly didn't want charity."

" A stranger to *you*, of course ? "

" To me, and to any person whom I count among
my friends—of course, Mr. Fitzalan."

And the girl, who had always plenty of dignity for
Tracy, walked back into the house with the air of an
empress. She was met, however, by Lady Rushcliffe,
who, having exchanged a few words privately with
the butler, and having thereupon divined May's un-
dignified errand, administered such a sharp rebuke
upon the impropriety of a young lady's making any
inquiry concerning feminine persons to whom she was
not introduced, that the poor child, while receiving
the lecture in proud silence, smarted under every
word ; and for the rest of the day observed towards

her adored cousin a reticence, a shy avoidance, which he, obtuse male creature that he was, never even noticed.

And this, of course, was the cruelty of it.

———

CHAPTER IV.

"That fawn-skin-dappled hair of hers,
And the blue eye
Dear and dewy,
And that infantine fresh air of hers !"

BROWNING.

TRACY was growing uneasy. For, on inquiry of Croly, he found that the butler ignored the fact that the stranger had asked first for "Mr. Speke," and then for "Mr. Fitzalan," and persisted in believing that the person she really wanted to see was the Earl himself.

If this belief should get abroad, and if the lady should disclose the fact that, it was on Tracy's suggestion that she came, that unhappy young man felt that his downfall would be irretrievable.

So, on the two days which followed that of her inauspicious call, Tracy roamed about the neighbourhood on the watch for the stranger; and failing to find any trace of her, began to hope that home-sickness had taken her back to the Strand.

This hope, however, was dispelled in the rudest manner. It was drawing towards evening on the second day, and Tracy was getting heartily tired of playing sentinel in the raw air of November, and wishing that he had left other people's business alone until the weather had grown warmer, when a figure, a long-coated, large-hatted figure came up to him out of the fog, and offered him a cheery greeting.

"Well met, well met, Mr. Fitzalan," said Dennis M'Rena, pressing his hand with apparent devotion. "The sight of your face in a servile, soulless country like this, is a good augury for the Cause."

3*

Tracy felt that he could have kicked Dennis and the Cause into the river with pleasure. Personal discomfort and a sense of things having gone very wrong with him had brought him low indeed. He felt at that moment that he was a rogue, and that he was sorry for it.

"Why don't you go back to ould Ireland then, Dennis?" said he petulantly. He would have added, had he dared, "instead of dogging my footsteps like a detective."

But Tracy had lost his nerve to-day, and could not even be impudent.

"Because I'm extending my field of operations. I've succeeded in making 'em feel in Ireland that life isn't worth living until you've put an ounce of cold lead into a vital part of somebody better off than you are yourself. And now," pursued Dennis cheerfully, "I'm starting to do as much for 'em over here."

"And whose thanks do you expect to get for that?"

"I don't look for thanks—at least not for a generation or two. When the people awakes to the sense of what it owes me, it will have to be content with offering up its gratitude on my grave."

"Is that the best reward you can offer as an inducement to one to throw in his lot with you?"

"No, Mr. Fitzalan. Your gifts are more brilliant, more striking than mine. You skim over the ground like a hare, while I grub along like the mole underneath. One great achievement, though, I may take credit for: Dennis M'Rena it was that first stirred your soul to thoughts of your country's wrongs; Dennis M'Rena it was that gave Tracy Fitzalan to Ireland."

"You lay it on pretty thick, don't you, Dennis?" said Tracy drily.

"No, sir, I do not," replied Dennis, lashing himself into fervour as he went on. "Old Ireland—bless her! has never lacked sons with a fist for an enemy's eye, and a bad word for that eye's owner. But though this, the infantry division, is as strong as ever, there is, at present, a lamentable weakness in the cavalry; in the ranks of those, that is, who can not only *call* a spade a spade, but can spell it, and write long columns of print about it. That, Mr. Fitzalan, is, as you know, the work I propose for you."

"But what's the figure, Dennis? The patriot is worthy of his—potato."

"What do you say, Mr. Fitzalan, to the leadership of the Irish party?"

"Say, that it may be a very snug berth, but it's occupied."

"Sure, that doesn't prove that it will never be vacant! You, sir, must work for the reversion. And when you sit in Parliament——"

Tracy moved uneasily. To have the letters M.P. after his name was one of his ambitions. He thought it would help him towards his greatest ambition of all—to "make a noise in the world." But there were difficulties in the way, want of money being the chief. For he did not want to sit at Westminster merely as one of the rank and file of the Irish Party; he wanted to make his own noise, not to help in keeping up the noise of other people.

"I can't sit in Parliament," he said shortly, his brogue coming out strongly to betray his excitement. "I have no money."

Dennis gave a sphinx-like smile, nodded, and took him by the shoulder.

"I'll find that!" said he confidently. "I tell ye I can wheedle the shekels out of a bank-safe; in fact it's my principal accomplishment. If you will do what I want you to do—and mind, the work itself, done as you will do it, will put you on the high road to fame, I'll engage to take a voyage out to America, and bring you back such a pocketful of dollars as will keep your patriotism warm for many a long month."

He had ventured on plain speaking at last,

certainly. Tracy played with his thin little moustache.

"And wh—what is it ye whant me to do?" he asked in a lower voice.

"I want ye to write a series of articles, in the form of letters to every man of note in England who is not of our way of thinking (and that's most of 'em, thank Heaven! or our occupation would be gone), turning 'em inside out, showing up every incident of their past lives which they would rather have kept quiet. In fact," went on Dennis, with a twinkle in his eyes, "laying bare everything which decency would have kept hidden."

"Can't you get some newspaper fellow to do it?"

"No. It would smell of printer's ink. For good sound abuse of any particular body of men, abuse with the genuine ring in it, you must go to a member of that body. For abuse of the English aristocracy, I come to you."

"Because I'm not a member of it? A bull, Dennis, a bull!"

"If you like," admitted Dennis good-humouredly. "But if Providence was merciful enough to let ye be born on the right side of St. George's Channel——"

"The left!"

"You'll admit," went on Dennis, without comment on his frivolous interruption, "that you're closely connected with the aristocracy on this side also."

This Tracy admitted willingly enough. But he had another objection to advance.

"I should like to write the letters," he said plaintively. "It's a sort of work that I could do, I am sure, but I don't think it would get me talked about in the right way, even if I could ever own to the authorship, which I couldn't do, for private reasons. Such work would never get me into the good graces of the respectable members of the party."

"No new man ever gets into the good graces of the respectable members of any political party. You've got to split the ears of the groundlings; and then when your name is in everybody's mouth, and you have become a public scandal, you see the error of your ways and settle down."

Tracy said nothing in reply to this, but after a little consideration he asked :

" Are you going to hold another meeting about here ? "

" Yes, on the second of next month."

Tracy had another question on the tip of his tongue ; but he glanced at Dennis out of the corners of his eyes, noted the expectant, sly expression of the agitator's face, and substituted a fresh one.

" What do you do after that ? "

" It depends upon you. I am due in Dublin on the fourth ; but if you decide to take the chance I've offered you, I can put off my return and stay here a day or two. In that case you might come over to Clough to settle matters."

Tracy listened, but did not look at him.

" I'll be over here on the night of the third to hear how you've decided," went on Dennis.

" That won't be any good. It is the night of the Cheston Infirmary Ball, and we'll all be away."

" I'll wait till ye come back then. Three, four, five o'clock in the morning is all the same to me, so long as I have a chance of doing me country a good turn." With a sudden change of tone, Dennis went on : " By-the-bye, ye're not always so cautious as ye are in this matter, Mr. Fitzalan. I was in Cheston to-day, and I met there a lady, who says you brought her down here, and——"

Tracy gave a moan. . Dennis, who had nothing further to gain by loitering here in the fog, left him to himself with a friendly suggestion that it would be well to send the fair one back to whatever place she came from, before rumours of her communicativeness. should reach the ears of Lord Malpas.

On the following morning, Tracy went over to Cheston ; and sauntering along the High Street, attracting by her appearance and manners no inconsiderable amount of attention, he soon found the person of whom he came in search.

" Glynn ! " he called under his breath, as soon as he came up to her.

She turned and nodded to him with a frank smile.

" You see, I haven't been long in taking your advice," said she.   And pulling out his note from her pocket, she showed it to him.   " You didn't say much, but it was enough for me," she added knowingly.

" *I* didn't say much !   *My* advice ! " echoed Tracy, feigning astonishment, but with scant success.   " I don't understand.   Let me look at that letter."

But Glynn only laughed again, as she shook her head and put the note back into her pocket.

" I know it was you, though," she said simply, " and that you've got some mischief in your mind against your poor cousin ; Speke is your cousin, isn't he ? "

" Yes."

" Well, it's a great shame, for he's worth ten of you, Mr. Tracy Fitzalan, Esquire.   And I don't suppose there's any truth in what you said about his going to get married, eh ? "

" No, no.   It was all a mistake.   I——"

" Oh, you *do* know something about the note then, after all ?   You've given yourself away this time, Mr. Innocence."

" There was an impression about a short time ago, that Mr. Speke was going to get married, certainly," answered Tracy, in whose cheeks a pink flush was coming and going, as in the face of a girl.   " But it was a mistaken one—entirely a mistaken one.   I—I think the best thing you can do now is to go back to town.   And I don't mind if I help you with the fare."

" Nor how soon I take myself off, I suppose !   But now I'm here, I think I won't go without a sight of my old man.   Who knows ?   We might make it up again."

" Come and have some luncheon, and let us talk it over," suggested Tracy persuasively.

He was anxious to coax her into giving up that compromising note. For if she should meet Victred, and show it to him—a possibility which he had over-looked until now—Victred's most useful friendship would assuredly be withdrawn from him. He was impatient, also, to end this *tête-à-tête* in the High Street, where he was exposed to the curious glances of a score of passers-by who knew him, and whose eyes turned at once from him to his companion.

" Glynn Dorien's " beauty alone would have at-tracted attention anywhere, independently of the striking bad taste of her dress. She looked young, but was in fact years younger even than she looked, her manner of living having impaired the freshness of a beauty, which, a few years before, had been almost child-like in its charm. There remained a pair of large, wide-open, black-fringed blue eyes, a nose just not straight enough to be severe, a red-lipped sen-suous mouth, a pink skin, and hair that was golden in the sun and brown in the shade. The expression of her face was extremely alluring, conveying, as it did, an impression of almost infantine innocence, which was, in fact, simply the result of an entire lack of moral consciousness. She spoke slowly, with a nasal twang which betrayed a want of refinement and a cockney origin.

This want of refinement was painfully evident in her attire. At a time when other women wore their skirts short and plain, hers was long and allowed to drag along the ground. From under a large be-feathered hat her hair hung down, its disorder con-fined by a net; while that vulgar impostor, "seal plush," was the material of which her short jacket was made.

Glynn shook her head at Tracy's invitation with a laugh.

" No, thank you," she said, " I won't go to lunch with you. And I won't go back to town until I

choose.   So, as far as I'm concerned, you're just
wasting your time.   And here's wishing you good-
morning."

She flounced away from him with these words, and
Tracy did not attempt to follow her.   He was quite
aware of a strain of headstrong obstinacy in Glynn's
character, and he thought that further interference on
his part would only render her more perverse.

"Good-bye.   You'll know your friends better some
day," was the plaintive farewell which he threw after
her.

Sauntering on towards the station, he watched her
as she walked on, and noted the look round of every
one who passed her.

"Of course, the story she tells about Victred is not
true," thought Tracy as she turned up a side street
out of sight.   "Why, if it were, even I should feel
compunction for having brought such an incubus
back upon him."

———

CHAPTER V.

" Hair in heaps fell heavily
Over a pale brow spirit-pure——."

VICTRED had heard of the mysterious feminine visitor
who had called at the Abbey.   But as he had to go
up to town on the very day of her interview with
Croly, to see his father on business for the Earl, he
took very little interest in the story, and had no idea
that it concerned him.

On his way back to Maleigh, when his visit to his
father was ended, Victred fell in with the ubiquitous
Dennis M'Rena, whom he found distributing leaflets
out of his big black bag to the passengers who were
streaming out of the railway station.

"Hallo!" said Victred, recognising the long coat
and big hat before he saw the agitator's face, "still
sowing sedition, eh?"

"And will continue to do so as long as I've a leg

to stand on, and a tongue to speak with," replied
Dennis cheerfully.

Victred glanced at the leaflet which had been
thrust into his hand. It announced in Dennis's own
high-flown style, that on the following night, the 2nd
of December, at Crossley Ridge, an open-air meeting
would be held, at which Red Jack, the champion of
the poor and the oppressed, would speak, and at
which all who were interested in the cause of
humanity and the progress of truth would do well to
be present.

Victred, although he considered Dennis a mischievous demagogue, was interested by a personality
which he recognised as no common one. So he stood
aside until the rest of the travellers had gone by, and
Dennis, having distributed his leaflets, not too profusely, but with a nice discrimination, shut up his bag
and rested from his labours.

"I see you don't give your invitations to everybody," remarked Victred, with his hands in his
pockets and a cigar between his lips.

"No.   It would be a waste of printing.   Never
give to a fat man.   *He* won't trudge out a mile or so
on a winter evening to hear me blaspheme at his
superiors!   He can do it himself at home.   Never
give to a man with a good overcoat, unless he's a
young swell like yourself who'd come from curiosity.
And never give one to a woman with a baby; she'll
give it to the child to play with, and he'll tear it up
into small bits and swallow half."

"Well, and who is Red Jack?" said Victred,
laughing.

Dennis threw up at the young fellow one of those
shrewd twinkling glances of his which said so much
and hinted so much more.

"Come and see him," said he shortly.

"Well, but I believe it's just yourself in a scarlet
shirt and a strong brogue!   Come now, guessed it
first time, haven't I?"

"Come and see," repeated Dennis, as he drew his

hat down over his eyes again, and gathered up his bag and his umbrella for departure; "you can't expect me to 'give away the show,' you know, can you?"

He had gained his object, and he went off, for he knew well enough that he had effectually stimulated the younger man's curiosity.

Victred was, indeed, glad of even the prospect of this small excitement, for he found himself in very uncomfortable quarters on his return to the Abbey. Lady May's fit of shyness had grown more acute than ever. Lady Rushcliffe had had time to strengthen her empire over the Earl, and her influence was all against Victred, while Tracy was still so perturbed concerning the result of his little plot, and so much occupied with private business of his own, that he kept as much as he could out of his cousin's way.

The day following his return being that appointed for the agitator's meeting, Victred made the excuse of a visit to pay to some people living at a distance, in order to avoid another quarrel with the Earl. On announcing his intention, he caught an angry glance from Tracy, who, however, made no remark. But his glance set Victred wondering whether "the tub-thumper's daughter," as he irreverently named the object of Tracy's admiration, would be present at the meeting. Of course Victred was a little ashamed by this time of his interference on the previous occasion. Reflection assured him that Miss M'Rena was, in all probability, a bouncing, buxom Irish lass of about twice the muscular power of Tracy himself, particularly well able to take care of herself, and very unlikely to be grateful for any interference from an outsider with the plans she had helped her father to concoct. Victred thought he should like to see this girl. She would probably have her father's keen blue eyes, and would certainly be saucy and amusing. He drew such a clear picture of her in his mind as the train carried him towards Clough, which is the nearest station to Crossley Ridge, that by the time he had got out the hope of seeing the girl was far the strongest feeling he had about the meeting.

Clough was a poor little place, with a small stone inn, which scarcely deserved even that humble name. However, here Victred contrived to enjoy a hearty dinner, for he was one of those healthy young men who can eat anything, anywhere, while retaining enough self-respect to grumble at everything put before him at a dinner-party, a ball-supper, or his club.

By the time he had finished, night had fallen, and it was time to set out for the place of meeting. Victred looked out towards the bleak moor which stretched for miles on every side of the straggling village. It was raining fast, and it was very cold. If there had been a train to take him back to Maleigh, he would have slunk off home without a second's delay. Miss M'Rena would certainly not tramp over the moor to give the meeting the moral support of her presence on a night like this; and as for her, and Dennis, and Red Jack himself, Victred would have given his last chance on earth of ever meeting any of them for a lift homewards even on a lorry.

But as in a battle the impossibility of turning back makes the coward a hero, so Victred, finding no way of retreat, buttoned his ulster about him, and set out through the rain at a smart pace for Crossley Ridge.

The ridge was a stony and bleak wall of hills, on the steeper side of which ran a rocky little river, punctuated by cotton-factories. Each of these bare, square stone buildings, with its rows upon rows of workhouse-like windows, pointed a long, gaunt black ·finger up towards the sky, which had been blue overhead before the long, gaunt black fingers, had come there.

The meeting-place was within easy reach of a dozen of these factories, which were bright with lights, like huge lanterns, when Victred began his journey. One by one, however, as he crossed the moor the lanterns were put out, as the hour for closing had come, and the "hands" were going home to their tea.

Ten minutes later, on reaching the plain stone bridge which crossed the river between two of the factories, the young man found that they were already trooping out again, some from their homes, others from the public-houses, and swarming, like summer flies, up the hill to the place of meeting. "Clatteradat! Clatteradat!" went the clogs, the sharp sound filling the steep stone street with noise. Meanwhile the air was alive with voices and hoarse laughter as the rough men, and the girls with shawls round their heads, climbed eagerly upwards.

Victred caught the words "Red Jack" in the strong Lancashire dialect which sounded on all sides of him. Some had heard him, and spoke of him with bated breath. "Eh, but a' spo-oke fine, that a' did! Like to tear yer heart aht a'most," some said. All had heard of him, and a throb of expectancy filled the atmosphere; and rain and cold and the rising wind were forgotten as they climbed. The enthusiasm was contagious. Victred, sympathetic Irishman that he was, felt delirious with the universal excitement when he reached the small circular plain at the top of the ridge, which was already thick with people. To beguile the time, the crowd commented freely on Victred's height; and saucy feminine faces peeped up at him from under their shawls, the girls making pretence of craning their necks and standing on tiptoe to be able to see what he was like.

Then a murmur rose on the edge of the crowd; and it swelled and swelled, travelling nearer and nearer to where Victred was standing, the crowd all turning their heads to look. Then it passed on like a breeze over a field of corn, and growing each moment louder, suddenly burst into a great cheer as, by the light of a flaming naphtha lamp, stuck on a pole and flaming in the wind, they all saw a face above them gleaming white against the darkness.

The first sight of the face gave Victred a shock, he scarcely knew why. It was so calm, so pale, so motionless, like the face of the holy dead. He felt that he wanted to cry out ; that something was lifting him for the moment above himself, above the narrow life of cigar-smoke and hunting prospects, club scandal and the odds on the favourite. He almost held his breath for the boy's first word ; for a boy was surely this "Red Jack," whose name was now being breathed about in hoarse whispers. No man could have a face like that, and the thick frieze suit he wore could not make him robust enough. He must be a lad of not more than seventeen.

"Eh, but a's a bit of a lad !" exclaimed many a voice in the crowd.

Then Red Jack held up his hand, and a hush came over them all as his first words struck their ears. Words! It was the face, the voice, which spoke, beguiling women of their sobs, firing the hearts of men, breathing through all the concourse that magic breath which makes a thousand creatures feel that they have one common soul. A half-tipsy scoffer on the outer edge of the crowd was savagely kicked and beaten. Victred felt a great throb of relief that Lord Malpas had not heard of the meeting. This crowd might have killed him if he had come that way to-night ; and Red Jack would not have stayed their hands.

The lad was a fanatic, that was undeniable. Yet, while you said so, you were carried away by his fanaticism. He had none of the ordinary agitator's statistics ; no painfully acquired scraps of perverted political economy. It was the stern reverent spirit of the Hebrews of old which seemed to break through the rich ringing notes of the fresh young voice. "God had given them the land," he said, " to make of it one great altar to His praise. But because they had forgotten that they were not beasts, but men, made in His image, because they had lost their sense of what was fair and good, God had put over them evil spirits in the guise of men, to drive them down, to keep their bodies in want, their souls

in sleep, while the God-given earth festered with the
evil wrought upon it.

"But," went on the voice borne clear on the air
like the sigh of a spirit, "the soul, that holy voice that
tells us we were not born to live in pain, die, rot, and
be forgotten, cannot sleep for ever. From end to end
of our beautiful earth it is waking now. Great
America trembles as she tries to shake her limbs free
from the shackles which bind her : she holds out her
hand to us, invites us to follow her example, and be
free. Russia stirs in her heavy sleep. France,
beautiful, brilliant France, has already opened her
eyes. My own country, your younger weaker sister,
cries to Heaven in her repentance, her misery. Give
back our land once more, she cries, to us who love
even its marshes and its stones. Let us lay our bones
in the earth which we have tilled, let our children
tread the ground our forefathers trod ; and if there is
not room enough in Ireland for Irishmen, send across
the seas the men who have lived upon our misery,
and leave us clinging to the land they have made
bare.

"You also," went on Red Jack, whose eyes were
by this time shining like fiery jewels in a face pale
with passion, "you also, you Englishmen and English-
women, must cry aloud till your soul wakes. No
more cheers for the spirit of evil, for my Lord of
Malpas with his vicious eyes. Let the maiden of
the people whom he looks upon keep her own eyes
pure from the pollution of his glance ; or rather, let
her nerve herself for a good deed, give him smile
for smile ; then, when the hideous mask, cast in
centuries of ill-doing, creeps close to her face, let
her take knife, revolver, what she will that is quick
and deadly, and purge the world of one monstrous
thing."

Victred shuddered. There was a hoarse, angry
murmur through the excited crowd. The Earl was
hated, and Red Jack's passion infected them. *He*
would have done the deed he advocated, had occasion

offered, without a second thought, without a qualm. They all knew this, and felt it almost as strongly as Victred himself did.

From this point the young man scarcely noted the rest of the speech, though the strange, clear voice rang in his ears just the same. Almost in a dream, he heard the voice cease, the cheering break out, saw that Dennis and the boy had disappeared, felt the jostling murmuring crowd disperse and melt away. Then "clatteradat, clatteradat!" went the iron-tipped clogs again—down-hill now. At last he was left quite alone, and found himself mechanically moving down-hill too.

He perceived suddenly the reason of the rapid break-up of the crowd ; the rain had begun to come down very heavily, and the wind had grown colder. He quickened his pace, crossed the bridge, and started across the moor.

Ugh ! What a nasty night it was ! He was coming to himself again, after the intoxication into which a face, a voice, had thrown him. For what was the speech, after all ? The mere fancies of a boy, a passionate child ! Inspired perhaps ; but then, that kind of inspiration "won't wash."

From these thoughts Victred passed to a hope that he would be able to find his way. The ground was getting very heavy, and the right road was growing difficult to distinguish.

Then, quite suddenly, going at a smart pace himself, Victred came upon the boy—nearly threw the little fellow down, indeed.

"Hallo !" he cried, and throwing out an arm, he caught and steadied him. "Why, there's nothing of you," he went on with a laugh. " I say, that M'Rena fellow oughtn't to let a little chap like you cross the moor all alone ! Where is he ? "

"He's staying at the Ridge to-night. I'm staying at Clough," said the little lad.

How frightened he was, how timid, now that the excitement of his speech was over ! He lagged on

4

the way too, as if his limbs could scarcely carry him further.

" How old are you ? " asked Victred abruptly.

" I'm eighteen."

" Really ?　You're the smallest lad of eighteen I ever saw.　They let you use your brains too much, so that the body suffers, I expect."

" I can't use myself up too fast in my country's service," answered Red Jack proudly.

It was a last flicker of energy, this haughty little speech.　The next moment he stumbled.　Victred had to stop, and wait for him.

" Let me give you my arm," said he.

But this plan did not answer ; between four feet ten and six feet four there was too much difference. At last Victred picked the little fellow up and carried him.　Red Jack protested, but feebly.　All the fire and the force had for the time gone out of him.　He was worn out.　Victred was moved to infinite pity and to a good deal of curiosity concerning this small creature with the burning soul.　How still the boy kept !　Now and then the big man who was carrying him stopped and tried to look into his face, almost frightened by this dead stillness.　Each time that he did so, the tired eyes opened, and Red Jack murmured, " Let me walk.　I can walk."

And presently Victred, coming to the edge of the village of Clough, took a peep at the pale face by the light in a cottage window.　He caught sight of one of the boy's hands, as he did so, noticed that the thick glove which covered it hung very loosely, and that the wrist was very small—ridiculously small—for a boy's.　This roused his suspicions.

" Let me down now, please," said Red Jack, " I am close to where I am staying."

Victred obeyed quite silently, so strangely moved by that suspicion of his that he could say nothing.

" That is my house," said Red Jack, pointing to a cottage close by.　" Thank you very much, sir, for your kindness."

Victred took the hand held out to him, very reverently, very pitifully. Then, as Red Jack moved away, he raised his hat.

Red Jack's secret was discovered. Without a moment's pause the murder-preaching agitator fled, never stopping until the cottage-door had slammed behind the little form.

CHAPTER VI.

" Thy vows are all broken,
And light is thy fame ;
I hear thy name spoken,
And share in its shame."
—BYRON.

VICTRED got back to Maleigh between one and two o'clock in the morning, having walked most of the way. Next morning at breakfast he was silent and abstracted, thereby filling the heart of his cousin May with misery so acute that she declined to eat. For this was the day of the Cheston Infirmary Ball, and Victred had not asked her for a single dance, though all the rest were chattering about the affair.

At last she broke down, and announced in full family conclave that she was not going to the dance. Her brother looked up sharply from his devilled kidneys.

"Rubbish !" he said. "Everybody from here must go. People expect it. You were crazy to go the day before yesterday. What have you got in your head now? Some sentimental nonsense, I suppose ?"

Victred glanced at the girl, and there darted into his mind the idea that he, in some perfectly innocent way or other, was the cause of her whim. Reddening awkwardly, as he so often had to do at poor May's sentimental vagaries, he said good - humouredly, affecting suddenly to remember some non-existing promises :

4*

" What, May, do you forget you are engaged to me for three dances? You are not going to throw me over like this at the last, are you? "

Her eyes glistened, her whole face glowed.

" I—I had forgotten. I—I didn't remember," she said in a low voice.

Victred did not know where to look, for the other ladies glanced at him with eyes full of demure mischief. Lord Malpas made a scoffing remark in an undertone to Tracy, who grinned, but did not look pleased. Lady May noticed none of these things. She had been whirled up into the seventh heaven of delight, and the day, after that, seemed never to end. For, with the humility which comes of an unreasoning, blind devotion, she kept out of Victred's way; she refrained from the joy of looking at him, in her gratitude for his gracious kindness. "Three dances! Oh, would the evening never come?"

When at last she and Lady Rushcliffe and Eugene had started on the long, cold, nine miles' drive to Cheston, the draughts which whistled about her ears failed to chill her, as she sat with her back to the horses, facing her brother and her future sister-in-law, full of the bliss which awaited her.

" First waltz, you know, May. That will be the next dance but one," were the words which greeted her on her arrival in the ball-room from Victred, who had driven over with Tracy in the dog-cart, and beaten the landau by half-an-hour.

That waltz was a dream of joy to May. The plain girl in white silk, with Indian ornaments of turquoises and gold, whose beauty seemed to draw attention to her lack of personal charms, was the happiest girl in the room.

She was too happy to think, too happy to see, too happy to notice a curious humming sound, as of half-whispered wonder, which was growing louder near the principal entrance, where an ever-increasing crowd, from the dancers and the non-dancers, was blocking the door-way, surrounding some centre of attraction.

"Hallo! What's going on over there, I wonder?" said Victred, as he proceeded with his partner towards the group.

It did not much matter to Lady May where she went, so long as she was with Victred. So they pressed forward together on the outer edge of the crowd. As they came near, a woman's coarse voice, in very unrefined tones, was heard saying stubbornly:

"It's no good trying to stop me. I've as much right to go in as anybody here, and I mean to. So there!"

Victred stopped. It almost seemed to May that he staggered. She looked up quickly into his face.

"Let us—let us go back," he said. "I'll take you to Lady Rushcliffe."

"Why? What is it?" asked May trembling.

"Somebody has got in who has no business here, I think," said he.

But Lady May resisted his effort to lead her away. There were changes in his face, in his voice, which filled her with vague fears. Before, therefore, he could take her back, the crowd had surged a little nearer to them, and a woman in out-door dress broke her way through, wresting her arm, with evidently considerable muscular power, from the grasp of an official who had been trying to remove her.

"No," she cried excitedly, "there's a gentleman here I want, and I mean to find him. Oh, there you are, sir, are you? Perhaps you're going to pretend you don't know me."

Lady May uttered a low sob. It was the woman who had made a disturbance at the Abbey, and the person she was addressing was Victred. May clung to her cousin's arm, but remained in every other respect quite composed, watching the angry creature before her with steady eyes. The intruder was evidently exasperated by the attitude of the young

girl. Victred turned to Tracy, who had just come
up, twisting his moustache and looking rather
frightened.

"Take her away," said Victred hurriedly, trying
gently to dislodge his cousin's hand.

"Yes, take her away, and tell her to keep her
hands off other folks' goods, or it'll be the worse for
her," cried the intruder, who was apparently excited
by something besides anger.

But Lady May stood her ground, with a feeling in
her heart that to leave her cousin would be to
abandon him to some horrible fate. For his usually
good-tempered face was rigid; the expression on it
was blank despair. The woman approached menacingly, with a gesture as if to tear the girl's hand
from her cousin's arm. This caused Victred to move
sharply, so as to interpose his person between them.

"Go, dear, go with Tracy," he said in a low voice.
Then, as the girl reluctantly relaxed her hold on his
arm, he seized the hand of the other woman to detain
her as she attempted to follow Lady May, and said in
a louder voice:

"This is my wife."

There was an irrepressible murmur among the by-
standers, followed immediately by a deep hush. As
for the woman herself, the open acknowledgment,
evidently unexpected, seemed to make her giddy.
Her defiant manner, her brazen impudence, fell to
pieces like tinder, her position of the aggrieved one
having changed in a moment to that of the aggressor.

"You had better come out," went on Victred
shortly; and, taking her by the shoulders he led her
quickly towards the door.

She went like a lamb, after one quick glance, full
of bewilderment, physical fear, and the cowed submission of a coarse nature finding its master in the
creature it took for its victim. Lady May looked on
like a stone, not caring that all could read in her eyes
the poor little secret of her love. If he looked despairing, she was heart-broken; for she was feeling,

in her sympathy for him, not only her own helpless anguish, but his shame.

Instantly, on Victred's announcement, the curious throng had begun to draw back, to disperse. His courage "in taking the bull by the horns" had compelled every one's respect. One susceptible lady, indeed, the wife of a town-councillor, burst into tears; and perhaps her murmured explanation to her companion gave the keynote to the feeling of her fellow-women:

"Such a—splendid—man—to—to be wasted on that—creature."

Without one word—perhaps he could not trust himself to speak—Victred took his wife to the nearest hotel, and asked for a room.

"One of your best," he continued to the waiter, in a hard tone; "it is for my wife."

The woman shrank back as her husband started to lead her upstairs.

"You—you are not coming—up!" she whispered huskily.

"Not to stay—be sure of that," answered Victred coldly, as he insisted on accompanying her up the stairs.

When they reached the room, in which the two recently lighted candles glimmered with but faint light, he let his hand, for the first time, fly up as if by a spring from her shoulder; and retreating to the door, stood with his back to it, his hand on the handle.

"Stay here till to-morrow," he said; "and I will come and see you again. You are staying here as my wife, so perhaps you will be satisfied with the disgrace you have already brought upon me, and will conduct yourself properly—or—or as well as you can. Good-night."

She gave a hysterical cry, and from her long, luminous blue eyes the easy tears of her type of womanhood gushed forth, as she bounded, like a graceful wild animal, towards him. She adored him,

she said; she would not let him go. He remained
quite still until she seized his hand and began to
cover it profusely with kisses: pulling it away from
her with a jerk which threw her back a step, he cut
short the fulsome expressions of endearment which
she was pouring forth, by just one fierce look, which
she understood and cowered under.

"Look here," he said, breathing hard, "I am trying
to treat you well, as I always have done—*always*
mind. But if I am irritated one degree more to-night,
I—I can't answer for myself. You understand. Stop
that."

It was not a dignified ending, but the homely words
were expressive. She let him go without another
effort to detain him.

Victred walked down Cheston High Street mechanically, and mechanically turned into the road for
Maleigh Abbey. It was a distance of nine miles; but
he reckoned that, in the mood he was in to-night, he
could do it in less than two hours. A certain paper,
which, on behalf of his father, Victred had succeeded
in inducing the Earl to sign that morning, was in his
portmanteau. If, as was probable, Eugene should
repent this transaction before morning, he would not
be above searching for and destroying the document
in his cousin's absence.

This was Victred's excuse for returning to Maleigh
Abbey, which, in the present state of his mind, he had
much better have avoided doing. His real reason
however, was a more belligerent, a more dangerous
one. He had been publicly disgraced that night, and
as he told himself, without fault on his part. But
Eugene and Tracy and Lady Rushcliffe would, while
hotly indignant at the exposure, magnify the scandal,
and heap up his shame upon him.

He wanted, hot-blooded young fool that he was, to
confront them, to defy them, to give back taunt for
taunt; in short, to let loose upon them some of the
passions raging within him which he had so far
managed to control.

When at last, under a misty moon, the ruined gate-house of the old Abbey came in sight, with the soft outline of the low hill behind, it seemed to him as if he had been transported thither in a few seconds. The gate was closed and locked, but Victred knew of a place where it was easy to get over the palings into the grounds. By this means he approached the house through the shrubbery, and got an earlier sight of it than he would otherwise have done. As the terraced steps came suddenly into view, Victred saw that there were two men on them. One, who was lounging on the balustrade, he easily recognised as the Earl : the other, standing a step or two below him, was the obsequious Jerry Coggin.

Victred stopped short at sight of them, cold with a violent chill. He felt quite suddenly that he did not want to meet his cousin to-night—that he hated him too much. As he stood on the edge of the shrubbery, his person scarcely as yet exposed to view, this feeling so took possession of him that he turned and was about to plunge again among the trees, when he came suddenly in contact with another man.

The shock of surprise was so great that Victred involuntarily uttered an exclamation, and before he had had more than time to recognise in the man the agitator Dennis M'Rena, a loud laugh from his cousin announced that he was discovered.

" At last, eh ? " said the Earl, in his most arbitrary tones. " I've been waiting for you. Coggin, fetch the skunk out ; bring him here."

The underling shuffled down the steps, not liking his task. But before he could get half-way across the intervening space, Victred had passed him. In another moment he had mounted the long double flight of steps, and was close to his cousin. In the moonlight Victred saw that Eugene was livid with anger, and that he was working himself up to keep it to a high pitch.

" So you're the fellow that had the infernal cheek to speak disrespectfully of the woman I'm going to

marry! Upon my word, if you hadn't brought such
disgrace upon the family, it would be laughable, that
it would. You, a sneaking humbug, pretending to be
too good for my guests, when you are not fit to sit
with the grooms."

Victred turned, in a hesitating sort of way, towards
the door. His cousin sprang at him, pulling roughly
at his sleeve and raising his voice.

"No, no, you're not going to slink away like that
yet! You want to——"

"I want to go indoors," said Victred, in a muffled
voice, "you have time for all this to-morrow. Let me
go, I say."

He struck his cousin full in the chest, not aggres-
sively, but to free himself. Eugene staggered back
as far as the balustrade. Infuriated by the push, he
went on, with head protruding from between his
shoulders, like a dog on a chain.

"Confound you, you shan't go till you know what
I think of your conduct in exposing me to disgrace,
by bringing that——"

Victred checked himself, as he was about to step
nearer. Clenching his fists which he held straight
down at his sides, he said in the same low voice as
before:

"Hold your tongue. She is my wife, really my
wife, I say. I married her."

There was a sudden break, almost a note of entreaty
in his voice. But Lord Malpas went blundering on:

"More fool you, that's all. And that won't prevent
me from saying that, though she may be good enough
for your society, she is not good enough for mine.
And it's the most infamous thing that ever was heard
of, to bring into the presence of the ladies of my party
a vulgar woman like that——"

He began the word, but he did not finish it. He
had gone too far. The devil's gleam shone in
Victred's eyes as he struck his cousin from his place
on the balustrade, with a force which flung the latter,
head first, down the lower flight of steps.

The very next moment he was shocked at what he had done, as he heard the crash of his cousin's body falling on the stone, and a short, gurgling sound, followed by perfect silence, perfect stillness.

CHAPTER VII.

" Per sua diffalta in pianto ed in affanno
Cambiò l'onesto riso e'l dolce giuco."—DANTE.

" EUGENE ! "

No answer.

"Eugene!" cried Victred in a louder voice. His eyes were fixed upon his cousin's form, lying motionless across the steps below him. But he did not go down to offer to help him to rise. For it was of no use. He knew what he had done; he knew that the attitude in which Lord Malpas lay was not that of a living man. He had killed him.

But although Victred was conscious of this awful fact, he did not yet appreciate it fully. He felt so little beyond a numbing sense that something had happened, that he was surprised to hear that his voice shook as he pronounced his cousin's name. Then, while he still stood staring in the moonlight at the dark heap on the white steps, he was startled by the sound of footsteps on the gravel. Jerry Coggin, too much frightened to come very near, too curious to stay away, had come limping up to within a few yards of the steps. On seeing the Earl's face he began to groan, and utter loud cries.

A sound above him made Victred look up mechanically. Tracy had thrown up his window; and his white face looked livid as he craned his neck to see what happened. After a few moments, he drew in his head quickly and shut down the window without a word. Victred went slowly down the steps and knelt beside his cousin's body. He had touched it, had made sure that the heart had ceased to beat, when he felt a hand on his shoulder. A cold sweat broke out upon him, though he could sarcely have told what he feared.

"An unfortunate business, dear me!" said Dennis's voice, cheery and buoyant as ever.

The tears rushed to Victred's eyes. The friendliness of the Irishman's tone and attitude, suddenly made manifest in this scene of silent horror, seemed to tear the younger man's heart. He looked up quickly at M'Rena, but at first his sight was too dim for him to see clearly. Therefore the shrewd calculation in the eyes of the demagogue escaped him.

"It's a most unfortunate business," said Dennis again.

"You were there? You saw——?" asked Victred hoarsely.

"Well, yes, I—I'm afraid I did. But never mind that. I will be out of the country to-morrow, and anyhow I'll take care to have seen nothing that can do ye any harm. Here's somebody coming. It will be better for you that I shouldn't be caught here just now. I'll see ye again though. And maybe I can be of use to ye in gettin' away—*you* know."

These last words he uttered in a whisper, which Victred, who had risen to his feet, bent down to hear. As the Irishman, who was not unskilled in the art of speedy disappearance, retreated rapidly behind the shrubs, the front door, which the Earl, on coming out of the house, had left ajar, was opened wide enough for Tracy to slink out. He was frightened, horror-struck. It was he, standing irresolute, pallid, in the doorway, who would have been taken for the man-slayer, and not the quiet man at the foot of the steps.

"Wh-what have you done?" he stammered, not venturing far beyond the shelter of the door-way. He had not seen Victred's blow, or the Earl's fall, but he had enough knowledge and imagination to understand what had occurred. "Have you—have you hurt him?" he went on, trying to speak as if he did not know,

" He is dead," said Victred shortly.

Jerry Coggin, creeping up quietly in the background, but keeping well away from the corpse, waited and watched for an opportunity of putting to the best advantage his own knowledge of the affair.

Tracy, whose nerves had been cruelly shaken by this gruesome disturbance of his night's rest, was a little reassured by Victred's apparent calmness. The latter did not, after all, seem dangerous or desperate. He might with safety be approached, Tracy thought. So he came to the balustrade, and looked down.

"Did you do it?" he asked in a whisper.

"Yes. He insulted me—and I struck him. I did not mean to——"

He stopped. There was a long silence. Jerry Coggin came a step nearer.

"Eh, but yer did do it, yer know yer did!" said he half apologetically, and glancing up at Tracy to find out whether he had the moral support of one of his hearers. "Yer stroock aht wi' yer fist joost like as it might be so "—and he illustrated his meaning with a feeble thrust into the air—" And—and yer looked *murder*, that yer did!"

Victred looked down at the little pointed-nosed rat's face, and shuddered. In a moment he saw what he had done in a different light, not as a ghastly, bitterly repented accident, but as the inevitable climax of a deadly hatred, reached just in time to prevent a marriage which might have proved destructive to his own prospects. He turned, leaning against one of the pillars at the bottom of the steps, and looked up at Tracy.

"You—you don't—think—*that*, Tracy, do you?" he said.

The voice was piteous, but the face looked heavy and sullen. The horror of his situation was succeeding to the horror of the deed. He felt benumbed. He had no words ready to his lips, he scarcely had thoughts ready to his mind. Something had happened which deformed the world, that was all he felt.

Tracy was intelligent enough to know that this was not callousness. An impulse of the ready, if shallow sympathy, which made men condone his bad principles, prompted him to reach his hand over the balustrade to his cousin, while the tears not only gushed into his eyes, but ran down his pale cheeks.

"No, no, old man, of course I dhon't. I shouldn't have thought you need ask me! We'll pull you through, never fear!"

Victred's hand, with which he had gripped that of Tracy, fell heavily at his side. For his cousin's very words implied the danger he was in.

"You don't think, do you," he asked again, "that anybody but that miserable mud-grubber there," indicating Coggin with a contemptuous gesture, "would say, would even think that it was anything but an awful—frightful accident?"

"No, no, certainly not," answered Tracy vehemently. "And as for you, you miserable skulking old ruffian," he went on, turning to Jerry, "you had better take yourself off and hide your miserable carcase in some rat-hole, till you learn the proper way to talk to gentlemen."

The underling was shuffling off without a word, when he was stopped, and the two gentlemen were startled, by a harsh voice crying:

"Stay where you are."

Tracy took the voice for that of a man, but Victred knew better. As the latter stood facing the house, he had seen a strange figure approaching the balustrade, a figure he did not know. It was clothed in grey flannel; the face also looked grey, and it was lined, withered, and ugly. Strands of rough, coarse, unnatural-looking hair escaped from a knot at the back of the neck. A more complete contrast to the trim, even-tempered Lady Rushcliffe of the day than this hard-faced, harsh-voiced virago of the night it would have been impossible to find. Her real age was as well concealed as ever. For whereas in her close-fitting gown, with her face exquisitely tinted,

and trained to a pleasant suavity, she looked ten
years younger than her age, which was thirty-five,
now, with her face distorted by base passions, she
might have passed for fifty.

"Stay where you are," she repeated fiercely, to the
frightened Coggin, who shuffled from one foot to the
other, uncertain what to do.

"Sh—sh," said Tracy. "We don't want to have
the servants up."

"But we do, and we will," cried she, in a still louder
voice. "This is a murder, yes, a murder I say," she
repeated vehemently. 'And it is not going to be
hushed up. *You*," and she pointed with a lean finger,
like a hungry hag, at the silent living man standing
below her with his eyes on the silent dead one. "You
murdered your cousin. You hated him, you always
hated him, and you've killed him to prevent his
marrying me, and injuring your chance of becoming
Earl. But you went too fast, too fast, and now you
will never live to be Earl, for — you — will — be —
hanged."

Victred listened, or seemed to listen, without a
movement or an interruption ; but Tracy was shocked,
and he showed his feeling in convulsive movements
of his limbs and the muscles of his face. He made
several attempts to interrupt her, calling her by her
Christian name. They had been close allies, he and
she, having discovered a happy similarity of tastes
and ambitions. This night, however, she had revealed
too much, and he was appalled by the thinness of the
veneer which covered the vindictive shrew.

"Emmeline, Lady Rushcliffe, consider. Pray, consider the family," said he, in the tone of one rebuking
a blasphemer.

But she only turned upon him with a hard, mocking laugh.

"The family ! What family ! Whose family ?
Why should I consider it ? *It is not mine !*"

The last four words summed up all the rankling
bitterness in the woman's mind. Rank, social position,

all that to her meant happiness, had in a moment
faded together out of sight. The death of Lord
Malpas was to her not the loss of a tenderly loved
one, but the downfall of her ambition. In the shock
of it she became honest, and forgot even the decent
show of mourning for the dead. The shameless
cynicism of her attitude in this respect moved Victred
out of the torpor which hung upon both mind and
senses. He looked up at her.

"Are you a woman," said he, "that you can think
of that now?"

She sprang a step forward, and passing Tracy,
leaned over the balustrade, her features distorted by
anger, and called imperiously to Coggin, who was
watching her intently out of his small cunning eyes.

"Did you, or did you not see this man kill Lord
Malpas?" she asked in the same loud hard voice.

"I did, your ladyship, I saw him throw his lordship
down like as you might fell an ox."

"And do you dare deny this man's testimony?"
she went on, turning to Victred.

"I don't deny it. But I deny before God that I
meant to—to kill him," answered the unhappy man
vehemently, but in a muffled dreary tone.

"I'm afraid a judge won't give you much credit
for your good intentions," returned she, with a laugh
which made even Tracy shudder. "Coggin, come up
here. I have an errand for you."

"No, no, no. Be reasonable. Listen, Emmeline,"
interposed Tracy in great excitement. "Victred is a
Speke, a member of the best family in the county.
Do you think the word of a low ruffian like that," with
a contemptuous gesture in the direction of Coggin,
"would weigh with a magistrate against my
cousin's?"

Her tone and manner suddenly changed. All the
fiery indignation she had shown seemed to die down
in her, giving place to a deliberate coldness and hard-
ness compared to which even her steely anger had
been a mild and agreeable manifestation.

"*His* word may not be of much weight," said she slowly, "but what about *mine* ?"

"Yours!" cried Tracy, startled. "But you—what did you see—hear?"

"Everything. Perhaps you forget that my room is on this side of the house. I heard the Earl reproach his cousin for his marriage. I heard Victred Speke retort, threatening to murder—mind murder was the word he used—threatening to murder him if he said any more about it. Lord Malpas began another remonstrance, and was cut short by the blow which killed him."

'Is this true, Victred?" asked Tracy doubtfully.

'No," answered Victred, without passion, almost as it seemed, without interest.

"Coggin," called Lady Rushcliffe to the underling, who had crept nearer to the balustrade, "is it true?"

"Ay, your ladyship!"

"I think, Mr. Fitzalan," she went on tranquilly, "even you will own *presently*, that the testimony of two eye-witnesses is not to be despised."

With these words she descended the steps, and with a partial return to the feminine grace of her every-day manner, threw herself on her knees beside the dead man. But it was too late to persuade either of the spectators that she felt any grief for the loss of the man himself. There was nothing convincing in the affectation of tenderness with which she wrung her hands.

"We—we must take him in," said Tracy to his cousin in an undertone.

Victred bowed his head. Lady Rushcliffe sprang up theatrically.

"You shall not touch him," she cried. "Are you not satisfied with what your hands have done to him?"

Victred, was, however, impervious to such taunts as hers.

Motioning to her with his hands to stand aside, he helped Tracy to raise the body, and in doing so dis-

5

covered that the Earl's death had been caused by the breaking of his neck. They carried him indoors and up to his bedroom, where Victred, like one stunned, stood looking at the lifeless form of the man who had hated him.

"Don't—don't look like that," whispered Tracy hoarsely. "You make my flesh creep."

"It wouldn't be so bad," said Victred below his breath, "if I had *cared* for him. As it is, I almost feel —as if that woman's words were true."

"Oh, nonsense: Come along. These are only morbid fancies, you know," said Tracy, hastily, as he pulled his cousin out of the room.

There were stealthy sounds about the house which betrayed the fact that some at least of the servants had been roused by the disturbances of the night, and were listening in remote corners. The rush of cold air up the staircase told Tracy that the front-door was still open, and he heard, muffled by distance, Lady Rushcliffe's strident tones.

"Go to your room, old man, and we'll decide what is best to be done in the morning," said Tracy to his cousin. "I must run down and get that awful woman to shut her mouth."

Mechanically, Victred went to his room. It was at the back of the house, and next to May's, and through the wall he could hear the girl's violent sobbing. At this sound, the young man's heart seemed to thaw within him; the dazed look on his face disappeared, and the tears rushed to his own eyes. For the first time he felt what it was that he had done, what a barrier his own act had set up between his past and his future life. Poor May was weeping her heart out because he was burdened with a worthless and vulgar wife; there in her little room, with her head buried in a pillow which was wet with her tears, no rumour of the scene which had had its climax in her brother's death had reached her ears. To-morrow she would learn everything, and her tears would be dried up with horror. Victred felt a keener pang, as this thought crossed his mind, than he had ever expected to experience at the hands of his half-despised little cousin. The horror within him, the biting remorse, yielded to grief in which there was more of sentiment. Here, outlawed as he felt he was, he heard for the last time sobs of tender, womanly pity for him. He sat down by his window and buried his face in his hands.

Meanwhile, Tracy had gone in search of Lady Rushcliffe. He found her standing alone by the stone balustrade, watching with hard keen eyes a retreating figure which was not that of Jerry Coggin. Tracy threw upon her a sharp glance of suspicion.

"Who's that? Have you been talking to him?" he asked, putting the second question quickly on the heels of the first.

"You know who it is, I suppose?" said she coldly. "He has gone for the police."

"The police! How dared you?" cried Tracy, in hot anger. "I would have thought, Lady Rushcliffe, you understood your duty as a guest better than that."

"I understand my duty as *fiancée* of a man who has been murdered," answered she deliberately; "and I mean to have the murderer punished."

"Well, luckily your messenger knows better than to fulfil such a mad errand. Dennis M'Rena would not dare to injure a cousin of mine."

Indeed Dennis, for the messenger was he, had stopped to see the upshot of this conversation, and was watching them in the moonlight by the bend in the drive. Tracy beckoned to him and Dennis began to move slowly towards them. Lady Rushcliffe laughed cynically.

"It is very generous of you, Tracy, to spare your rival. That man has just told me that you and Victred Speke are, to use his own expression, both "sweet on his daughter.'"

Tracy's face changed.

"He told you that?" said he, in a low voice;

5*

adding quickly : " Nonsense, Victred's never seen the girl ! "

" Yes, he has.   On Crossley Ridge, so this fellow says, last night.   You remember that Victred went away yesterday afternoon, and did not return until nearly two o'clock this morning ? "

Tracy did remember, and his pink and white face grew ashy grey, while his whole body shook like a leaf.

" Let him go," he whispered at last hoarsely ; " let Dennis go for the police then ! "

Lady Rushcliffe uttered again her harsh little laugh, as she signed with her hand to Dennis to go on his way.

He seemed to hesitate for one moment ; and then quickly disappeared behind the shrubs of the drive.

CHAPTER VIII.

" My friend was already too good to lose,
   And seemed in the way of improvement yet,
   When she crossed his path with her hunting-noose
   And over him drew her net."
                                        —BROWNING.

WHILE the pitiful sound of poor May's sobbing still reached his ears at intervals through the wall, Victred sat by the window with his head in his hands until his fingers grew stiff with the cold.   Then a gentle tapping on the pane aroused him and made him look up.   A man's head, which he recognised at once by its enormous hat, was close to the window.

Victred pushed the sash up.   Dennis had climbed up by the ivy, which grew thick and strong on this, the oldest side of the house, and was clinging to the window-sill.

" Look here," whispered the agitator, " I've got a gig waiting outside.   That woman's in earnest.   The police will be here before morning.   She's sent that loafer Coggin to Cheston, not altogether trusting me. Come away with me ! "

"No," said Victred doggedly; "I'll take the responsibility of my own acts."

"Then you'll take a rope round your neck, me bhoy!"

Victred moved restlessly.

"Well, why not, if they can prove I deserve it?"

"Well, when you've been hanged, it won't be much consolation to feel that you didn't."

"What do you mean—when I've been hanged!" said Victred surlily. "You know very well no jury would bring it in more than manslaughter!"

"I mean that the gentle lady downstairs, whose chance of becoming Countess of Malpas you have destroyed, is ready to swear anything to be revenged on you. And you know what chance a man has against a woman with a jury!"

"*She* wouldn't have had much if the jury had seen her to-night!"

"No, but what they will see is a slender creature in deep mourning, bowed down with sorrow, choked with tears (which she won't shed, mind—because crying spoils the complexion), who gives her evidence reluctantly but straight to the point. Come, is this true, or isn't it? Because I can't stay here, hanging on by the eyelashes, all night."

"Yes, it's true enough, but——"

"But what?"

"What am I to do? Where can I go? Besides, to slink away would be to confess myself guilty."

"Well, you are guilty—to the extent that you've killed him. It's penal servitude at least."

"I—I suppose it is."

His voice shook: for the prospect was not pleasing.

"Come away with me then. It will give you time to think things over at any rate. To-morrow your chance even of that will be gone."

Victred debated with himself for one minute. Then he nodded.

"All right," he muttered in the rapid whisper in

which they had held the whole of their conversation,
" I'll join you outside."

Without another word, Dennis, with his usual
promptitude, dropped down upon the grass below
and ran off towards the road outside. Victred began
hastily to put some clothes into a portmanteau. With
that clearing of the brain which results from the
taking of a decisive action, he used a nice discrimination as to what he should, and to what he should not
take. He changed his clothes, for he was in the
evening dress in which he had been to the ball, and
put on the thickest suit he had, in view of a cold
drive. Then he held a review of his boots and shoes,
and chose the strongest. Next he packed his dress-
ing-case, and, after debating whether he should want
his razors, or whether he should let his beard grow,
he decided to take them, as they were a nice set and
he could sell them if they were unnecessary. He
even remembered where he had put some tooth-
brushes which he had mislaid. When the necessaries
had all been packed, a more difficult task of selection
began, and sentiment, that accursed sentiment, proceeded to make havoc of convenience and common
sense. The " Shakespeare," which had been a school-
prize—which represented a hard-fought battle and
had been valued by him accordingly, was it to go or
not ? With a pang he said no : it was big and bulky.

On the other hand, a little damaged terra-cotta
bust of some classical celebrity whom he had never
been able to identify, must have a corner found for it
among the socks. Memory connected the little
worthless thing with his dead mother, by means of
some half-forgotten incident of his childhood. The
slender-handed lady, with tender brown eyes, rose up,
a dim but sacred figure in his mind ; and he blessed
God that she had not lived until this day. For his
father he cared comparatively little ; a cold-faced,
cold-mannered valetudinarian, of strict principles and
reserved habits, it struck Victred as almost laughable
that he should have such a delinquent son. How-

ever, he paused over a framed photograph of that father, asking himself whether he should take it with him. He decided to take it, without the frame. " It might prove a means of identification, and save the coroner trouble," he said to himself bitterly.

The other trifling treasures, which he was in the habit of carrying about in his luggage, he had to leave behind ; so in order that his sentimental weakness should not be discovered after his departure, he re-opened the window, and threw the rest of the things out, one by one ; a book into the cabbage-bed of the kitchen-garden, his writing-case into a clump of laurel ; a brass calendar-frame (a present from a girl) alone failed to reach a hiding-place, and fell, bent and broken, on the edge of a gravel walk. They were all chance-shots, as the shadows cast by the moon among the ruins were so black ; but fate did fairly well for them.

Out of the book, before he threw it, he drew a book-marker, with " Many happy returns of the day," worked in silk on perforated card-board, an old gift wrought in May's clumsy fingers when she was nine. This he took with him, with a tender thought of the silly, devoted girl in the next room.

He heard her sobs no longer ; she was asleep, poor child, most likely. After a moment's hesitation, he wrote in pencil, on a leaf torn out of his pocket-book, the following words :

" You are a silly little girl to trouble your head about me, and you will be ashamed of yourself to-morrow. God bless you, May, and send a good fellow to love you and take care of you. Good-bye. Mind, you will hate me to-morrow, and you will be quite right. Good-bye."

He did not sign this message, but he slipped it between the leaves of the " Shakespeare," and put the book under the mat outside her door. Then he carried his portmanteau downstairs.

Tracy opened his bedroom door as he passed. The lamp which burned at night in the corridor showed Victred the change to undisguised malice and dislike in his cousin's face when he saw who the disturber was.

This sight amazed Victred. He turned back to knock at Tracy's door. There was no answer, but when he knocked a second time, he heard the key turned in the lock. Utterly puzzled by his cousin's change of attitude towards him, Victred, knowing that he had no time to lose, reached the front door and went out of the house, with his head bent and his brows contracted, a fugitive and an outlaw.

He made himself the excuse of a short cut to the road, that he might throw one glance of farewell towards the window of his only friend, the girl who loved him. May was not asleep. She had heard Victred moving about the house and closing the front door, and she had opened her window and was peering out into the darkness. The moon was at this moment partially obscured by clouds, but Victred could dimly see the white face of the girl, who was still in her ball-dress, as she leaned across the ivy. She did not see him ; he did not want her to see him. With a sharp prick of some vivid sensation, whether of pleasure or pain he did not know, he turned and went quietly away.

He found Dennis waiting in a gig outside the grounds, and he got up with his portmanteau after the interchange of a very few words. It was not until they had started at a brisk pace along the road towards Accrington that Victred, who was sitting with folded arms, and his head on his breast, asked:

" Where are we going to ? "

" Clough."

" And what do you propose to do with me ? "

" Well, we can't do much at first but lie close and see if it blows over. My Lady Spitfire may be ashamed of herself to-morrow morning, and set herself to undo the mischief she's already done."

" I don't think it's likely."

" To tell the truth, no more do I. Still, as it's only
the wicked that fleeth when no man pursueth, we'll
wait and watch the turn of events. I was going to
Dublin to-morrow, but I can put that off."

Astonishment at this sacrifice roused Victred com-
pletely.

" But why, why should you do this for me, a
stranger ? " he asked.

Dennis laughed.

" Ah, well, maybe you'll be useful some day," he
said. And again Victred noticed that look of far-
away scheming cunning in the shrewd, humorous
eyes, which had repelled him before. " Any way
there's no denying you've rid the land of a nuisance."

Victred shuddered.

" My cousin's doings provided you with an excuse
for agitation, at any rate," he said.

" Ye-es, I grant you that," said Dennis imperturbably. " But really that wasn't reason enough for
him to live."

" He was part of a system which remains the
same now he is gone. My innocent and well-mean-
ing old father will make just as bad a landlord as
he did."

" So much the worse for your father, and so much
the better for 'the Cause.' Every bad landlord is a
nail in the coffin of the old system."

" And what do you intend to replace the old system
with ? "

" Time enough to think about that when the first
part of the work is done."

" And don't you think you may do as much harm
by the way as any of your bad landlords ? "

" No, sir, I don't. But if I did, I should go on just
the same."

" Now that speech you made at the Nab the other
night was fustian, you know, rank fustian."

" Sure, don't I know ut ? What's the good of
jumping as high as a house to get over a two-foot

wall ?   Where fustian's good enough, why waste anything better ? "

"That doesn't sound as if your democratic sentiments
went very deep."

"It's on account of the misdeeds of your class that
these wretched serfs are incapable of understanding
anything but fustian."

" Then why are you befriending a member of my
class ? "

"Because by your own deed you belong to it
no longer." Victred's heart seemed to stand still ;
it was as if he heard his own funeral knell.   All
his sentiments, sympathies, tastes, and preju-
dices rose in revolt as the agitator went on :
"Socially, at least, you are outlawed.   Whether
you like it or not, you are at war with society,
because society is at war with you.   You have
become one of us."

" No," protested Victred stoutly ; " I have broken
the law by a horrible accident.   You do it syste-
matically and with intention.   There is all the
difference in the world between us."

" But the difference is not all in your favour.   We
act upon principle, you from passion.   Anyhow,
although the starting-point is different, you will soon
go by the same road."

Victred sank into sombre silence.   Was life, any
life which would be tolerable to an honest man, indeed
closed to him ?   If so, why not go back, give one's-
self up, and at least have the satisfaction of facing the
penalty of one's own act like a man ?   But then the
false witness of the revengeful Lady Rushcliffe and
the time-serving Coggin might bring upon him a
penalty which he felt he did not deserve—the shame-
ful felon's death.

The gig travelled fast.   Accrington was passed, and
the little lonely village of Clough reached, in less than
an hour.

"Go in quietly," said Dennis, as he handed him the
door-key of the cottage where he was staying, "into

the front room. Jack is in the back room ; we must not wake him."

The one word " Jack " fell upon Victred's ears with bewildering effect. He had forgotten her, altogether forgotten, in the stress of the night's events, the little fragile creature with the inspired eyes, who had filled his thoughts during the whole of the preceding day. He entered the house as softly as a thief, full of such a sense of his own unworthiness as he had not felt even when writing the farewell note to his cousin May. He opened the door of the front room, a poor little apartment with a deal table spread for one person's supper. In the grate was a dying fire, and before it was one of the high wooden rocking-chairs without which no Lancashire cottage is complete. He sat down and hung shivering over the red embers, lost in thought.

With a dull sense that the end of all things was come, he let his mind wander through the scenes of his past life : the death of his mother, and the consequent sense of the coldness and emptiness of the whole world ; the increase of this feeling when his father repulsed his shy, boyish approaches ; how Letty, the great Norfolk dairymaid, had consoled him with frantic hugs, which dealt bruises to the body, but balm to the mind ; Harrow, Oxford—Ah, there was the plague-spot!

It was in his first year that he had met Louisa Brett, holding the equivocal position of barmaid and principal attraction at a small public-house which was a favourite resort of the rowing-men. She was then not more than sixteen, exquisitely pretty, passing for more than her real age on account of the assurance of her manners and the early development of her figure. He fell in love with her at once, as did most of the frequenters of the place. But the difference between him and the rest lay in this, that she did, in a shallow but effusive sort of way, fall in love with him.

The acquaintance ripened quickly ; so did the love.

Then who was the tempter and who the tempted is not easy to say. The girl yielded at once, being little more than a beautiful animal, with caprices and impulses of passion. The real fall came later, when Victred Speke, full of remorse, burning to atone, and still in love, married her, and tried to raise her to his own level.

As well have tried on a kitten. Indeed, the kitten, when it reaches mature cat-hood, has a dignity and a sense of responsibility to which Louisa would never attain. The poor thing found the restraints of education and decorum, which her young husband tried to impose upon her, intolerable. She sighed for the "chaff" of the "Seven Stars," or even for the less violent delights of her father's fried-fish shop at Hornsey Rise. Victred was jealous with the frantic jealousy of twenty; and under the hot blasts of syntax and suspicion her short but fierce passion for him died quickly down. She developed new faults, became secretive and untruthful, and took to watching him furtively out of her long eyes, in a manner which maddened him. For, like all handsome eyes, those of Louisa seemed to express much more than their owner was capable of thinking or of feeling. And, when he tried to find out what was in her heart or in her mind, the only answer he could get was "Nothing"—which was generally the truth, though he could not believe it.

Of course she was vulgar, but it was not her fault. Neither was it Victred's fault that her vulgarity irritated him. It is really a trifle to eat shrimps whole, and to call them s'rimps; but when these deeds are committed by one's own wife, the trifle becomes a tragedy. Again, the transposition of the aspirate is consistent with the possession of all the virtues; and he might have known that there is no devout cult of the letter " H " at Hornsey Rise. Nevertheless, Louisa's sins of omission and commission in this particular weighed heavily upon Victred's soul.

Still, in spite of occasional exhibitions of impatience, and of a too lively educational zeal, Victred behaved pretty well, acknowledged to himself that the blame of the whole affair was his, and still worked on towards an ideal atonement. Even when her ever increasing coldness towards him found expression in sulky silence, or in jarring taunts, when disgust was rapidly bringing about the wane of his own affection, he struggled on in his sensible determination to stick to her, and to make the best of her.

Quite gently he remonstrated with her leaning to feathers ; tenderly he strove to prove that coloured glass ornaments, set in brass, add nothing to the power of beauty.

" Oh, nonsense," said she ; " they're just as ' showy ' as real ones, and much cheaper."

And she was satisfied that she had made out her case.

But Victred was not yet convinced that the task he had set himself was a hopeless one. He would take her abroad, to some town in Germany or Italy which was an art centre, where they could live cheaply, where the very atmosphere would refine her. There, being unknown, he would feel less keenly her initial social mistakes, and would be more indulgent over them. And then, when her education was completed, which, he argued, having heard much of the mental quickness of women, would be very soon, he would bring her back to England, the accomplished wife of a proud husband, and they would live happy ever after.

Then Louisa destroyed all these carefully laid plans by running away from him. Victred found the following note, written on a well-thumbed half-sheet of his note-paper, which she had folded very small, on the sitting-room table of the lodging which he had taken for her :

" DEAR VIC—" (she would call him Vic, not being able to get on without a nick-name)—" I have 'ad enough of this so I am gone I 'ave gone back to mother at Hornsey Rise! I cannot stand haveing potrey read to me it is only a long buzz buzz to me an will never be anything else so now you know—I dont know why you married me Im sure I never wanted you too an it don't suit me an no more it does you by the looks of you—Anyhow Im gone an I dont want to hear any more from you unless you prommise to give up teaching me things I cant learn and let me dress as I like an see people an talk has I ave been used to. You left your purse on the drawers so I have taken all but five shillings which I have left I do not give my adress has I want some piece and quiteness but if you write through the seven Stars they will send it on.

" Your afecttionate wife,
." LOUISA."

"Poscrip—I could have eld out another month if it hadent ave been for the potrey, but when you took to that I said to myself chuck it."

That letter caused the scales to fall from Victred's eyes. She had been conscious of no wrong; she had craved no atonement. He had been living in a fantastic air - palace, peopled with phantoms of womanly feeling, feminine delicacy, restored honour and self-respect; and now his wife was gone, and the phantoms proved to be phantoms indeed.

He did not try to follow her; but he wrote, as she had directed, through "The Seven Stars," informing her that as long as she lived with her mother he would make her an allowance, and to that end she could send her address to his lawyer, whose name he gave. Then the mother herself came to Oxford to see him; and Victred, though at first appalled by his own action in taking to himself a relation who would have passed for the washerwoman, was soon forced to acknowledge that in all the finer feelings with which he had mentally endowed her daughter,

Mrs. Brett was infinitely Louisa's superior. She was very quiet and respectful, expressed gratitude for his honourable behaviour towards her daughter, but was not hopeful as to his chances of domestic happiness in the future.

"You might have knocked me down with a feather, sir, when Louisa bounced in and told us as how she'd married a gentleman. And I wouldn't believe it, no more didn't her father, till we'd seen her marriage lines. And I tell you I was sorry, sir, for unequal marriages like don't answer, as I know well. But I'll do the best I can for her, sir, and maybe if you'll have a little patience I'll bring her round and get her to come back to you. But she's a wilful creature, sir, as ever trod shoe-leather, and gives a power of trouble. And here's thanking you kindly for seeing me, and wishing you a good-day, sir."

She was only too anxious to hurry away, and Victred followed her to the door to ask if it would be of any use for him to come and see his wife.

"Dear me, no, sir," answered Mrs. Brett hastily, " I —I don't think as it would do any good, but more likely harm. She seems that bitter against you at present, sir, and ten times as flighty and wilful as before she were married. Good-morning, sir."

So Victred let her go.

In the four years that followed he never once saw his wife, never once heard from her, and, truth to tell, he soon began to acquiesce in the expediency of this arrangement, although he made a point of honour of writing from time to time, asking her to come back to him. The mother always wrote a respectful note of thanks in return for the quarterly allowance made to her daughter: but beyond a brief mention that she was well, she gave no details about Louisa.

And Victred had grown reconciled to his enforced bachelor's life, and had even become something of a misogynist, when the abrupt appearance of his wife, at Cheston Town Hall, led to the committal of the act which had cut him off from his kindred, and his kind.

Still brooding over these past events, by the fire in Dennis's cottage sitting-room, Victred heard the agitator enter the house softly, and go up the stairs. Then he heard him moving about overhead. But soon the sounds grew fainter in the young man's tired ears, and before many minutes had passed, he sank, with his head on his breast, into an uneasy and unrestful sleep.

Ugly visions floated in his mind, born of his despondent waking thoughts. They gave place, however, presently to a feeling of rest, of solace, which seemed to spread its balm through every weary nerve. It was his dead mother, surely, who was hovering over him, whispering in his ears.

"Poor boy," said the voice, "he is so tired, he looks so unhappy. I should like to stay with him, to comfort him. Poor, poor boy."

A shiver ran through Victred's frame, not of horror, not of shame, such as he had felt many a time that night; but a thrill which brought warmth into every frozen vein. He seemed to feel in a moment the weight lifted, which had oppressed his spirit even in sleep. He threw himself forward, suddenly, with his arms outstretched, and a cry upon his lips.

Then a more material shock awoke him.

He had fallen from the rocking-chair against the table. The vision was gone. But as he stared stupidly before him, he saw the door softly shut.

He started up, and would have crossed the room. But at the second staggering, sleep-heavy step he took, he heard the slamming of the front door. The next moment a dark object stood outside his window in the faint dawn. He had only to turn to see that the object was a human form. One step nearer, one more look, and with his whole being throbbing with a strange excitement, he recognised the little white face of "Red Jack." She was in her boy's dress, rough frieze coat and round felt hat; but at that moment, as, still only half awake, he stared into her great brown eyes, it seemed to him impossible that any one should doubt that the tenderness and pity he saw there were those of a woman.

Dennis was, however, only a few steps behind. Victred had only exchanged one glance with the girl, when her father, nodding hastily to the young man, drew " Red Jack " away by passing his hand through her arm. Victred hurried, stumbling, to the outer door. The cold dawn of a winter morning was showing, in their most desolate aspect, the bleak moors and the barren hills beyond. From the cotton factories the long shrill wail of the steam-whistles was summoning the " hands " to their dreary toil. The clogs were beginning to clatter on the stones. Down the hill towards the station, without a look behind, went the two figures, the little one at a trot keeping pace with the big one's stride.

Victred shivered as he turned away, feeling that he was an outcast indeed, when even Dennis M'Rena threw him over, and stole away from him in the darkness.

CHAPTER IX.

" Pansies let my flowers be :
    On the living grave I bear,
Scatter them without a tear ;
    Let no friend, however dear,
Waste a hope, a fear, for me."

—SHELLEY.

WHEN the two figures were out of sight, Victred sank again into the chair from which he had risen. As he did so, a note directed to him in a man's handwriting, which had been left on the table, caught his eye. He opened and read it :

" I will be back this evening, and by that time, if I find things are shaping badly, I will have found a place for you to go to. Meantime lie close and keep up your courage. Burn this.—D."

6

The fire was out, but Victred lit a match and
burned the scrap of paper. Then he buttoned his
coat and went out, passing the landlady, who wished
him " Good-morning," and let him go without comment. It was evident that her erratic tenants had
accustomed her to mysterious visitors.

He took the road back to Maleigh, and reached the
village while it was still very early. People, the
people he knew and who knew him, looked at him
askance, he thought. Still he went on in the direction
of the Abbey gates until a man who was ostler and
general help at one or two of the inns of the village,
after following him some time in silence, came up with
him, saluting him respectfully.

" Axing yer pardon, sir, but Ah wouldn't be going
to t' Abbey just now, if Ah was you."

Victred stopped short, and looked down into the
man's wrinkled face, which was eloquent with com-
passion and fear.

" Why not ? "

" Well, sir, there's teales goin' about, an'—an' the
police is there, and that Lady Rooshcliffe makin' a
great bother."

" All right. Thank you for the hint. Good-
morning."

Victred took a by-path that led towards Cheston,
and walked on as if in a dream. To be getting out
of every one's way like a hunted beast was a curious
sensation : the seriousness of his own danger was
already deadening his sense of remorse at what he
had done. Now his principal feeling was wonder at
the smallness of the cause which had led to such a
tragic result. Eugene had spoken insultingly to him,
but that was nothing ; he was always insulting everybody. He had spoken insultingly of Victred's wife ;
but she had been his wife only in name for four years,
and Victred could scarcely believe that Eugene's coarse
expressions wronged her. But in that reckless mood
in which, feeling saturated with misfortune, a man
courts interviews which at any other time he would

shirk and avoid, Victred never paused until he reached the hotel at which he had left his wife on the preceding evening.

"Mrs. Speke is in the coffee-room, sir. There's a young lady with her," said the waiter. "Lady May Speke I think it is, sir. She has just gone in."

Victred was startled by this information. Such a headstrong freak as this he would not have expected of his languid, melancholy cousin. He was rather nervous as to the upshot of a meeting between two such strongly-contrasted women, the one refined, sensitive, emotional; the other coarse in feeling, manner and language.

He could not even hear the sound of their voices. There was an alcove in the dark passage into which the coffee-room opened. Standing back in it, he waited, with more anxiety than he had thought himself capable of feeling in his present condition, for the women to come out. It was not long before the door of the coffee-room opened, and May's tall, lean, stooping figure appeared in the dim light of the doorway. By her side was Louisa, resplendent in feathers. The latter, in spite of a whipered "Sh-sh!" from her companion, was still talking.

"He 'asn't been such a devoted husband that you need have expected he would fly here, I can tell you," she was saying in a loud hoarse whisper. "But there, it's knocked me all of a heap what you've told me, that it has. And I do thank you kindly for what you've done and what you've promised. And I will say this, that——"

The rest of the sentence was lost as the two women turned into the front hall. A few moments later, Louisa returned alone. She was so busy peeping at something she held in her hand that, in the obscurity of the passage, she ran against Victred, who had come out of the alcove to meet her. She uttered a short scream, and as she started back, something fell from

her right hand to the ground.   By the chink Victred
learned that it was money.

"Come in here a moment," he said quietly, opening
the door of the coffee-room.

Subdued as his manner was, she was so much
frightened that she did not even look for her lost
coin, but passed at once into the room, with a shrink-
ing manner, and proceeding almost to the end of the
apartment, turned sharply, and watched his approach
with furtive eyes that did not travel further up than
his boots.

"What did my cousin come to see you about?" he
asked, stopping short some paces away from her.

"To find if you were here, I think.   And to
find out if I was really your wife, too perhaps.   So I
showed her my marriage lines, and she looked at 'em
as if she wished they'd been hers," added Louisa,
venturing upon a short laugh.

"Anything else?" asked Victred, cutting her
amusement short.

"Well, she's a nice lady, regular tip-top, and no
pride nor anything.   And she said if I wanted for
anything I was to write to her; for you were like a
brother to her more than a cousin, she said; and
nothing was too good for your wife no more than it
was for you."

"Anything else?" asked Victred in a lower voice,
turning towards the nearest window, with a lump in
his throat.

Louisa hesitated.   Glancing at her, he saw that she
was regarding him with wide-open startled eyes, and
that the bright colour came and went in her cheeks.

"Anything else?   Did she tell you anything else—
about me?" he asked slowly.

The woman's nostrils dilated with agitation as,
after one glance towards the distant door, as if mea-
suring her chance of escape, she answered :

"Oh, I—I daren't say it."

"Did she say that I had done anything—strange
last night!"

"She said that you—you—had"—her voice sank to a whisper, "had *killed* your cousin, the Earl!"

But it was evident that the enormity of the crime was so much increased in Louisa's eyes by the rank of the victim that the story seemed to her scarcely credible.

Victred remained silent for a short time. May knew what he had done then; and in the face of that knowledge, she cared for him enough to hunt out the woman he had married and to offer help for his sake. But for his wife's presence he would have sobbed. Her voice, in a hoarse whisper close behind him, startled him and caused him to turn round.

"Is it true then? Oh, is it true?"

"Yes," said he shortly. "My cousin accused me of having married a woman of light character, and I was fool enough to resent what was, I suppose, only a statement of the truth."

And he cast on her a contemptuous glance. But she did not receive his speech with cynical laughter, or with an outburst of indignant and vituperative denial as he had expected. Her face altered strangely; some deeper feeling than he had supposed her capable of, than indeed she had been capable of four years ago, surged in her bosom and burned in her eyes.

"Vic," she said suddenly, in a gasping, strangled voice, which betrayed the creature utterly unused to place any check upon her feelings, "why did you marry me? I was never the wife for you, let alone you being a gentleman and me out of a fried-fish shop! Why did you do it, I say?" And she stamped her foot. "Look here, it wasn't good for *me*, no more than it was for you!"

"Very likely. But we need not trouble our heads about that now. I suppose," and he gave her a searching glance, under which she had the grace to hang her head—"I suppose I could set myself free by making a few inquiries. And I suppose I should if I were in a different position. As it is, it would

very likely be impossible for me to come forward,
and in any case my freedom would be of no use to
me.   As for you, perhaps I am not wronging you in
supposing that you couldn't be any more free than
you are."

"You can suppose what you like," said she sullenly,
but with an undernote of serious intensity that was
quite new to him.

It caused him to look at her again.   And then he
saw that it was not the seemingly shallow creature of
four years ago, the restless, heartless girl whom no
devotion had ever touched, who stood before him
now.   With the loss of her beauty's first freshness
had come a meaning in the great eyes, a passion in
the lines of the sensuous mouth, which fascinated his
attention, but repelled his sympathy.   The change
caused a strange comparison to dart into his mind :
the cubs of wild beasts are harmless, playful creatures in their immature state, with no worse faults
than caprice and the cruelty which consists of ignorance of their own powers for harm.   It is not until
they attain full age that their innate untamable
savagery shows itself.   And this woman before him
was the wild animal arrived at maturity.

They looked at each other with direct glances of
deliberate curious interest for the space of full three
minutes.   Then she suddenly ran forward, clasping
her hands, and speaking still in a whisper, with passionate earnestness.

"Look here," she said, "come to London with me.
Let me hide you.   Nobody shall ever find you, I
swear it.   Trust me for that.   And oh !   Don't turn
away like that !   I won't come near you there : I'll
tell nobody who you are, and who I am.   But I'll do
this to show you I do feel something for the way
you've treated me.   I do, and I'll show it."

She saw that she was pleading in vain, that her
offers, her entreaties only repelled him ; and again
the light of passion in her face gave place to sullenness.

"Thank you," said he, "I am going abroad. Your allowance will be paid as usual. But I warn you I shall have stricter inquiries made as to how you are conducting yourself."

He turned abruptly, without leave-taking, and walked straight up the long room to the door. He felt humiliated by the woman's offers, with the suspicions which he now entertained of her rankling in his breast.

As he reached the door, he felt her hot, moist hand thrust into his. She was shaking with an overwhelming torrent of most genuine passion.

"Don't leave me like that. Just a word! Give me a kiss, Vic, just one? I'll never affront you by owning myself as your wife again, if you'll remember it just this once. What? What? You'd kiss that long, whey-faced girl, I'll bet, if she asked you!" And a flash of real jealousy, as distinguished from the sham emotion of the preceding night, shot from her great blue eyes, "Oh, if you knew how sorry I am, how bad I feel about you, you wouldn't be so hard!"

"I'm not hard," said Victred.

And it was true. He bent down and kissed, not without a feeling of repulsion, the red, sensitive lips on which his soul had once hung in all the frenzy of a lad's first strong passion. She was not satisfied, but she felt that against such indifference she was powerless.

"Good-bye, Vic," said she.

"Good-bye," said he.

And so he left her.

CHAPTER X.

" So farewell hope : and with hope, farewell fear."
                                                    —MILTON.

THE smoke-cloud which generally hangs over the
cotton towns was dense above Cheston as Victred
Speke came out from the hotel into the High Street.

He turned to the left, which was the way to the
station, but without any definite idea as to where he
was going. Presently he felt an arm drawn through
his, and he was dragged rapidly out of the stream
of passengers into a side street. It was a very quiet
street, leading into a dull square where minor cotton-
lords and ladies lived : so, without fear of exciting
remark, Dennis led his captive a little way, and then
stopped short and shook him by the arm.

"Man alive!" he cried, in a tone of mildly indignant remonstrance, "ye mustn't go about with a
face like that on ye! Why, your face alone would
hang ye, if ye were to run against a policeman!
Pull yourself together, man. The stations are
watched; there *is* a warrant out, but I'll show ye a
way of keeping clear of them all, if ye'll not go and
give yourself and me away by your black looks."

"Was I looking black?" said Victred.

"By the powers, but ye were! and wh-what about,
now? Ye've done no worse than a man does out
west in Colorado without giving it a thought, more
than saying, 'Lucky it's he, and not I!' You've no
cause for all this remorse, I tell ye."

Victred blinked like an owl in the sunlight, and
then began to feel in his pockets for his cigar-case.

"Remorse!" he said, raising his eyebrows. "Well,
to tell you the truth, I don't feel any ; at least I
don't feel much, about my cousin's death."

"That's right. Spoken like a man."

"I did," went on Victred, in explanation, "until

they began to make it out murder. That pulled me round. It was such rot."

"So it was, me dear bhoy, so it was. But you—you seemed a trifle upset about it last night."

"Why, yes. And you yourself jumped to the reason. I didn't want to be hanged."

"And this morning you see things differently. You *do* want to be hanged?"

"Not precisely. Only when the day gets a bit warm, when such sun as there is has been on the roofs a little while, one feels better than one did at four o'clock—in the fog."

"True, very true. Then why disguise yourself with a haggard eye and a bandit's walk, as you were doing when I met you?"

"Was I? Oh, that was another matter altogether. I'd just been seeing a woman—seeing the last of her."

Dennis's face fell. He frowned disapprovingly, and shook his head.

"Ah, that woman! One never knows when one has seen the last of her. That's the worst of it."

Dennis looked at the young man with interest. He would have liked to hear more of that story.

But Victred was looking at his watch, and had apparently no more to tell.

"What's the time?" said Dennis.

Victred flushed a little, and took out his watch again with a laugh, for he had forgotten to notice what the time was.

"Twenty to twelve," said he.

"You didn't forget to wind it up last night then?" said Dennis in surprise. "Well done. Now, where are you going?"

"To a cigar-shop."

"Have you had any breakfast?"

"No-o, I don't think so. No, I don't want any."

"Better try and eat something. Besides, it will fill up the time while we talk over what you had better do. There's a little shop I know round here; not exactly Piccadilly or Boulevard form, but—it's out of the way."

This was significant; and Victred, with an unpleasant sort of internal convulsion, realised that here, in that warm light of day of which he had spoken so confidently, he was in danger of arrest by the police. He let Dennis lead him to the little coffee-shop which he had mentioned, tried with docility but without much success to eat something, and listened to his companion's suggestions.

"What were you thinking of doing now?" began the Irishman gravely.

"I thought of getting out to Texas or Manitoba. I have money enough to pay my passage, and to get some sort of outfit, if you could get a cheque cashed for me."

"Well, that wouldn't be much use just at present, for of course New York is just the place everybody will expect you to go to. And you're such a d——d casy figure to identify!"

Victred reflected for a few moments, and shook his head.

"I've no more ideas," said he. "Have you?"

"I have one, but you won't like it."

Victred gave a short laugh.

"I don't suppose I shall. But what is it?"

"You must give up all thought of cheque-books. Keep what you have for an emergency. Your best chance is to bury yourself."

"Then why not be hanged first?"

"Bury yourself in a social stratum where men of your class are never found. It will only be for a time. The business will blow over."

"But won't that be just the way to draw attention to myself?"

Dennis smiled and shook his head.

"Not where I propose to take you. Now then, are you ready to try my plan?"

"Why, yes. In fact I must, since I have none of my own!"

"Come on then. I know where we can get a trap to take us over to Burnley. You know Burnley?"

"Yes."

"Ah! But you don't know the part I'm going to take you to."

They left the coffee-shop together; and, Dennis's knowledge of by-ways being extensive and peculiar, they had soon reached the outskirts of the poorest quarter of the town of Cheston. Here they got the "trap," which proved to be a hooded market-cart. The agitator made his companion get inside and they started on their long thirty mile drive. The cart had no springs, and for the first few miles Victred was occupied in trying to accommodate his person to its peculiarities. When physical suffering had chastened him into resignation, he began to take note of outside things again and to remark the sincerity of the welcome which Dennis received along the whole route. He was known and greeted heartily at every wayside inn, at many a little nondescript shop. At Blackburn he became the centre of an eager, excited group of factory "hands," to whom he addressed a short, inflammatory speech. In many cases the welcome he got was not so serious; he was received with a laugh and a slap on the back. The one notable thing was that every one was glad to see him. With a joke for those who took him in jest, an elegant tirade for such as took him in earnest, Dennis M'Rena made his journey a triumphal progress.

They changed horses a little way beyond Blackburn. As Dennis then advised him to "stretch his legs a bit," Victred came into the little beerhouse, and was struck afresh by the familiar confidence with which the agitator was treated.

"I see," said the young man when they had started off again, "that to be your friend is a valuable passport, Dennis."

Dennis nodded good-humouredly.

"You might have a worse."

" But what is it you propose to make of me ? "

"Well, in the first place I'm going to introduce you to a lady."

" A lady ! "

"Yes, a *real* lady, all over diamonds."

Dennis looked out before him over the horse's head, with a serious mouth but laughing eyes.

Victred was rather angry. Of course he thought that M'Rena was making fun of him. Finding that his companion received this remark in silence, Dennis looked round at him, and then took a letter out of one of his pockets.

"She's an old flame of mine," he said, with another merry look. "She'd do anything for her Dennis."

Victred took the offered letter, which was a trifle greasier, a trifle more soiled in the folding than a lady's letter ought to be, and in response to a nod from its favoured owner, opened and read it. It began, " Dear Den," and was signed " Mariane de Mowbray," and referred to some business transaction in which they had been partners.

" Mariane is not faultless, but she has her good points. And she's a capital woman of business," said Dennis with fervour, as he received his letter back. " Maybe you won't like her at first, maybe you will. Maybe she'll grow upon you. Robert—that's her husband, he's not a bad sort either ; but you needn't trouble yourself so much about him, if you and the grey mare get on all right." Victred showed little interest in these details. Looking upon the proposed hiding-place merely as a temporary refuge, he did not care what it was like ; and being prepared to find it in every way distasteful, he was in no hurry to anticipate its discomforts.

Daylight had long since given place to darkness when the cart reached Burnley. It was Saturday night, and the streets were thronged by a rough crowd. The mill-girls had discarded their shawls and their clogs, and shone resplendent in holiday array, which was a cheap imitation of the most

marked eccentricities of the prevailing fashion of a
year before. One especial feature, a freak of local
taste, was the prevalence of feathers of a disagreeable
orange-brown. The male compeers of these ladies,
though making of necessity a less brilliant show, had
washed their faces, and in many cases put on smart
Sunday clothes of quite a dashing cut. And the
lads in their twos and threes, and the lasses in their
twos and threes, surged in a slow-moving stream
through the town and about the market-place.
Here the naphtha lamps flared above the sweetmeat
stalls and at the entrance to the pea-saloons, where
hot peas, trotters and baked potatoes formed the
popular—and satisfying—menu. Here you could
indulge in the giddy delights of the steam roundabout
and be whirled round and round till you were sick,
on an everlastingly jibbing wooden horse, to the ear-
splitting music of a steam orchestrion. Here you
could throw balls at a row of fluffy figures, each of
which seemed by its breadth to offer a tempting
target; but the balls went through that delusive
fluffiness, and only a practised marksman could hit
the small stick in the middle and bring one of those
fluffy figures down.

Dennis had put up his horse and was elbowing his
way with Victred through the crowd. He was evidently searching for somebody.

" Is this where you expect to find the diamond-
bedecked lady ? " asked Victred ironically.

But Dennis nodded quite seriously. As he turned
to look at Victred, a tall handsome and rather well-
dressed man touched him on the shoulder.

" Hallo, Dennis ! "

" Hallo, Bob ! Missis about ? "

" Yes. She's started a show of her own. You
knew, didn't you ? Giant, dwarf, and fat lady."

" H'm. That's playing it rather low down, isn't
it ? "

Robert put his hand up and twirled a long, silky,
fair moustache. He shook his head deprecatingly.

He was a simple creature, full of transparent cunning and supernatural astuteness; and he never gave a direct answer to a question, having always to think out what guile might lurk within the most innocent inquiry.

"It pays, it pays. She's an energetic woman is the missus. The dime museums on the other side gave her the idea, and she's doing very well. Been going on two years now. One must go with the times, you know, go with the times."

And Robert twirled his moustache again, and looked at Dennis out of the corners of his eyes, to see whether, in his own phrase, he was being " got at." From Dennis his gaze travelled to the tall young man by the agitator's side. M'Rena hastily withdrew his arm from Victred's, with a few words of muttered apology, and spoke apart with Robert for some minutes. Victred remaining staring stupidly at the jostling figures, as they passed into the lamp-light, at the flying·roundabouts, at the white-aproned, plump women who sat so quietly at the doors of the modest temples of pleasure where you could see a Waxwork Exhibition, or a " Ghost Show" for two-pence. He had had scarcely any sleep the night before; his long, jolting drive had made him ache in every bone; he was therefore conscious at that moment of no more acute danger than that of falling asleep on an overturned barrel, which he had appropriated as a seat. But his unusual height had already begun to draw upon him the attention of the crowd. "Eh, but he's t' Giant as has gotten away from t' show!" cried a girl, giving the signal for a chorus of comments. This he would not have minded a bit if the masculine portion of his audience had not early manifested an inclination to try their aim at this broader target than the fluffy figures, with cab-bage stumps and odds and ends of the market refuse.

So Victred, rousing himself from his stupor, made a rush at the nearest marksman, and seizing his hat, ignited it at a naphtha lamp that was high above the aggressor's head, lit a cigarette with it, and then politely offered to return the blazing head-gear to its owner. There was a shout of laughter. The crowd, now on the side of the ready-witted Irishman, pressed jeering round their crestfallen comrade.

"Eh, but t' big 'un had tha that time!"

"Eh, a' did get t' best on it, that a' did!"

In the midst of the laughter the forlorn giant regained his uncomfortable seat. Dennis and Robert found him a little later with his head on his hands and his elbow on a mussel-stall, more than half asleep. The blare of the orchestrions, the cries of the stall-owners, the bang-bang of the shooting galleries, were becoming merged into an indistinct din which acted on his tired senses like a lullaby.

"Let me introduce you—Mr. Robert de Mowbray," were the words uttered close to his ear, which made him wake with a start.

"Poor chap! He looks done up," said the gentleman with the Norman name, whose accent, by-the-bye, betrayed that some of his less remote ancestors must have had their broad lands in Whitechapel.

Dennis was trying to shake Victred into the full use of his wits.

"I have spoken to this gentleman about you. He is in want of a good actor with a fine appearance. Told him you are the very man," said Dennis in his ear.

Victred stared at his friend.

"Very man for what?" he said blankly. "Not the stage! Why, good Heavens, I——'"

"Are the very man," insisted Dennis authoritatively, as Mr. Robert de Mowbray was drawn into a minute's conversation with a passing acquaintance. "Think I don't know what I'm talking about? Now, I've got to go and look for Mariane, and I shall leave you with de Mowbray. Whatever he asks you if you can do, mind you say yes at once—whatever it is, mind; and whether you understand him or not."

"All right," said Victred hazily.

This proposition had been sprung upon him so suddenly that he had no time to formulate objections. Otherwise he would have demonstrated clearly to Dennis the impossibility of his adopting the stage as a profession when he had never even taken part in an amateur performance.

Dennis had disappeared, and a moment later Mr. de Mowbray sauntered up. In the meantime Victred had had time to resolve to take the agitator's advice. "They can only find me out," thought he, "and I dare say they're not all Salvinis."

Mr. de Mowbray gave him a nod by way of introduction.

. "So you want a shop?" said he.

"Yes," said Victred readily.

He was delighted to find that Dennis had been mistaken. He was not wanted to act, but to sell. He was sure that he could make up parcels and give change, and do all the business of a shop as well as anybody.

"Been out long?"

"Some time," said Victred.

"What was your last shop?"

This was a puzzler. He must mention some place a long way off, or discovery might be swift and sure.

"Who were you with last?" went on de Mowbray, breaking the pause.

"John Green of Newcastle," answered the aspirant.

"Don't know him. Been used to portables?"

Victred thought this might perhaps mean that he was not too proud to carry home the parcels. So he said readily :—

"Yes, oh yes."

"What's your line?"

"Line?"

"Yes, what's your line of business?"

Another puzzler. For if he said "Greengrocery" or "Drapery" and it should turn out that he was wanted to sell sweet-stuff, he might be told he wouldn't do,

So he said, "Oh! anything," as if his experience had been too vast for him to particularise.

"Responsibles, I suppose?"

"Yes."

He fancied he saw a doubtful look on de Mowbray's face, so he hastened to say:

"I can turn my hand to anything—make myself useful in fact."

De Mowbray nodded.

"Yes, of course. You wouldn't be much use in a portable if you couldn't. Are you a good study?"

"Yes," answered Victred, but with less assurance.

He was getting more puzzled. The use of the word "study" seemed to him new and peculiar. And surely "study" had something to do with the learning of parts, not the carrying of parcels.

"You can wing a part, I suppose?"

Again without the slightest notion of what he was pledging himself to, Victred assented.

De Mowbray went on:

"And you can pong a bit, of course?"

"Certainly," said the bewildered applicant, Why should he stick at a trifle like this?

"Mind," continued de Mowbray impressively, "I don't have any fluffers in my show who just get through and never give a cue. And I don't chuck things on anyhow. Every piece is a production, sir, just the same as at 'Enry's show or Gus 'Arris's."

To this, happily, Victred could assent with a free mind. But he was getting more and more puzzled as to what de Mowbray's business really was. He seemed to be a sort of Jack-of-all-trades.

"You've got some good props, I see," said de Mowbray, looking admiringly at the other's clothes.

Victred thought he was alluding to the length of his legs and he acquiesced with a smile.

"What's your figure?"

Victred was about to tell him his chest measurement, and inform him that his height was six feet four, but de Mowbray did not wait for his answer.

7

" I pay salaries, you know," said he. " None of your ' sharing terms, houses checked ' here."

The applicant shook his head appreciatively at this announcement. But he wondered what sort of a house it might be that had to be checked. He could understand checking a runaway horse, or a mad bull, but a house——Why then, it must be the house that was " portable," he supposed.

"Of course I don't know what you can do yet."

Victred thought that his chances seemed to be getting less. A happy thought struck him.

" I can play the piano pretty well," said he.

"Can yer, though ? "

De Mowbray, who had begun to move slowly on with the crowd, stopped short and looked at him more hopefully.

" Can you vamp ? "

Victred did not know what this might mean, any more than what the other accomplishments were to which he had pledged himseelf. But he thought he had taken quite enough upon himself, and that an occasional denial would be more convincing than this eternal dull assent. So he said he couldn't vamp.

" Perhaps you've never tried," suggested Robert.

Victred admitted that he had never even tried.

" Well, come and see what the missis says. She has a rare eye for finding out what a man can do."

Whereupon Victred felt that he did not want to see the missis ; but he could not help himself. De Mowbray dragged him along through the crowd till they came to a booth, more brilliant than all the rest in lights and gilding, on the platform of which Dennis was standing, talking affably with a lady who was sitting at the turnstile. Such a lady too ! Not one of the homely-looking creatures in apron and shawl whom Victred had noticed in charge of the other places of entertainment. But a gorgeous Being in black satin, with a large black Gainsborough hat, profusely trimmed with ostrich feathers, an enormous gold locket suspended from her neck on an equally enormous gold chain, a silver horse-shoe brooch two inches across, and a display of diamond rings, on not over-clean fingers, which gave one a comfortable feeling as to the financial stability of the establishment. "This," thought Victred, as he went up the steps with the Being's proud husband, "is the grey mare."

"That's the missis," said Mr. Robert de Mowbray, nodding in the direction of the Gainsborough.

The fair Mariane was a short brunette, of Jewish type, with a hard square face, a long, narrow, straight mouth, and a long, narrow, straight nose, which hung down over it. Victred thought her repulsive, and learned later with surprise that she was still considered something of a beauty. But he had nothing to complain of in her reception of him.

No sooner had she turned her head from Dennis to see who it was that was coming up the steps, and caught sight of her husband and his companion than, springing up from her seat, she pointed at Victred a forefinger on which shone a diamond half-hoop and a great single stone, and cried, in a tone of triumphant excitement :

" *The* very man ! "

But Victred had already been told that evening that he was " *the* very man," and nothing had come of the announcement ; so he merely raised his hat, and waited for the lady to deliver herself further.

" Eh, what ? what ? " said her husband, in a hesitating, nervous manner peculiar to him.

"Come in here," went on the lady imperiously, jerking the Gainsborough and all its nodding plumes in the direction of the interior of the booth. Behind Mrs. de Mowbray was a curtained recess, very small and narrow, into which she ushered the three men.

" What's your height, young man ? " she asked with authority, standing at the entrance, so as to keep one eye on the turnstile.

" Six feet four," answered Victred.

7*

"Then if you're a steady fellow, I can give you a shop."

Victred began to understand that a shop did not always mean an emporium for the purchase of goods.

"Thank you, madam," said he.

"Been long in the profession?"

Victred hesitated an instant. Then: "What profession, madam?" said he.

There was a roar of laughter from de Mowbray, in which even Dennis had ruefully to join. Mrs. de Mowbray put her be-diamonded hands to her black satin sides. It was quite the best joke they had ever heard, to meet a man who did not know what *the* profession was!

"Why, you're an amateur!" cried Mrs. de Mowbray. At least she *said* "amature."

"No, indeed I'm not," said Victred. "The fact is, I'm a complete novice."

But that was a distinction without a difference to the show folk.

"Never mind," continued Mariane indulgently; "you'll do for me, if you won't for the boss. That is, if you ain't too much of a swell for what I want."

"No, indeed, I——"

But she interrupted him with a knowing shake of the head.

"Oh, don't tell me! *I* know. Come now, make a clean breast of it. You're a gentleman, a gentleman in trouble!"

Victred grew red and white, hot and cold. This was worse than he had feared. He would never have expected from this woman so much discrimination. He cast a helpless but angry glance at Dennis, who might surely have come forward to help him in the plight he was in.

"Look here," went on Mrs. de Mowbray, thrusting her tongue into her cheek, closing one eye in the most pronounced wink he had ever seen, and putting against the side of her nose one of those terrible fingers whose sparkling ornaments emphasised the vulgarity of her movements, "*I* know, so what's the good of talking? You're one of the young sparks out of some swell draper's shop, Sharp and Tighe's, at Cheston, very likely—and you've been putting your fingers in the till to go horse-racing! Bless you, *I* know! I could have told you as soon as I set eyes on you! And I ain't often wrong, am I, boss?"

The "Boss" was in ecstasies of admiration over the missus's penetration, while Dennis had to go outside to give vent to his feelings.

"Well now, I never should have thought of it!" murmured the obtuse Robert, gently shaking his head in profound amazement.

But Victred was in a tumult of rage. He was on the point of exploding with a vehement expression of opinion, when he suddenly felt M'Rena's arm pressing his side from behind, and heard the agitator's voice addressing Mariane in demurest tones.

"No, no, no," said he gently, "you're wrong about the till, Mariane, I can answer for that. We may plead guilty to having had ideas a little above our station, and even to having gone so far as to be shopwalker at a fancy stationer's, eh, Fred?" And he pinched the arm of his companion, who nodded submissively. "But we preferred Art, and so gave it up, and sought to become an Art*iste*."

Mrs. de Mowbray gave another wink, and shook her head waggishly.

"Right you are," said she. "But, mind, I shouldn't have said anything if you'd have liked to have owned up. Young men will be young men. Only I must have no side, you know, if you come here. Are you steady? I don't mind a man's being a little bit 'on' Saturday nights, but I won't have your prossers and your loafers. They're no good to *me*."

"I can give him a good character as far as that goes," put in Dennis, who was in mortal fear that the young man would speak.

"That's all right. For it's the very thing that I've just given my giant the sack for."

"Giant!" echoed Victred, bewildered.

"Yes, at a pound a week, and money sure. And let me tell you, young man, that it would be a long time before you'd be worth such a screw as that in any other branch of the profession."

"I know that, madam," said Victred humbly.

"Yes, and don't 'madam' me, for I don't like it," continued the lady, who was not used to having her plans opposed in any way, and who began to scent "side" in the young man's hesitation. "Is it 'on,' or is it 'off,' and be quick?"

"It's 'on,'" said Victred quietly.

Dennis's merry face lengthened with astonishment. Mariane looked at Victred with the softening expression of one who has done a good stroke of business.

"What's your name?" said she. "We can settle to-morrow what we'll call you in the bills. Of course it must be Captain or Colonel something."

"My name?" said Victred. "Oh, my name's Fred."

"Fred what?"

"That's it—Fred Watt."

"Colonel Watt of the United States' Army," murmured Mariane. "That'll do for the bills."

Dennis, scarcely yet knowing whether Victred meant to stick to his bargain, or whether he had engaged himself "for a lark," took a hasty leave of Mariane, and drew the "giant" down the steps on to the stones of the market-place.

"I say," said the agitator, looking up curiously into the young man's sleepy face, "you're not serious, are you? You don't mean to——"

"To be a giant? Yes, I do. What the woman said was quite right. I'm not worth a pound a week at anything else. And if am worth a pound a week to stand up and be looked at, why on earth shouldn't I earn that pound a week?"

"Mr. Watt! Colonel!" called out Mrs. de Mowbray in a loud, husky whisper, as she came to the front of the booth and stooped down to speak to him, "you'd better come back here to sleep. I can put you up. It won't do to make yourself cheap by staying at an hotel."

"Oh, I shouldn't think of it!" began Victred.

But Dennis interrupted him, shaking him by the arm and whispering:

"She means a pub."

"Because," continued Mrs. de Mowbray, "we've another week to stay here, you know."

Victred was about to beg her to show him a resting-place, whether bed, bench, or bare ground he did not care, immediately. But at that moment Robert de Mowbray ran down the steps, and slipped his arm familiarly, even, so it seemed to Victred, affectionately, into his.

"Come and have a drink," said he.

And those five magic words, so Victred soon found, formed, as it were, the motto of show-life; the basis of friendship and the bond of peace.

CHAPTER XI.

" Who doth ambition shun, And loves to live i' th' sun;
Seeking the food he eats, And pleased with what he gets,
Come hither, come hither, come hither :
Here shall he see No enemy
But winter and rough weather."

—SHAKESPEARE.

TIRED as he was, Victred passed a by no means comfortable night. For the bunk which he occupied in the living-carriage was underneath that of the dwarf, a mis-shapen and vicious little man, who came to bed drunk, and amused himself for two hours by singing "comic songs" which would have brought a blush to the cheek of a grenadier. From time to time a female voice, husky but plaintive, from the next compartment, alternately implored and commanded the "Major" to be quiet, applying to him certain striking epithets quite new to Victred, and threatening to wring his neck in the morning. These remarks were accompanied by a series of forcible thumps upon the partition, which convinced Victred that the unknown lady possessed the muscular strength to carry out her threat.

At last Victred struck a match, and looked at his watch, and found that it was past two. So he got out of his bunk, struck another match, and put his face into the bunk above.

"Don't you think you've made that row long enough?" he insinuated gently.

"Garn! Sh't up! S'hgarn makin' it s'long'sh I like," replied the dwarf, who was of Metropolitan origin.

"I think not," rejoined Victred more sweetly than before. "At least, if you do want to go on screaming that filth, you'll do it outside. Now, I give you two minutes."

He went to the door of the van, and pushed it open. The dwarf sprang up in his bunk, and assailed him with a torrent of half-unintelligible abuse, which he uttered in that peculiar, explosive manner, with a pause to gather fresh energy between each two or three words, and a climax of emphasis before each pause, common to the natives of lowest London.

"A long, ——, ——, ——, as thinks 'ishelf a bloomin' toff, acomin' t' turn honesht folksh out o' their beds—middle o' th' night! Garn! Garn! Garn away! Who are you when you're t' ome?"

Victred did not tell him. What would have been the use? The "Major" would not have believed him. But when the two minutes were up, the young Irishman lifted the still voluble dwarf out of his bunk, and gave him a gentle swing against the opposite wall just to prepare himself for a further throw. Then he carried him to the door, and gave him a swing over the wooden steps.

"You can be very comfortable there under the

canvas till morning," said he, "and you can sing as much as ever you like."

Meanwhile the "Major" was struggling, kicking, yelling for mercy. A good deal sobered by his fright, he was appealing to his captor's manliness not to take advantage of a poor little dwarf not a quarter his size. But this appeal seemed only to make the "giant" more ferocious.

"Yes," said Victred, giving him another shake, "you've been using that snivelling cry for any number of years, I know. To sneak out of the treatment you deserve for making yourself a nuisance. Else you would have been pounded into a jelly long before. I'll give you one more chance—only one. Do you hear?"

He flung the abjectly protesting creature back into his bunk; and then had to smother his laughter on perceiving that the poor wretch was for a long time too much frightened even to lie down again, lest his moving should disturb the monster underneath.

When Victred awoke next morning the dwarf was gone. He had fled to Mrs. de Mowbray to represent that, not for five pounds a week and a benefit, would he spend another night in the company of the murderous ruffian whom she had just engaged. Mrs. de Mowbray, who loved a joke and was not too tender-hearted, laughed till she cried at his terrors, and said she was glad she had some one to keep him in order at last.

Meanwhile Victred, on his side, was resolving that he must ask permission to lodge elsewhere; the limited accommodation of the living carriage was not to be endured again. The cold was intense; the arrangements for washing were better adapted to the dwarf than to him. He stepped out of the van, blue-nosed and shivering, and was met by a smiling lady of stupendous breadth, who wore a bonnet with strings hanging loose. By her husky voice, when she greeted him, he recognised the neighbour who, on the previous night, had threatened to wring the " Major's "

neck in the morning. There was no possibility of
doubting that he was in the presence of the divinity
whom the bills announced as " Madame Elaine, the
Fattest Lady in the World." Haply the patrons of
the show had never heard of " the lily-maid of
Astolat," or there might have been suggestions made
that the title was " wrote sarcastic." For not only was
this latter-day Elaine plump, but she was also red.

She invited Victred very graciously into a second
and smaller van, which was fitted up with a stove, and
she asked him if he would have some breakfast. As
she poached the eggs very deftly, understood the art
of tea-making to perfection, and made him sit close
to the stove till he was warm, Victred felt that he
would not have exchanged her overpowering presence
for that of a dozen lily-maids, however fair, and however lovable.

She beguiled him with conversation which gave
him a curiously reminiscent feeling. Surely he had
heard dames of higher degree talk much as this
plump lady talked, if with clearer voice and a more
profound knowledge of grammar.

"What that there dwarf has made me suffer, Mr.
Watt, me being brought up with notions and my
uncle the biggest butcher in Market Cross, Tranberry,
and quite the gentleman too and kep' his gig and
everything in the 'ighest style; an' me his favourite
too!"

Visions of Bayswater teas floated before Victred's
eyes, and he seemed to hear the casually-met matrons,
in mantles of heavily jetted brocade, dragging in by
the heels a reference to "my cousin the Admiral," or
"my son's dearest friend, Lord So-and-So," with just
as much relevance as this poor "freak" alluded to
the glories of "my uncle the butcher."

"If I 'ad only a little bit more courage than what
I 'ave, Mr. Watt," she went on, "I declare I'd up and
ask Mrs. de Mowbray why she doesn't get another
dwarf." As a matter of fact Madame Elaine, who
was scarcely so shrinkingly timid as her words im-

plied, had made the suggestion to her manager in very plain terms, and there had been many exciting verbal encounters between the two ladies over the matter. " Why, it's a disgrace to Mrs. de M., an' her such a perfeck lady too, with everything first class an' no stint, and with me, an' I'll make so bold as to say you too, sir, with social statuses to be kep' up, an' us to 'ave to associate with such as 'im ! But there, p'raps your coming may make a difference. She knows a first-class article when she comes across it, do Mrs. de M. An' me been with her ever since she started the ' museum,' an' says she to me, ' Madam Ellen,' says she, ' I mean to keep this exhibition tip-top, and I mean to keep *you*.' "

Victred's quiet manner of listening, or appearing to listen, quite charmed the fat lady, who was not used, poor thing ! to much deference. He found it hard to get away. And when, after hotly refusing his offer to help her to wash up the breakfast things, she suffered him to go, it was with a tender smile on her expansive features that she watched him through the booth.

For Victred had caught the sound of Dennis's cheery voice, and guessed that the agitator was in search of him. M'Rena met him at the entrance to the booth, and breaking away from Mrs. de Mowbray, who was only a trifle less gorgeous of raiment than on the preceding evening, he drew the young man into a corner.

" Are you going to stay here ? "

" Certainly. I told you so last night."

" What ! As giant ? "

" As anything they like. Why not here as well as anywhere else ? It won't be for long, as you said yourself."

" H'm. Well, yes, I know I did, but——"

" But what ? "

" I begin to be afraid—it won't be quite so easy to —to get you off as we hoped."

Victred felt that his throat was getting dry,

and his mouth parched. He knew all that Dennis
meant.

"What makes you think so?" he asked.

"Well, it's true that there's a warrant out against
you for one thing."

Victred looked curiously into his companion's face.
He did not know how it came, but a suspicion of
Dennis's disinterestedness shot through his mind.

"Do you think I've cut my own throat in getting
away? Will I go back?"

"If you like. But what do you get by going
back?"

"What do *you* get by my keeping away?"

The ungrateful words were out of Victred's mouth,
uttered on the impulse of the moment, almost against
his will. The next moment he was ashamed of them.
But Dennis only laughed.

"Well done," he said. "Give a dog a bad name
and hang him. You didn't ask these questions yesterday, when you thought the police were dogging
you. Stay here or go back, as you like. If you go
back you run a fair chance of being hanged. If you
stay here I'll come back at the proper time and de-
mand your soul in fulfilment of our bargain. Mind,
I'm in earnest, so look out. Of the two evils, choose
whichever you prefer. I've a train to catch, so ta-ta."
He shook hands with the half-penitent, half-bewil-
dered Victred, and turned to say, when he had got a
few steps away: "And it's a compliment I'm paying
ye in wanting your dull Saxon soul at all, mind that
now."

In a moment he had run up the sloping planks to
the pay-box and disappeared.

Victred remained in deep thought. The gloom of
the canvas-roofed booth seemed to help him to a clear
consideration of his case. Yesterday and the night
before he had believed in the agitator's disinterestedness towards himself; to-day he doubted it. Yet he
could not tell why. What had Dennis to gain by
advising him against his interest? He, Victred, was

not clever like Tracy, so that his brains might be worth purchasing. Search as he would, the poor giant could find no reason for his mistrust.

As for his suggestion of going back, he did not seriously entertain it at present. He would hear first what the vindictive Lady Rushcliffe had to say at the inquest. If she were really ready to swear his life away, it would be madness to go back. And Victred did not care enough for the old existence to make a strenuous fight for it. The burden of his unacknowledged wife had hung for years about his neck, clogging his energies and embittering the cup of life to him. He would stay where he was, get new experiences, and perhaps find gain in his loss after all.

Victred found his experiences new indeed.

It was a great relief to him to find that he was not to exhibit himself to gaping crowds in his own proper person, but in a disguise—a "make-up" Mrs. de Mowbray called it—in which his own father would never have recognised him. In the first place his face and hands were changed to a rich bronze with Armenian bole. A wig of long, curly, black hair, a black beard, and a ferocious black moustache with drooping ends, gave him a wild and rather picturesque appearance. A pair of high boots, with an ingenious arrangement of lifts inside by which he almost stood on tip-toe, added considerably to his height. Leather trousers, a red shirt, and a huge sombrero hat completed an equipment in which, as Madame Elaine said enthusiastically: "'e looked a Mexican Colonel or Cow Boy, every hinch of 'im!"

He was a huge success. He even felt a little personal pleasure in the magnificent appearance he presented, and a little pride in the outspoken admiration of the factory girls, which found expression in ill-spelt *billets-doux*, and in small presents of violent-coloured neckties and bad tobacco.

And thus the adaptability of the human creature was proved once more.

CHAPTER XII.

" The sweet season that bud and bloom forth brings
With green hath clad the hill and eke the vale ;
The nightingale with feathers new she sings ;
The turtle to her mate hath told her tale."
                                    —THE EARL OF SURREY.

IN spite of his stoical determination not to care, it
was with a shock that Victred read, in a local paper,
an account of the inquest held on the body of his
cousin, Lord Malpas.   For the jury returned a verdict
of " wilful murder " against Victred Gerald Speke, for
whose apprehension, so the account continued, a
warrant had already been issued.   But when he came
to the details of the inquest, and found that it was
the false evidence of Lady Rushcliffe and of the
servile Jerry Coggin which had brought about this
result, his anger grew so hot against both of them
that he started up with an impulse to go back to
Maleigh, not to clear himself, but to do something
vaguely awful to repay the obligation he was under
to them.

A very few minutes, of course, were required for
the evaporation of these intentions.   After all, though
the fact in print looked so much more serious than
it had seemed by word of mouth, he had known
what was going to happen.   The only real surprise
for him was the evidence of his cousin Tracy.   For
the latter, while admitting that he had not witnessed
the blow or the fall, seemed to lay stress upon the
ill-feeling which had existed between Lord Malpas
and Victred : and the manner in which he described
his first view of the body and of Victred standing by
it, implied that his own impression was unfavourable
to the latter.

Victred read and re-read these details with a
puzzled expression of face.

" It must be the way those d—d stupid reporters

have put it down that makes it look so odd ! " thought
he. "Of course Tracy never thought I did it on
purpose ; why, he told me so, and he shut up old
Coggin, and spoke out his mind to that she-devil.
I've a good mind to write to him, and——-"

Suddenly he remembered Tracy's curious change
of front: how he had looked out of the room when
Victred was on his way out of the house. And then
Victred, never suspecting his cousin's good faith, felt
his body grow wet and cold, as he said to himself
that it must have been his own stealthy departure
from the Abbey which had bred this horrible suspicion
in the mind of the other.

"What a fool I was not to explain to him, to ask
his advice. He's got three times the brains I have,
and he would have helped me. But then he locked
the door upon me and wouldn't answer. Why, that
woman must have been at work upon him while I
was in my room ; and susceptible as the beggar is to
a petticoat, he must have been persuaded. After
he'd seen her on the terrace ! I can't understand it."

And Victred, sore at the defection of his cousin,
whom, without exactly respecting, he had been fond
of, resolved to take the first opportunity of seeing
Tracy, and "having it out" with him. He would
have liked, too, to see May again. The girl's loyalty
to her fantastic passion could not but move him
deeply. But on the whole he felt that he was not
strong enough to go through the ordeal of an interview with her after what had happened. She must
remain a memory with him, a memory partly tender,
partly sad, and partly ludicrous, but still the plea-
santest thing to dwell upon in his whole life. When
she married, however, he might manage to let her
know how much he wished her happiness. Suitors
for a girl so well dowered as she was would not, he
knew, be wanting. Indeed, Tracy was not the only
young fellow who had asked for his good word with
her.

And then Madame Elaine came up, and with fawn-

like and kittenish grace coquetted around him and
his newspaper until he gave her the latter and went
out for air.

There was no denying that, as the winter went on,
the two ladies of the establishment persecuted him
with their attentions. Victred, who was not only
soon reconciled to his new life, but began to find
some enjoyment in it, hated them both like poison :
hated the plump, perspiring Elaine, and schemed to
avoid the breakfasts and teas with which she sought
to beguile him ; hated still more his hard-faced
manager*ess*, her continual, generous offers to "stand
treat," her unsought confidences concerning Bob and
his " carryings-on," her jewelry and her jokes.

These hatreds he cherished in spite of an undeniable
but gradual deterioration in tone, which took place
in him during the course of the first five months of
his life in the booth. This was inevitable ; as a
sense of irresponsibility is the key-note of Bohemian
life, while the *mot d'ordre* of the gentleman is, and
always must be, *noblesse oblige*. It was not that he
sank far or irretrievably : nobody about him noticed
the slightest change. Nothing ever could or would
bring him down to the level of the men who were
now his companions : his education, his traditions
forbade that. He could never, as many of his class
do, in losing caste, lose his prejudice in favour of
clean linen, and a clothes-brush, and an abundant
supply of soap and water. It brought tears to the
eyes of the " Major " to see a man waste on his
washerwoman shilling after shilling which might have
been spent in beer. This was an offence against the
dwarf's code which caused him greater disgust than
his songs now did to Victred. It was not that the
giant liked these effusions better than he had done
before : but he was used to them.

For Victred had soon made the acquaintance of
Mr. de Mowbray's Dramatic Company, with whom
intercourse was only possible in the tap-room of a
public-house. When he wanted a walk, he had to

take it by himself, unless he bribed one of the company with visions of unlimited beer at a certain destination. So he began by inexpressible contempt for these men, which dwindled when he found himself longing for some human society other than that of the "Major," Madame Elaine, and Mrs. de Mowbray.

And presently he had to acknowledge that, when the domestic horizon is bounded by the walls of one room in the smallest and dingiest of hostelries, the fancy of the occupier when it lightly turns to thoughts of bars is not to be marvelled at. Treated like the sparrow, either as a mischievous outcast or an amusing vagabond, to whom one throws crumbs while laughing at his antics, the booth actor, like the circuit actor of bygone days, is alternately patronised and insulted, "treated" and snubbed, until he has taken to heart his most fitting philosophy: "Let us eat and drink, for to-morrow we die."

So Victred had to recognise that "the pub is the vagrant's club," and to understand that the over-dressed young cads whose fathers sold butter and ham, or manufactured cotton, and whose pocket-money enabled them to "stand treat to the actor-chaps," were his social superiors and eminently conscious of the fact. It made his blood boil to see how servile the actors were to these cubs, with whom he himself would have nothing to do.

The "heavy man," an old fellow between sixty and seventy years of age, who had been a fine actor in his day, and who knew to a nicety the art of making "points" where there were no "points," took Victred to task one day for his "high stomach."

"Now that young fellow who was standing treat to-day at 'The Finisher-off's Arms'—you contradicted him flatly more than once, and then you marched out of the place without touching the drink he'd ordered!"

"Well, I couldn't stand his impudence. Why, he was insulting you to your face, you a man old enough

8

to be his father "—grandfather, Victred might have said !—"and with more brains in your little finger-nail than there are in all his family !"

"Well, boy, but I don't mind. I'm past the hot-headed time of life, and the airs these young sparks give themselves only amuse me. And "—here the old man's voice assumed a tone of real bitterness—"he would have ordered drinks round again, only your behaviour had disgusted him too much !"

"Very well, Jumbo. I won't ever again be annoyed when I see you badly used."

"Well, boy, you'll oblige me if you'll keep that promise," rejoined the old fellow with a twinkle in his eye.

For Ben Russell, commonly called "Jumbo," had a sense of humour. For this, together with a certain old world chivalry the man had, and for his stories of the past circuit-days, which he told with a pathos and fun which made him a *viva voce* Mürger, Victred loved him. So with the rest. He might be angry with them, he might hate them, he might despise them, he might be disgusted with them, and then some act of kindness, some impulse of strained generosity, the discovery of hardship bravely borne, or of devotion freely given, would soften his heart and show him that attractive other side. Or perhaps, it would be some act of crack-brained folly, which, exhibiting them in their character of overgrown children, reconciled him to the fact that it was useless to expect figs from thistles.

But he was glad that he was not a member of the company. For intercourse with them brought always a reaction of low spirits and self-disgust.

The attractions of Mrs. de Mowbray's " Museum " being less lasting than those of the " portable," with its extensive repertory, the former had to move from place to place much more frequently than the latter ; and, as the spring came on, Victred found his pleasures chiefly in long, solitary walks, discovering unknown beauties in a region which he had associated with nothing but factory-smoke, clogs, and general ugliness.

They had pitched their tent on a piece of high waste-ground above the pretty Yorkshire town of Wakefield, when Mrs. de Mowbray made an announcement to Victred which struck him for a moment dumb with a strange mingling of sensations. He was fastening the canvas roof on, and had a rope in his hand.

"By-the-bye, I've had a pretty piece of news to-day, on top of the bad business last week. It never rains but it pours. Dennis's daughter will be here on Saturday night, and I've got to take her along, and such a nuisance as the girl is, always talking about nothing but 'father, father,' or else going about with a long face enough to turn the luck against us. What are you staring at?"

Victred had dropped the rope.

"Dennis's daughter!" echoed he.

"Yes. I suppose you've heard of her. She goes about Ireland with him through the winter, lecturing and speechifying or something. Then when the summer comes he carts her over to me (at least he did last year, and he's going to, this), and I have to drag her along till the short days come and he wants her again."

Mrs. de Mowbray paused and looked thoughtful. An idea had struck her. Victred was considering the news with a feeling that something was going to happen which ought to be stopped. Although his impression of little "Red Jack" was no longer so vivid as it had been, he remembered enough of the sensation her pale spiritual face and weird passionate eyes had caused him, to be shocked at the idea of her living among such surroundings as those of the booth.

"Odd idea to send her here? Don't you think so, Mrs. de Mowbray?" he suggested.

"Why odd? Her father and me's been partners in a business at Hull this many a long day. He

8*

knows there ain't any lady in England who the girl would be better with than with me. I'd like to know how the idea's odd, Mr. Watt?"

"Oh, no, you misunderstand me. One would have thought M'Rena would have put his daughter where she would have—have something to occupy her—something——"

"You've 'it it!" cried Mrs. de Mowbray, with an emphatic gesture. "You've 'it the right nail on the 'ead straight off! She does want something to do, and she shall 'ave it. The 'Major's' been sickening for days, you must have noticed it. Last week he couldn't eat anything, and yesterday and to-day he can't drink anything; so you may guess that it's serious, such a boozer as he is: it's my belief he's got a touch of the ague, like what he had last year. I'm thinking of sending him to the Infirmary. They'll keep him some time there——"

Mrs. de Mowbray stopped short, smiling to herself at her beautiful new plan. Victred, rather nervously, said :

"Well?"

"Well. She shall be the dwarf. Dennis's daughter shall be the dwarf. And there you are—slap-up!"

She emphasised her conviction with a thump on her knee. Victred grew red and white. But he knew better than to state to Mrs. de Mowbray the grounds of his objection to her plan ; he could not tell her that his soul revolted from the thought of exposing the little fragile fanatic, with the ethereal eyes, to the gaze of the bumpkins, whose coarse jests fell harmless on the less sensitive ears of Madame Elaine and himself.

"She isn't nearly short enough," said he ; "she can't be very much under five feet."

The manager*ess* gave one of her preposterous winks.

"Oh," said she, "we can manage that. I'll have a cut opened in the stage so her feet can be below, and have a pair of shoes fastened round her ankles. Or she can double herself up some way. All freaks are faked, more or less. Look at you and Ellen. She wouldn't draw a cent if it wasn't for the india-rubber air-belt. And if it wasn't for your big hat and your boots, the public would throw eggs at you for a do."

Victred said nothing more. The proverbial woman's will was wax to Mrs. de Mowbray's. He waited with interest and even some impatience for Saturday.

The last show was over on Saturday night, the audience had clattered out, and Victred, still in his giant's dress, sat down on the edge of the stage to smoke a pipe. Presently the "Major," who was indeed so ill that he had scarcely been able to drag himself through the little travesty of military drill which formed his performance with Victred, came halting up to his big companion, and pulled his arm down and whispered in his ear.

"I'm goin', did you know? I've got the sack. I'm a-goin' to the Infirmary to-night, an' you'll never be able to pitch into me no more. She says I'm no good no more, an' she's got old Paddy's girl instead o' me. You'll like that better, I dessay. She's a bloomin' toff compared to me. Jest your sort. Well, ta-ta, I shall be in the bloomin' churchyard by time the show comes round 'ere again. Ta-ta."

"I'm going to see you to the Infirmary," said the giant.

With a mist before his eyes Victred took the poor "Major" up in his arms and carried him to the cab which was waiting for him outside. For Mrs. de Mowbray could treat well those who had served her to her satisfaction, and she was crying loudly at the cab door as the dwarf was put inside.

"'Ere, Major," and as she thrust something into the dwarf's hand Victred heard the chink of gold, "that'll help you to get yourself little extry comforts. And we won't forget you, my dear, when we come this way again."

And she threw her arms round the poor freak's neck and hugged him warmly. Victred was about to get into the cab, when Mrs. de Mowbray thrust him aside, and declared her intention of taking the "Major" to the Infirmary herself.

But the "Major" looked at Victred with disappointment.

"Good-bye, Fred," said he, "you're a rum 'un as ever I come across. But you ain't 'alf a bad sort. Gord bless yer, Fred, Gord bless yer."

Victred couldn't say anything; he just nodded two or three times, and squeezed the dwarf's horny little hand. Then the cab started off, and he went back slowly into the booth.

Forgetting that he still wore his giant's boots, he walked carelessly, stumbled over a board that was lying under one of the living-vans, the sides of which formed the walls of the booth, and went sprawling on his face. But this was not the worst of it. Stretching out his arms in an instinctive effort to save himself, he struck a girl standing under the canvas, who with difficulty saved herself from falling to the ground. His dismay was overwhelming when he perceived, as he with much trouble got himself and his ingenious stilt-like boots into a perpendicular position, that the lady to whom he had introduced himself so unconventionally was "Red Jack."

The naphtha lamps had been extinguished; but a little oil-lamp, in a bracket on one side of the proscenium, gave enough light for him to see the girl, dressed in a dark skirt and a black jacket, as she shrank away. Her pale face was wearing just the same look of extreme fatigue as on the night when he carried her across the moor.

"I beg your pardon," said he in crestfallen tones. "I—I did not see you, and——"

"And it's Saturday night. I know," answered the girl coldly.

Victred retorted with great heat: "It might be any

other night as far as I am concerned, Miss M'Rena ; I'm as sober as yourself."

Jack raised her tired head slowly and looked full in his face. Then the old look of fanatical enthusiasm, the look which had impressed and fascinated him during her wild speech at Crossley Ridge, came gradually back into her tired face, the light began to glow in her black eyes ; she clasped her little thin hands and held them against her breast.

"Oh, I know, I know now who it is "—she began in a slow, dreamy tone—" I must not say your name, but I know it. My father told me. He told me "— she went on, with ever-rising enthusiasm — "how, though you were born a gentleman, rich and with hopes of high rank, you gave up all, all, because you loved your poor country better than wealth, ease, better than life itself ; how you hated to be happy while your countrymen were oppressed ; how you left the home of your birth to live and toil with the people ; how you were proud to live under the stigma of having killed an enemy of mankind, even though he was your own kin. Oh, sir, I honour you, I revere you. You are a king among men. Bend down. Let me kiss your face."

Such an invitation, from any other girl's lips, Victred would have accepted with alacrity. But Jack was different. He grew hot, and cold, and almost frightened, as the little elf-like creature held out her hands, and stared at him with her great eyes. He would have liked to laugh it off, and remain unkissed ; but he did not dare. Stooping hastily therefore, and with much bashfulness, he received the imprint of her lips upon his cheek.

He almost shivered as he raised his head. The touch of her lips seemed to sting, to burn.

CHAPTER XIII.

" If one could have that little head of hers
Painted upon a background of pale gold,
Such as the Tuscan's early art prefers."
—BROWNING.

THE oil-lamp which lighted the booth burned dimly, smoking the glass ; the wind blew coldly under the canvas walls ; but it was not with the cold that Victred shivered, as he stood with his big felt hat rolled up in his hands, looking down at Jack. Her kiss seemed to burn still on his lips, not like a kiss of love from a beautiful girl, but like the brand of a hot iron. It was uncanny, that kiss; he wished she had not given it him. Just as his heart was opening wide to the little fragile-looking girl, whose coming was to him as the first appearance of the mouse to the prisoner, she rose up in the panoply of her enthusiasm as patriot and preacher, and as it were threw back his pity and his tenderness with great blows.

He was for the moment quite confused by her misplaced enthusiasm, as much unable to laugh at it as he was to sympathise.

"So, so you're—you're going to be the dwarf?" he said, stammering. "It's too bad of your father ; he ought not to let you do such a thing."

Now to attack her father, even in the lightest manner, was almost as infamous a crime, in Jack's eyes, as to attack the great Cause of which she and he were the prophets. She answered with energy:

."Whatever my father does is good and right. We have to sacrifice ourselves to the work. In the summer he travels abroad, visits foreign centres, collects materials for the next winter's campaign. He could not take me ; I should be in the way."

There was an unconscious note of regret in these last words, which moved Victred to persist in his protest.

" But at least he might provide for you better than by letting you travel about the country in a show-wagon, to be stared at by a lot of rough mining brutes ! "

Victred's democratic sympathies were entirely undeveloped. The divine people, whom Jack worshipped so enthusiastically, were in his eyes just " cads," considered collectively, necessary for the tillage of the soil and for the service of *nous autres*, but otherwise very little nearer his own level than dogs or horses. The closer acquaintance with the masses which he had lately been forced to make confirmed him in this view. Individually, he had met some among them, and did not doubt that there were others, who stood out from the rest, and merited his esteem by good sense or good feeling ; but on the whole his enforced study of them had resulted chiefly in the discovery of characteristics, of which the love of beer, of dirt, and of noise, and the free use of language of monotonous nastiness, were the chief.

Jack was appalled by the depth of moral corruption revealed by his ill-considered speech.

"Brutes ! " she exclaimed. " Rough mining brutes ! You, with the courage and the heart to strike a bold blow in the cause of freedom, you speak of the suffering, toiling millions as brutes ! "

The little creature hurled the words at him as if each one had been a blow. Habit had made inflated language, whenever the Cause was in question, as natural to her as inflated thought. Victred did not immediately answer. That this girl should take it for granted that his cousin's death was no accident was horrible. He began to think, with a regretful pang, that the madness of the everlasting " Cause " was going to put an end to all his hopes of companionship. At this point it occurred to him that Jack's spurt of energy was rather feverish, and her voice hoarse. They might perhaps agree better on the safer ground of mere material themes. He must offer some apology, he saw that ; then they

could make a fresh and haply a more successful
start.

"Well, I didn't mean the word offensively," he began in a very meek voice.

"You don't call the word 'brute' offensive when
applied to a human creature? Would you not call
it offensive if applied to yourself?"

"Why, yes," admitted Victred with a gentle sigh,
as if he saw that he was condemned to an argument
in which he would be made to have the worst of it.

"Then you think yourself superior to the 'rough
brutes,' as you call them, to the men who labour with
their hands, to the bulk of your fellow-men, in fact?"

Victred hesitated. "If I 'climb down,'" he said to
himself, "and satisfy her by telling a lie, we shall start
wrong; I shall have to go on telling her lies, until
some day I shall forget, and then there'll be an ex-
plosion, and I shall stand convicted of bad faith, and
there'll be the —— to pay. Hanged if I won't tell
her the truth at once and have done with it.

"Yes," he answered in as gentle and deprecating a
tone as he could possibly find, "I do consider myself
their superior. If I didn't, I'd shoot myself."

Jack had to wait a minute to take breath in the
face of the unblushing confession of such a creed.
Then she laughed ironically, with a pretty, musical
little laugh which she often used very effectively in
her speeches at crowded meetings.

Folding her arms she asked, with her head a little
on one side:

"And on what grounds do you base your assumption of superiority? Or rather admit at once that
you have no grounds, that you, nursed in luxury and
educated in ignorance, have always taken your
superiority for granted, without giving the matter a
second thought."

"But I haven't," protested Victred. "I've thought
about it a great deal; and the more I've thought
about it, the more I've become convinced that I'm
right."

Jack stood before him, or rather below him, immovable, majestic, deeply in earnest, swaying with bodily fatigue, but with her mind absorbed in readiness to hear and confute his answer.

And the lamp smoked, and the wind began to blow more keenly, and the voices, some rough, some shrill, of the revellers on the fair-ground outside came to their ears with more distinctness than ever in the silence inside the booth.

"Well?" said Jack at last.

"Well," returned Victred gently, "I am fonder of soap and water, less fond of beer, my vocabulary is larger and much better chosen, and I take some sort of interest, occasionally, in things outside the range of my daily life. Those are some of the points which make the class I come from superior to the other."

"But all those things are superficial."

"They count though, other things being equal."

"Yes, yes, *other things being equal*," repeated the girl earnestly. "But are they? What virtue has your class to show that can compare with the uncomplaining patience, the cheerfulness under toil and suffering which are the heritage of the poor?"

"If uncomplaining patience is their great virtue, why do you try so hard to destroy it?"

"Because such toil, such suffering as theirs are unworthy the dignity of men."

"So that by giving them less to do and less to suffer, you would *raise* the class that toils with its hands nearer the level of the class that does not. Is not that an admission of the superiority of the class you detest so much?"

"But it is a false and evil superiority, not based on any personal merit of its possessor!"

"You may say the same of any sort of natural superiority—exceptional beauty or health, or strength or brains."

"There is no such thing as 'natural superiority.' Personal defects are the results of ages of *un*natural conditions of life. As knowledge spreads among the people, when we shall have freed them from the yoke which is upon their neck, and given them time and opportunities for the self-culture you think so much of, they will learn to avoid those conditions which result in ugliness, ill-health, mental inferiority in themselves and their children ; the world will be peopled by strong, handsome, intelligent men and women, to whom their lightened burden of daily toil brings only enough fatigue to secure happy, healthy slumber. Then it will be your boasted gentlemen, your aristocracy, your plutocracy which, pampered and lost beyond redemption by the self-indulgence of ages, will supply the world with its idiots, its weaklings and its cripples ! "

Jack was happier, more at home, in long flights of this sort than in give-and-take argument. Her voice swelled, her eyes glowed, her little upturned face flushed, and her tiny hands swept the air with impassioned gestures, as she delivered this speech with all the fire of irresistible conviction.

Victred rolled up his hat and tapped his knees with it. He was standing with one foot on a barrel which was one of the supports of the front bench, and leaning his head on his hand rather disconsolately. It would be a great bore if she went on like this much and often, he thought. But the poor little speech-maker imagined she had made a great effect, and she looked at him exultingly. When he did not speak she fancied it was her picture of the fate in store for him and his "class" which had struck him dumb. Still, she was inexorable. Tapping her hands lightly against each other, and letting her voice fall to a dreamy whisper, she added :

"Then indeed we shall have our revenge ! "

He looked at her in bewilderment and pity, watched the rising and falling of her bosom, the nervous movements of her tired limbs. And then, glad to find relief for his tender feelings in anger, he threw himself into a passion of indignation against Dennis, to whose selfish exploitation of his daughter's

enthusiasm she owed, Victred felt sure, her fragile
physique as well as her general impracticability.

"Does Mrs. de Mowbray know you have come?"
he asked rather shortly.

"Oh, yes. She was very kind, and she told me I
looked tired and had better go to bed."

"Well, that was very good advice, I think. Why
didn't you take it?"

Jack laughed a little in an embarrassed way. She
seemed, when once it was no longer a question of the
Cause, to shrink into a childish little creature, with
purposeless reticences and spasms of shyness. At
last she said, hanging her head:

"Madame Elaine was in the way, sitting on the
steps. And—and she looked so disagreeably at me
that I didn't like to ask her to move. I am to sleep
in Mrs. de Mowbray's own carriage, and she doesn't
like it."

"No. Miserable old porpoise! She's jealous."

"It's only natural. You see, she's been with Mrs.
de Mowbray a long time, and she's very fond of her."
Victred laughed ironically. "It was just the same
when I was here before."

And the regeneratrix of humanity, with a weary
little sigh, sat down on the lowest of the three rickety
steps which led up to the stage of the booth, and
shivered.

"You're not going to sit here in the draught for a
couple of hours, till that wretched old woman goes to
bed?"

"I shan't have very long to wait. They're counting the checks now; when that's done they're going
across to the hotel together. Mrs. de Mowbray
offered to take me too——"

"What! Into a public-house? Infamous!"

"Why? I've been in them with her before."

"Well, you won't go in one with her again, at least
while I'm here." Jack raised her head quickly,
astonished at his tone. He went on, without giving
her time to make any comment: "May I bring my

supper, and cook it in here? I've got a little stove,
and you can warm yourself by it. You look as if
you were cold."

"Of course you can bring it. But I'm not cold,
thank you."

Her manner was haughty now, as well as cold and
shy. She resented his pitying, protecting tone, and
above all his amazing assumption of authority over
her movements.

Victred hurried off in search of his stove. Outside
the booth he was met by the fair Elaine, who was
looking even moister and pinker than usual. He
would have avoided her, but her large, flabby hand
was laid upon his arm even as he recovered from the
shock of the meeting. Mrs. de Mowbray, who delighted in teasing her obsequious humble friend, had
found a great opportunity in the coming of Dennis's
daughter, and Elaine was longing for a sympathetic
bosom on which to weep.

"Only to think, Mr. Watt," sobbed out she, after
expressing pleasure at the sight of his "kind face,"
"only to think that I, after all this time, and the
friend I've been to Mrs. de M., and the way I've
taken her part and said always whosever fault the
fault was it was none of hers—to think that I should
be cast aside now for a chit of a girl, a little sneaking
baggage that knows how to worm her way, and to
fawn and to flatter, which thank goodness I don't,
nor couldn't demean myself so much as to try."

The wily Victred thought he perceived his advantage, and he affected to be moved by this tale of her
woes.

"It's too bad, it is indeed, to turn you over just for
a fresh face. If I can do you any good, by keeping
the girl out of Mrs. de Mowbray's way, I will, rely
upon me."

Elaine wiped her eyes, and sobbed out that he was
a gentleman, he was, and it was no more than she
had expected of him. But still she did not relax the
grasp of her adhesive fingers. After taking a few

minutes to recover her breath, she bashfully murmured that Mrs. de M. (pronounced dee-em), had promised to "stand her a drink," but "had been so taken up with new-comers and interlopers" that she seemed to have forgotten all about it; and Elaine distinctly hinted that it was the plain duty of a gentleman that was a gentleman to rectify her employer's omission. On this occasion, however, Victred was not to be beguiled; he would have been delighted, he said, to escort her himself to "The Clogger's Arms," but unhappily he had made an appointment, which he had only just time to keep.

"Oh, don't let me keep you then, pray," said the fat lady snappishly.

And, releasing his arm, she gave Victred the opportunity to raise his hat and leave her. He hurried to the living-carriage, and in a few minutes was back again inside the booth with his stove, which he put down on the ground close to the raised stage. The smoking lamp was almost out: on the steps where Jack had seated herself Victred could see something huddled up, something which did not move at his entrance. He struck a match, guessing rightly what had happened.

Tired out with her journey, the girl had fallen asleep.

At the first moment that his eyes fell upon her, Victred experienced a great shock. Her hands hung down at her sides; her head, thrown back, rested on the stage above her; her face was entirely colourless, and he could not see a movement of her body. Was she dead? She seemed to him so tiny, so fragile, so utterly unfit in body for the strain to which her father caused her to be constantly exposed, that he would not have been surprised to find that life had indeed, at this first moment of release from the strain, left the little body. And he asked himself, when, taking one of her cold hands in his, the twitching of the muscles told him she was alive, whether it would not have been better for her to die like that, full of faith in her father, belief in her great mission, than to go on living till the inevitable moment of disillusion came.

Victred lit a candle which he had brought with him, and examined the face attentively. The features were small and delicate, extremely beautiful, but with a beauty which appealed only to the eye of refinement. And even more striking than its beauty was the exceeding childish innocence of the face: as Victred gazed upon it and thought of the utterances of fierce sedition which he had heard from those childlike lips, a smile of infinite pity crossed his face, and he murmured below his breath: " Poor little thing ! "

Then he seated himself on a barrel beside the stove, and with great care and science set himself to grill chops. And in a few minutes, roused either by the hissing noise or by the smell of cooking, or by the genial warmth, Jack awoke, sat up, and stared blankly at her companion across the red glow.

" Who are you ? " she said at last, without any fear , but with much wonder.

" I'm the cook," cheerfully responded Victred, who had taken off his flowing black locks and Wild West' moustache, and now shone only in the paler light of his natural beauty.

Jack sprang up.

" I remember ! " she gasped. " You called them brutes ! "

Victred sat back, gridiron in hand, in dismay.

" You're not going to begin again about that now ! "

Jack hesitated. She was looking from the chops to the loaf, from the loaf to the other items of the feast, with earthy, animal interest. She sighed.

" Supposing we have supper first, and discussion afterwards," suggested Victred, giving a last turn to his second chop.

To his joy she seemed inclined to consider this proposition.

"Will you hear what I have to say, then?" she asked cautiously.

"Of course I will. And I will feel much more inclined to agree with you when I've had my supper, you know."

But Jack did not smile at this flippant remark. She sat down on the steps again with a little sigh, and watched Victred while he turned out his chops on a dish, and then diffidently produced from the corner of the stove three huge baked potatoes.

"I got these," said he, with an apologetic laugh, "from a man outside; I thought it would save time."

"And they're so nice," said Jack. "I should have often gone near to starving if it hadn't been for the baked potato man."

Victred felt a choking sensation in the throat as he looked at the enthusiastic little drudge whom her father did not seem even to feed properly. There was no sacred fire burning in the white face now. She looked cold and pinched, grave and quiet. He handed her a plate with another apology. There seemed to him to be a want of imagination about his choice of chops to feed such a fairy-like creature.

"I didn't know what to get," said he. "The oysters one gets in these towns are as big as tables; three of them are a load for an able-bodied man. I dare say you would have liked butterflies' wings better, only it's too early in the year for butterflies."

Again Jack did not laugh. She looked up gravely from her plate.

"Butterflies' wings!" she echoed. "Why, I have had nothing to eat since breakfast!" Seeing the shocked expression on Victred's face, she went on: "We had a little under-estimated the expense of the journey. I found I had only my fare from Southampton, where I left my father."

Victred said nothing: he dared not. He watched her furtively and in silence as, almost too tired and faint to eat, Jack went slowly on with her supper. He was wondering how he should set about converting

9

her to the knowledge that she was wasting her life
and youth and health in the service of the most selfish
parent that ever existed, and the most shadowy
Cause that ever was held.

She, on her side, was wondering, sleepily wondering,
poor child, what argument would be the strongest and
most effectual to rouse him from his sluggish apathy
in the Cause of suffering humanity. At last, after re-
flecting deeply, with her eyes on the glowing stove-
lamp, she suddenly threw back her head with a
movement which he knew to be common with her
when addressing the People.

He rose at once from the barrel from which he had
been furtively watching her, and began to collect his
batterie de cuisine.

"And now," he said, "I'm sure old Elaine will be
out of the way. You'd better make haste off to bed."

Jack held out her hand to him.

"Good-night," she said. "Thank you very much
for your kindness." Then she let her hand remain in
his while she said simply : "I think I am glad you
won't let me speak to you now. I feel so tired,
so heavy, I might not be able to convince you.
But I shall some day. Promise me," she went on
earnestly, as a sudden fear darted into her innocent
mind, "promise me that you will not avoid me.
Promise that you will let me say to you what is in
my mind, in my heart, and that you will listen."

And Victred, with a smile but with a tremulous
lip, promised that he would.

———

CHAPTER XIV.

"Untouch'd by love, the maiden's breast
Is like the snow on Rona's crest;
So pure, so free from earthly dye,
It seems, whilst leaning on the sky,
Part of the heaven to which 'tis nigh."

—SCOTT.

"HOW old are you, Jack?"

"Eighteen."

"As much as that?"

"Nearly. I shall be eighteen in September."

"Why, you are a woman!"

"Well, what did you think I was?"

And Jack smiled, an accomplishment she had already learned in the fortnight since she joined the "show."

"I looked upon you as a child."

The smile instantly faded from the girl's face. She had not by any means forgotten her intention of converting this kind-hearted and estimable man to the worship of The People, and he had got into the way of listening to her so attentively, with his hat over his eyes and his pipe between his lips, that she had come to consider his conversion as an event much nearer than in reality it was.

"And do you think a child could speak as I speak, and feel as I feel about The Cause?"

Victred tilted up his hat and looked at her with a tender smile on his lips. He did not yet dare to tell her the truth on this point.

"Well, you are very clever," he said, "and you have been very well taught."

"You think one can be taught to *feel!*"

"*You* think so. It is what you are trying to teach me. 'Feel for the toilers,' you say; 'put yourself in their place and feel for them.' Only I'm a stupid learner, and can't or won't learn. You are a clever learner; you could, you would, and you did learn."

9*

There was silence.   They were sitting on a stile in
the sunshine, and each, after a long winter of trouble
and anxiety, was feeling joy and new life in the
return of spring.   The river, shallow and turbid, ran
in front of them.   On the right rose a gentle hill, on
the summit of which, though not yet in sight, was a
famous old mansion, the object of their walk.   It was
the first time they had been so far together, and each
felt a little pleasant excitement in the expedition.

There was another long silence, during which Jack
considered her companion's face thoughtfully.   He
was puffing at his pipe and his eyes were following
the course of a barge which was being propelled at a
great rate down the muddy river.   At last a little
smile began to flicker about that side of his face which
was visible to her.

"How easily you take life!" said she.   "You are
always smiling."

He turned his full face to her, and the smile grew
broader than ever.

"It isn't life that makes me smile, it is you," said
he.   "You are· so absurdly unlike any one else,
Jack."

"How?   How am I unlike any one else?"

But he could not tell her that her calm, straightforward, and yet absorbed study of his own face was
what so much amused him.

"Oh, well," he said, hunting for an answer, "any
one else wouldn't let me smoke my pipe."

"Oh, I don't mind it.   I have had to sit, even to
speak in a room where hundreds of men were smoking
at once, not nice tobacco like yours, but tobacco that
seemed to poison the air and choke one."

"Yes ; The People's taste in tobacco will have to
be reformed with the rest of its education," said
Victred mischievously.

He expected a fiery outburst for his sneer, but to
his surprise Jack only reddened a little, and looked
steadily into the budding hedge beside her.   He was
filled with compunction directly.

" I mustn't tease you about your favourites, must I ?" said he, "or you will never come out with me again."

She turned upon him eyes full of surprise.

" It is very good of you to bring me out," she said. " And it is I who have no right to bore you with that one subject. Unfortunately, it is my only one," she added with an ingenuous little sigh.

It was Victred's turn to be astonished.

" You are going to give up trying to convert me, then ? "

" Yes," she answered rather sadly. " I am going to leave it to my father. I have come to the conclusion that the most I can do with you is to prepare the way for him."

" You think he will have more influence with me than you ? "

" Yes. You see you are so much better educated than the people I can influence, that you want a man as well educated as yourself to convince you. Besides, you know I'm a girl, and that destroys any influence I might have."

" Does it ? I should have thought it would increase it. I've often wondered why you masquerade as a boy, when as a woman you would excite still more attention."

" Too much, my father says. Then it is so much easier for a man and a boy to get about the country than for a man and a girl ; and by a change of sex I can sink my identity when I'm not wanted. My father says the mystery keeps up my market value," she added with a little laugh of pride in her usefulness.

Victred said nothing to this for a long time. He was so much interested in that barge that he got off the stile and walked a few paces down the lane in order that he might be able to follow its course a little further. Presently he came back, and stood a yard away from Jack and began pulling the young shoots of hawthorn off the hedge.

" That's all very well at present," he said at last, continuing the talk where it had left off, " while it's only a question of what your father and you choose. But presently there will come along the evil genius Man in the form of a baneful but beautiful creature like myself, only more so ; and *he* won't let you go wandering over the face of the earth in—in his own costume, I can tell you."

Jack looked at him with superb disdain, disdain which gave a curve to her lips and sent a becoming little flush to her cheeks.

" Do you really think so little of me as to suppose that there exists a man in the world who would get me to forsake The Cause ? "

Victred nodded slowly and emphatically.

" I'm sure of it," said he.

Jack smiled serenely.

"Well," she said, "you are wrong.   There is no room in my heart for a man.   And if one were ever to succeed in thrusting himself in, with the help of my love for my father and my love for The Cause I would thrust him out again."

Victred laughed.   He was glad to hear her talk like this.   Since to him love was anathema, it was pleasant to find a companion who was in the same mind.   Only he had misgivings, from which the girl was free.

They went up the hill and inspected the beautiful Tudor house, with its mullioned windows overlooking a stately terrace.   And then they were tempted to wander further, Jack taking an extravagant delight in the spring-like green of the fields and trees which astonished Victred, who had imagined that her cross-country life would have familiarised and even satiated her with the charms of wood and field and lane.

" Do you know," she said with sudden gravity, stopping with her hands full of weeds and grasses, with not one of which she seemed to be acquainted, " that I have never, *never* been for a walk like this before ? "

"What! Not with your father?"

"No. He doesn't care for the country; and besides, it is only in the winter that we go about together, when it is cold and bleak; and then he never can spare the time to walk. And when he leaves me in lodgings by myself, as he often has to do for two or three days at a time, he likes me to keep indoors— and so do I, for I'm afraid to go about alone."

"Afraid!"

Jack hung her head. The admission had slipped out, and she had instantly desired that it should pass unnoticed.

"What are you afraid of? Surely not of—the People?".

She blushed.

"No, no, not really afraid, of course. And it is very silly, I know. Especially as I pass for a boy. But——"

"But you are afraid all the same? Well, I am glad to hear it. You can regenerate mankind quite as well without being so very strong-minded."

She looked up at him askance, in some doubt of his seriousness. But he was so grave as to leave himself open to no reproach. And then, as he saw by her lagging steps that she was getting tired, he got her a glass of milk at a little shop before they turned their faces again towards the town.

With that day began a season of pure delight for both of them; a season of wanderings in the sunshine, over treeless moors and along the banks of rocky stream or trim canal. Often they would sit down beside a lock, and watch the barges as they came through; or they would find a still pool wherein to practise a delusive sport which they called fishing; and on Saturday, the great gala-day with all showfolk high and low when "the ghost walks," they would go straight to the market-place of the town they happened to be in, and Jack would choose herself a rose or a whole sixpenny bunch of more modest flowers from one stall, and sixpennyworth of almond

rock or barley sugar from another. And then they
would trip off to the station and, all out of Victred's
modest guinea, take two third class tickets to some
place where there was an old castle to be seen, or
an ancient church. And if there was no fee for
seeing the interesting building, they saw it, both the
outside and the inside ; but if there was a fee, they
saw the outside only. In any case they were perfectly contented ; and after devising and carrying out
a plan by which the hunger and thirst of two persons
could be allayed within the limits of a shilling, they
would return tired, dusty, silent, happy, in time to don,
the one his red shirt, leather trousers, big boots, and
magnificent coiffure ; the other all the glories of a
cotton velvet page's suit trimmed with spangles, from
under which, by the ingenious device of Mrs. de Mowbray, peeped a pair of shoes which were tied, not on
Jack's feet, but round her ankles.

Of course every day was not Saturday. After the
reckless dissipation of that one grand outing they
had to retrench ; and day by day, as the hole in
Victred's guinea grew larger, their pleasures and their
needs grew more modest, until Thursday found them
debating how ninepence could be made to spread over
two days' expenses ; while on Friday, if their walk
brought them to a bridge where there was a halfpenny
toll to pay, they had either to turn back or to "run
for it."

It was Jack's constant lament that she brought
nothing to the exchequer, for she got no salary, only
her food and her little cot in Mrs. de Mowbray's living
carriage. She knew that Victred, who had to pay
all his own expenses except that of lodging, had
the hardest of struggles to make both ends meet,
and it cut her to the heart that he should spend
money on her. To Victred, however, this fact of her
dependence on him for every halfpenny was a source
of infinite joy. He limited the number of his pipes ;
he had a meat dinner every other day, and on the
alternate ones contented himself with bread and

vegetables; he washed most of his own clothes, not
with the best results; and for some weeks things
went on merrily enough.

At last, however, one dreadful, never - to - be -
forgotten Saturday, when there was a haze over the
hills and a damp mist enveloping everything, Victred
sauntered up after "treasury" to where Jack was
sitting on the steps leading to the pay-box. They
were staying in a big, ugly, Yorkshire manufacturing
town; but there were lovely walks outside, and all
the week they had been promising themselves an ex-
cursion to an historical abbey a few miles off.

"Jack," said he, bending his head to the level of
her ear, "I can manage the flowers. Can you do
without the sweets?"

Jack burst out crying.

"I knew it," she sobbed, below her breath, "I knew
it. Boots?"

Victred nodded.

"I've managed a long time," he murmured softly,
"with brown paper, one layer glued over another. As
long as the weather's dry it answers capitally. But a
damp day plays the—I—I mean it doesn't agree with
make-shifts at all. Yesterday I could have been
traced the whole way—brown paper footprints—and
scraps of brown paper pulp."

Jack dried her eyes in a dashing manner and
sprang off the steps.

"Never mind the flower," she said; "I don't want it.
Go and get the boots. We couldn't have gone to the
abbey to-day in any case; it's too damp. Go, go,
go."

"Well, will you wait till I come back?"

"I've got some sewing to do for Mrs. de Mowbray.
I'll take it inside and wait for you there."

"Inside" meant inside the booth, the canvas walls
of which formed their shelter whenever the weather
was too bad for wandering about the country. Many
an hour they had spent there together, Jack with
her sewing, and Victred, with a needle and thread,

trying to equal her deftness as he mended his own clothes.

It goes without saying that the open predilection of these two young people for each other's society, their constant companionship, did not pass without remark in their own circle. But that circle was so extremely limited that what in a larger community would have excited much comment seemed but the natural forgathering of the only two young people in the "show." Mrs. de Mowbray looked upon Jack as a child, and had a genuine respect for Victred; besides which she did not care to exercise the strict duties of a chaperon, except by fits and starts. The male staff of the show, besides Victred, consisted of two men who sometimes appeared respectively as a "man-snake" and a "bearded lady," but whose duties were principally those of "handy-men," alternately check-takers, money-takers, carpenters and chuckers-out. These harmless necessary beings were stigmatised by Elaine as "low creatures;" and undoubtedly they did leave something to be desired on the point of refinement. But in the camaraderie of life on the road, they considered themselves as being also "pro.'s," and occasionally amused themselves by saluting Jack as "Mrs. Watt."

Jack took the joke without prudery and without annoyance, and told Victred to his face that she hoped every wife hadn't as much trouble in keeping her husband in order as she had. Victred laughed a forced laugh, and said he hoped not. He was in love with her, and by this time he knew it. The touch of her little hand thrilled him into silence; to watch her face, to listen to her voice, to get a smile from her by what passed with them for wit, to see the flush of health week by week grow in her pale cheeks—these were now the pleasures of his life. All he had asked was that they should continue, that the winter should not come to take her away, that no censorious eye should read his secret, no over-busy tongue pour the poisonous knowledge into her innocent ears.

For Jack knew no more of love than a child does, or if she had reached the outer gates of the enchanted ground, she was ignorant of the fact. All the passion of her young heart, the fervour, the heat of it, were bestowed on that unresponsive phantom, The People. Wrapt up in this devotion, she believed herself invulnerable, and had dropped straight into constant companionship with a handsome and attractive man, with no more fear either for herself or for him than if he had been one of the middle-aged and grubby patriots, her father's friends and contemporaries, of whom she saw so many.

The subtlety of the danger lay in the fact that Victred did not make love to her, did not put on an air of effusive respect, while paying her exaggerated compliments, and looking at her in a way which made her blush, as Mr. Tracy Fitzalan did. He treated her as she liked to be treated, as a friend, a comrade, with only just so much gentleness and consideration as was due to the fact of her inferior size and strength.

And yet there hovered about them always the fascinating danger of a word or a look or a touch which should open her eyes. Now, for instance, as she looked under the canvas watching for his return in his new boots, there was a look of tenderness in her eyes which made Victred's heart bump uneasily against his side when he caught sight of her.

She looked up in his face with a smile, and then down at his boots.

"Oh!" cried she, with an accent of deep disappointment.

"Don't you like them?" he asked in an aggrieved tone. "They're soldier's boots—such a bargain!"

"They're not nice enough, somehow, for you," she said ingenuously.

Victred laughed, touched by something in her tone.

"Why, I think they're nice enough for anybody, Jack. "I'm quite proud of them."

"Oh, yes, yes, they're very good and strong, I know. But they're just ordinary men's boots, and they don't seem to go with the rest of you somehow."

He did not point out to her her delightful inconsistency. He longed to lift her up in his arms and kiss her for it. He laughed a little, looking away from her out upon the wet stones of the market-place, and there was silence for a few minutes. Then he said in a mock-serious tone:

"The worst of getting anything new is that it shows up all the old things so. Now when I tried on my boots I was ashamed of my socks."

Jack sprang up from the bench on which she was sitting.

"I can knit socks," she cried joyfully. "I'll make you some. "Oh, but——" Her face fell. "There's the wool."

"Oh, I can get that," said Victred, "if you really will be so good. I'll get it—next Saturday."

But Jack had set her face doggedly.

"No, you shan't," said she. "I'll get it myself, *myself* I say." And she stamped her foot. "I won't be always sponging on you——"

"Don't say that, little Jack," interrupted Victred. "When you leave off taking your share of my guinea, I—I'll chuck it into the gutter, or down old Russell's throat, or—or give it back to Mrs. M."

Through his playful tone there peeped out the danger signal, in a little huskiness, a little uncertainty of utterance. Jack patted his hand gratefully.

"You shan't be driven to such straits as that," said she softly. "But I'll get the wool myself all the same."

"How?"

"Never mind."

And she pursed up her little mouth to intimate her royal pleasure that the subject should be considered closed.

The following week was a mysterious one. These two faithful friends avoided one another, and gave weird and fanciful explanations of the hours of their absence from each other. Jack's spirits drooped, however, as the days went by, and it became evident that her secret enterprise was not prospering. By Thursday it was clear that she had taken a great resolution, and on the evening of that day, just as Victred was going to dress for the show, she rushed panting up the steps of the living-carriage he was entering, with a paper parcel in her arms, out of which tufts of wool of nondescript colour were bursting.

"Look, look, I've got it! I said I would!" she panted, in a whisper which went off into a little shriek of delight in the end. "The wool, the wool! Don't you see? Oh, you shall have some lovely socks now!"

Victred sat down on the steps to be near her level, and she planted her parcel triumphantly in his arms. He did not thank her; he did not express any pleasure. On the contrary, he looked up with quite a stern frown upon his face.

"*I* know what you've been up to," he said with a little tremor in his voice, which may, of course, have been indignation, but which set her crying:

"Oh, don't, don't speak like that, don't, don't."

"I know!" he repeated sternly. "That spoon of your mother's—I missed it at tea last night. You were trying to make up your mind whether you could spare it, and you—you—Oh! you are a wicked girl!"

"Sh—sh! I didn't sell it outright," whispered the girl tremulously, "I only—*you* know."

Victred did know. The girl's resource had been his many a time already during his wanderings.

"I tried to get some work to do at the shops first," she explained, trying to lessen her guilt in his eyes. "But nobody would give me any. I think they knew I belonged to the 'show,' and believed that I should steal the materials. So then I grew desperate, and— and——"

"Well," said Victred doggedly, "you've only come
to the same thing in the end as if you'd come to me;
for you will have to get me to give you the money to
get it out on Saturday. And I shall want a lot of
coaxing, mind you, because I consider you've behaved
badly."

At first poor Jack was rather crestfallen at the
thought that she would not be allowed to consum-
mate the sacrifice of her one treasure, the silver spoon
that had been her mother's. But Victred brought
strange and subtle arguments to bear, and suggested
that the spoon should be his until she could get the
money to pay him back, and that meanwhile he would
lend it to her to eat her porridge with.

And comforted but a little confused by his reason-
ing, Jack consented, and went off to don her cotton
velvet suit.

CHAPTER XV.

"There are mincing women, mewing
Of their own virtue, and pursuing
Their gentler sisters to that ruin
Without which—what were chastity?"
                                        —SHELLEY.

AND The People, The Great People all this time?
The divinity was not forgotten, although Jack's worship had indeed of late grown somewhat intermittent.
For the introduction to a new life, a life in which
there were pleasures as well as duties, joys to be
savoured as well as trials to be borne, was at first
rather intoxicating; and in the fascinating companionship of one single representative of the tyrant
classes, the down-trodden masses ran the risk of
losing their foremost place in her heart.

The weeks of early summer were the first taste of
happiness, real unalloyed happiness, which Jack had
ever known. She had passed a dull youth, first as
a pupil and then as a pupil-teacher, in a school in
Switzerland, where the instruction was sound, the

diet meagre, and the discipline rigid. During the two subsequent years of travel with her father, her whole time had been given up to an education and a discipline more rigid still ; while her first stay with Mrs. de Mowbray had been a season of acute loneliness and of misery more acute still.

The making of Victred's socks was an epoch in the young people's lives. To watch the progress of the work under the girl's busy fingers, to fill her with tortures of doubt as to the correctness of her measurements, to hail the completion of each sock with astonishment, to affect to regard it as too good to wear ; through all these phases Victred passed again and again, amusing himself and filling the little worker with delight.

Meantime the mystery of his movements continued to excite Jack's curiosity. Saturday came and went. Jack got back her spoon, causing a fresh strain, as Victred had prophesied, on his finances ; the next week advanced. Still he gave no explanation of his unaccountable absences until Friday came, when he suddenly dazzled her eyes by holding up before them two silver coins.

Jack gasped.

"Not," she murmured incredulously, "not *half-crowns !*"

For the possession of any but bronze money on a Friday was unheard of, almost portentous. Victred, after having allowed her ample time to feast her eyes upon his treasures, dropped them into his pocket, and jingled them affectionately.

"What shall we have for supper to-night, Jack ?" he asked with affected carelessness.

Jack laughed ecstatically. There was something so amusingly new about such a question on a Friday, which was usually with them a day of abstinence of the strictest sort. For when Victred abstained from flesh for lack of funds, Jack, who dined with Mrs. de Mowbray, abstained also for sympathy. Supper the proprietress did not undertake to provide for her charge, and the dwarf would have gone hungry to bed but for her friend the giant, who saved up his choicest bargains, and exerted his best culinary efforts for this the crowning feast of the day.

"Don't let's waste it on supper at all," said Jack thoughtfully, after a long pause, during which, with her chin in her hand, she had considered, in all its bearings, Victred's new position as a capitalist. "Let's—let's *save* it; and then, when something dreadful happens again, new shirts—or a week with the other crowd, you will be able just to put your hand in your pocket, and—and there!"

She made a gesture with her hand, to signify the pouring out of boundless wealth. Victred looked disappointed.

"Oh, I say, Jack, you don't think I would ever have worked like a slave at the books of a miserable old ironmonger this week and more just to *save* the money, do you?"

From which speech it will be seen what inroads Bohemianism had already made in the young man's principles. Jack dropped her knitting, which she had been continuing mechanically, into her lap, and looked at him with round eyes.

"*What* have you been doing?" faltered she.

"Doing the books of that old rascal who sells sixpenny saucepans at the corner-shop opposite 'The King's Head.'"

"Doing his books! How clever of you! I didn't think you could."

A cloud passed over Victred's face.

"Well," said he apologetically, "he couldn't do them himself at all, you know. They were in an awful muddle."

"And you put them all straight!" exclaimed Jack with admiration.

"N—no, not exactly," admitted Victred sadly. "But he'll never find it out unless somebody comes and tells him. He says he's expecting his nephew, who is a ' great scollard,' and he wanted to put things straight before his arrival. If the nephew arrives before we leave the town, I am a lost man ! "

Jack did not laugh. Instantly in her mind the illiterate and not too sober ironmonger became a type of The People, whose ignorance was taken advantage of by the better-instructed.

" Then you cheated him ! " she cried tragically.

" No, I didn't. I did ten shillings' worth of work and charged him five shillings. If I had done what he expected me to do, I should have been underpaid with five pounds. That is how things right themselves in this world," he added in a philosophical tone.

But Jack still grieved. A woman is either honest or dishonest : she knows nothing of the man's intermediate state, and never tries to compound with the devil. That night Jack ate her sweetbread with a sigh, and then between mouthfuls of angel-cake murmured, " that poor ironmonger ! "

It seemed to her that it was a punishment for her participation in Victred's guilt that Madame Elaine was particularly disagreeable to her that evening. The fat lady, who possessed that excess of sentiment which seems to be the heritage of all creatures of abnormal stoutness, had never forgiven Victred what she chose to consider his defection. It was quite true that he now never carried her parcels for her, if he met her on her marketing rounds staggering under a load of half-a-pound of sausages, a loaf, and a couple of cabbages which she had picked up a bargain. He was always with that little ha'porth of misery, who, any one could see, was only just playing with him, and would chuck him up as soon as look at him if a man earning his thirty bob a week should come along ! Not that there could be more than one man in the world with a taste for such a skinny piece of goods ! And when there was a woman about too, a real woman of flesh and blood, and not a mechanical doll wound up to walk to one everlasting tune, who would have cared for him, aye, and looked after him

10

too, and cooked his dinners, and not wanted him to spend all his money careering about the country with her, like some people that had no thought for a man's pocket nor for his stomach either !

Reflections such as these had long rankled in Elaine's mind, and she had even allowed herself to hint pretty plainly to Mrs. Dee-m that such goings on as those of Dennis's girl were a disgrace to a respectable show.

"I'm sure the way she follows that young man about is perfectly sickening ; and one of these days, mark my words, there'll be a scandal, and we shall have to suffer, you and me too, ma'am, for being mixed up with a little trollop that can't make the men keep their distance ! "

But Mrs. de Mowbray did not at the moment want to be bothered to look after Jack. She had, as she herself would have put it, "other fish to fry." A theatre in a big desolate Lancashire cotton town was to be let cheap, and she was revolving in her mind the question whether or not she should take it. So she chose only to laugh and to tease her obsequious companion.

"We all know *you* can keep 'em off, don't we, Ellen ? " she answered with great jocularity. "Sort of atmosphere of reserve about you, my dear, that freezes 'em up, eh ? Never you trouble about the girl ; she's under my eye, and she'll come to no harm while I have the care of her."

And the lady had dismissed Elaine with a nod, and returned to calculations of the price of the bargain upon which she had set her heart.

Unluckily, however, fate since that day had been unkind to Mrs. de Mowbray. An unexpected competitor had out-bid her, and she had lost the chance which had seemed fair in her eyes. Of course this event told upon her temper, and for some days Elaine had been on the watch for an opportunity of dropping afresh into her employer's ear a word which she felt sure would now fall upon better ground.

This opportunity came on the Friday when Victred burst upon Jack with his unexpected wealth.

It happened that Madame Elaine was very fond of sweetbread, and also that, on this particular evening, she had drawn so heavily upon her weekly stipend as to be unable to treat herself to so much as a modest "half-pint" wherewith to slake her perpetual thirst. So that when Victred, in a rapid aside just before the show opened, informed Jack of what was in store for her, the wrath of the plump one overflowed, and big tears rolled down her cheeks which she had only just time to dry before the curtain rose.

When the show was over, and the last of the rough spectators had gone, and when Victred had let down one canvas wall for ventilation, Elaine, with angry, jealous eyes, saw the little stove brought out, and the feast prepared, before she took her own departure in search of Mrs. de Mowbray. She found that lady at the pay-box, counting the evening's earnings in no very good humour. She snapped at the Fat Lady, and threw out dark hints that if business didn't improve, she should "chuck up the show," and turn her attention to something more profitable.

Here was Elaine's opportunity; she rushed at it.

"Well, if things are bad in front, they seem to be very good for some folks behind;" she said, with the laborious effort of a stupid person inclined to be vicious.

"What folks?" asked Mrs. de Mowbray shortly, as she bit a doubtful sixpence.

"Oh, some folk I could name but will not, knowing well as there are some folks such favourites as they can do no wrong, which not happening to be one of those lucky ones myself, I might get myself into trouble perraps."

So she spoke, wagging her head the while, and embracing the most prominent part of her voluptuous figure.

"Well, please yourself," said her patroness shortly.

Without being an intellectual colossus, Mrs. de M.

10*

could give the fair Elaine many points. And she knew that the latter was bursting with her piece of scandal. In a very few moments, to the accompaniment of a flood of tears, out it came. She had not been used to be treated with much consideration, since the time when she was the favourite niece of her uncle the butcher (etc., etc.); but to see the way some people turned up their nose at the good food provided for them and must needs go persuading men to buy downright extravagant suppers, over which they made game of the show and everything else, why it made the loyal Elaine perfectly sick, that it did! And him that was a gentleman, she didn't deny it, teaching that insignificant chit to think herself too good for anybody in the show; and him encouraging her in it, and running down in the very hearing of Elaine herself ladies that were not too proud to go into a hotel to have a friendly glass with a gentleman.

"Which, Mrs. de M.," ended Elaine triumphantly, as she at last saw the wished-for expression of hard, vicious anger on her patroness's straight mouth, "I take it to be a reflection, not only on myself, which I should not so much mind, but on you whose bread they eat."

Mrs. de Mowbray, without relaxing her features, uttered a disagreeable laugh.

"I'll give my lord, and my lady too, a lesson," she said.

And although she entered into no further explanation, her hearer felt entirely satisfied.

On the following evening, when the performance was over, Mrs. de Mowbray sent a message to Jack by one of the assistants, that she wanted to speak to her.

"Don't be long, Jack," said Victred, suspecting nothing. "Supper will be ready in exactly two minutes and a half."

Nodding and smiling happily, Jack ran off.

The two minutes and a half passed, five, ten,

twenty, half an hour. Victred at length began to suspect that Mrs. de Mowbray, with the love of ponderous mischief which distinguished her, was detaining Jack on purpose to annoy both her and himself. So he went to the pay-box, and found it deserted. Bob, the most incompetent and the laziest of the two handy men, was smoking his pipe on the steps.

"Where's Mrs. de M ? " asked Victred sharply.

Bob repressed a rising grin.

"Where she is most nights when the show's over."

And he nodded in the direction of "The King's Head" at the corner of the market-place.

"Old Ellen's there too, *and* Miss Jacqueline," added Bob.

Victred gave him a nod by way of acknowledgment for the information, crossed the market-place in a few rapid strides, and dashed into the private bar of the crowded public-house. There he found Mrs. de Mowbray, in her best black velvet hat, the one with the longest feathers, leaning against the counter, laughing loudly, and gesticulating freely with her dirty, be-jewelled hands ; while Elaine, mollified by rum-and-water, played dutiful chorus to her patroness ; and Jack, shy and silent, tried to hide herself behind them to escape the attentions of a young, dissipated-looking, flashily-dressed man, whom Victred knew well as one of the habitual bar-loungers of the town.

On Victred's entrance, the girl uttered a low cry of delight, relief. He pushed past the dissipated-looking man, making him stagger ; and drawing Jack's hand through his arm, was leading her away, when Mrs. de Mowbray, with a furious gesture, laid a detaining hand upon the girl's shoulder.

"'Ow dare you ? 'Ow dare you ? Jacqueline, stay where you are," thundered she in a voice which was husky with rage. "She's in my charge, not yours, you long-legged puppy, and a deal safer with me than you when all's said and done ! "

" Her father will be judge of that," answered Victred in a low voice, most anxious to avoid the vulgar brawl which Mrs. de Mowbray seemed just as anxious to promote.

Now these words of Victred's contained a threat which infuriated while it frightened Mrs. de Mowbray. Dennis was too useful a friend to be offended ; and it was just possible, now that there was a tale-bearer at work to make the worst of things, that he might object to certain details of her guardianship about which Jack herself was too submissive to complain.

" Her father knows very well that she can go anywhere with a lady," almost shrieked Mrs. de Mowbray.

As she still held Jack tightly by the shoulders, Victred was obliged to answer.

" Certainly. She can go anywhere where a lady can go."

" And perhaps," rashly went on Mrs. de Mowbray with an ironical laugh, " perhaps you don't consider that I'm a lady ? "

Victred looked down contemptuously at the shrieking virago.

" Of course not," said he with a shrug. " You haven't even the feelings of a decent woman.

Inarticulate with rage, she released Jack's shoulder in order to make a personal attack upon the wretch who had so insulted her. But Victred, seizing the opportunity of Jack's momentary freedom, whisked her through the doors and out upon the market-place before the blow had time to fall.

———

CHAPTER XVI.

" Of all the heavenly gifts that mortal men commend,
What trusty treasure in the world can countervail a friend ? "
—NICHOLAS GRIMOALD.

BEFORE they had exchanged a word, and when Jack had thanked Victred for his rescue of her only by the grateful pressure of her clinging hands on his arm, she fled away from him, and left him to enter the deserted booth alone.

There was desolation indeed. In his haste to find Jack, Victred had forgotten to warn Bob to look after his supper. Half a dozen rough little urchins had found their way under the canvas, and helped themselves to Victred's broad beans, bacon and baked potatoes, to Jack's ginger-beer and bit of pastry, and now they were warming themselves at his stove ; for although it was July, they were in the midst of one of those spells of cold weather with which an English summer so often breaks its monotony. At Victred's coming they all rose and fled, clattering off in their wooden-soled boots, tumbling over one another, and finally leaving one squealing mite in the hands of Victred, who gave him a shake and then gently placed him on his feet to show him that he was not killed, as he had at first supposed.

Then Victred sat down with his head in his hands, much troubled. He had insulted his " manageress " ; he would be sure to get his notice within a few hours. Then what would become of Jack without him ? And what, oh ! what would become of him without Jack ? During the past few weeks life had rolled on so easily, so happily for both of them, that all the black clouds that hung over the existence of each seemed to have melted away. The accusation which hung over Victred, the woman who had disgraced him, were both forgotten ; and even the all-absorbing Cause, which was Jack's inspiration and Victred's bugbear,

had sunk of late to a secondary place, and left the
girl free to enjoy some of the sweets of life and
youth. Now all these cares rolled back again upon
him, and one of them, the existence of that terrible
"old man of the sea," his wife, swallowed up all the
rest by its magnitude.

As long as he enjoyed Jack's society without
hindrance, he had been able to content himself with
her straightforward, sisterly affection, and to keep his
own growing passion under such complete control
that no suspicion of it had ever troubled the young
girl's mind. But now this threat of enforced absence
from her, and the coarse speech of a spiteful woman,
showed him more clearly the real nature of his feeling
for Jack, and made it more difficult for him to hide it
from her.

Two little hands, placed from behind, suddenly and
softly one on each of his, as he sat holding his head
and considering the situation, made him start.

" You have a guilty conscience ! " cried Jack.

" Quite true."

" What is your dark secret ? "

" Well, I've let a parcel of rascally boys steal our
supper for one thing, and I've insulted the manageress
for another."

" The first I can't forgive, because I'm hungry ; the
second——" involuntarily she began to laugh a little ;
" well, you were rather unkind, weren't you ? "

" I didn't say anything but the simple and obvious
truth," said Victred stoutly. " I shouldn't think twice
about it except for the consequences. Of course I
shall get my notice to-morrow."

But Jack, jumping upon the stage and sitting upon
the edge with her feet dangling, smiled a smile of
superior wisdom.

" No, you won't."

" Not after telling her before everybody she was
not a lady ? Why, that's the greatest insult in the
world to a woman who hasn't the slightest pretensions
to be one ! "

Still Jack smiled confidently.

"Yes, yes, but you don't understand these—these *persons*," said Jack with a twinkle in her eyes. "Persons—ladies who go into bars, are sure sooner or later to hear themselves called by a good many ugly names. Why, I've heard Fred" (this was the carpenter and chief handy man) "call Mrs. de Mowbray to her face words that I shouldn't care to repeat, when they were simply having a little disagreement about the time it took to do a particular journey! By to-morrow morning she will merely look upon to-night's incident as a 'few words," and if you'll ask her 'what she'll take,' she will consider it quite sufficient apology."

"Do you mean it?" cried Victred aghast.

"Indeed you will see that I'm right."

"But the awful thing she said—hinted!"

"What was that? Oh, that I was safer with her than with you. She wanted to say something nasty, and she never thought twice about it, I'm sure."

Victred marvelled, but was scarcely convinced. It was not until the following morning when, coming unexpectedly face to face with Mrs. de Mowbray, he was greeted with the words: "Well, got over your tantrums yet?" uttered with an air of jovial bantering, that he, accepting the proffered olive-branch with some awkwardness, had to own that Jack knew more about show life and show manners than he did.

As Jack remained perfectly easy with him, the slight feeling of constraint which the incident had engendered in Victred soon wore away, and for a brief fortnight, during which they visited two fresh towns on their way southwards, the happiness of the two young people was almost as unalloyed as ever. When Jack bemoaned her neglect of The Cause, Victred assured her with some truth that she could not serve it better than by devoting all her thoughts to building up her strength for the next winter's campaign. As for himself, he would not think; there was misery behind; there was misery ahead;

in the meantime he would take care of Jack and be happy.

The ultimate destination of the show was London, where Mrs. de Mowbay was to meet the "boss," and a great consultation was to be held as to the future movements of both.   Plans were in the air for giving up the "freak" business altogether, and taking to a higher class of entertainment.   In London, too, Dennis was to meet his daughter, in all probability to fetch her away.   Victred's horizon therefore was bounded by the arrival of the show in London.

They had travelled down, by slow stages, as far as one of the big Midland towns, when Jack greeted Victred one morning with a rather lugubrious face.

" Anything the matter, Jack ? "

" N—no, not exactly the matter."   Pause.   " I've had a letter from my father."   And she showed a lengthy communication on blue foolscap, written all over in a tiny, neat hand.

Victred's face fell.

" He is coming to take you away ! "

"Oh no!   He is sending some one to see me——"

" Well ? "

" Some one I don't much like."

· " Who is it ? "

" Your cousin, Mr. Fitzalan."

Victred felt as if he had been seized by the throat. Without at all respecting Tracy, he had been very fond of him ; and his cousin's conduct at the inquest, in giving evidence against him, had troubled him very much.   At first he had tried to explain it away by ascribing it to bad reporting ; but the more he thought about it, the more clearly he remembered the circumstances of his last sight of Tracy's face, and the look upon it, the more apparent it became to him that his friend had in some way become his enemy.   As to the reason, there could only be one—Victred's having prevented his *tête-à-tête* with Jack when she was left alone in the cottage at Clough.   In these circumstances he felt that a meeting with Tracy would be exceedingly awkward, especially in company with the young girl who was the cause of their estrangement. He guessed shrewdly enough that the wily Dennis, using his pretty daughter as the most innocent of decoys, had arranged Tracy's visit as a means of reviving the clever young Irishman's energies in The Cause.

"Does he know I'm here?" he asked, after a few minutes' thought.

"I don't think so."

"Well, then we won't let him know. Nobody would recognise me in my make-up, and I'll take care he doesn't see me without it. When is he coming?"

"He will be passing through here to-morrow, and will break the journey to see me and give me my father's messages. He will be here in the evening, and go on again the next morning."

"Give you your father's messages! His letter does that," said Victred irritably.

A little look of mystery and importance came into the girl's face.

"Well, it isn't only that," she said in a low voice. "My father says he seems to be growing cool, and that I am to rally him to The Cause."

Victred moved impatiently.

"Your father should be able to do that if any one can," he said shortly. "I don't see what you can say to him that your father can't."

"Ah." She looked very wise with that childish wisdom which knows only the outside of things and thinks it the whole, "but my father says he is peculiarly susceptible to feminine influence."

"Well, that is just why he has no business to send him," said Victred angrily. "But I suppose you like to feel your influence?" he added with a pang of unmistakable jealousy.

Jack's face suddenly flushed, and a look of maidenly trouble came into her grey eyes.

"I don't very much like talking to Mr. Fitzalan," she admitted reluctantly, "even though he is, I believe, truly attached to The Cause."

"And why not?" asked Victred dictatorially.

"Why not?" she echoed. "Well, well, I hardly know. Except perhaps that—that——"

"Well."

"He is always wanting to talk about himself, for one thing."

Victred recognised this as an old habit of Tracy's, especially with women.

"And he wants me to talk about myself, or about him, when all I want to talk about and all he *ought* to want to talk about, is The Cause."

"Well," said Victred, somewhat mollified, "he's been spoilt. Most women like to talk with him about anything he likes. He is a great favourite with them."

"Is he really? More than you?"

"Oh, yes."

Jack looked at him inquiringly for a minute, and then shook her head.

"I don't believe that. At least, I think it is only very silly women, or—or women who are not nice, who would like him better than you."

"Why? I'm so modest that it won't do me any harm to know."

"Except just that one thing that you don't care for The People and he does, you are much *better* than he is."

"Oh, Jack, I'm not better than anybody? If you like me because you think that, little one, you'll hate me some day."

Jack smiled faintly, her eyes fixed upon him the while with much intentness.

"No," she said obstinately. "Whatever you may say, you are better than he. *You don't pity yourself.* All men," she went on didactically, "deny that they are good. And as far as I can judge they are generally right. Those that are not bad say that they are bad, and those that are bad say that they are worse. *But it is only the bad ones that pity themselves.*"

Victred burst into hearty laughter. To see that tiny creature, that absurd mixture of shrewdness and simplicity, laying down the law with a wise forefinger raised, filled him with amusement.

"You have a great deal of knowledge of the world, Jack," he said, only half in fun. "I've got just two and eightpence left. How shall we spend it?"

And they began an elaborate calculation, subdividing that handsome amount into fractions, whereby every halfpenny should be made to yield the largest possible amount of substantial profit and pleasure. That afternoon they made a frugal picnic in a field a little way out of the town; and returned, tired, dusty, and with slow feet, Jack hanging on Victred's arm, just in time to dress for the show.

It was about ten minutes before the last performance when Victred, with a curious sensation, saw his cousin Tracy, in a light suit, with a cigarette in his mouth, lounge into the booth, and place himself close to the stage, leaning against it with the air of a man who finds his surroundings and his companions profoundly novel, amusing, and absurd. He did not scruple to raise his hat to Jack as coolly as if nobody but he and she had been present; then, after letting his eyes travel once from her to the giant, from him to the fat lady, and from her over the whole audience with a look of undisguised contemptuous amusement, he fixed them steadily on the "dwarf," with an audacious admiration which made Victred tingle from head to foot, with a desire to fling him on his back sprawling among the benches full of the factory-hands he so openly despised.

The moment the curtain fell, and the rough audience of wooden-shod hobbledehoys and be-shawled girls began to fight for exit just as they had fought for entry, Tracy calmly lifted one corner of the curtain and got upon the stage.

"Why, my dear little Jack, what an age it is since I last saw your small face!" he exclaimed, taking both her hands in his and wringing them and clasping them with affectionate familiarity, while Victred re-treated to the remotest corner, unwilling to disclose him-

self to his cousin and so enter upon a scene of useless reproach and wrangling.

" It is a long time, Mr. Fitzalan, but I am glad to
see again such a staunch friend to The Cause," she
answered, dropping her voice to a whisper on the last
words.

" I should think you must be, after weeks spent in
this sort of thing!" said Tracy with a shrug. And
glancing in the direction in which Elaine, after vainly
trying to attract the distinguished visitor's attention,
was slowly disappearing, he added : " That's a sweet
little thing that has just toddled off! You've got to
put up with odd friends now, Jack."

" Very good ones, some of them ! " answered she
promptly, turning her head so that her words carried
balm into the ears of the silent giant in the background.

" And you don't wish to hear the latest from Papa ? "
asked Tracy, who found Jack too demure and self-
possessed, and thought he should have a better chance
with her if he had her all to himself.

" Of course I do?"

" Then come for a walk as far as the castle. The
perfume left by our kind friends in front is perhaps a
shade too strong of fustian, pease-pudding, and stale
tobacco, don't you think so? Very nice for a time,
of course; but in the end cloying, decidedly cloying."

Now the influence of weeks of constant and happy
companionship with Victred suddenly made itself felt
in a manner for which both he and she were unpre-
pared. They had taken all their pleasures together ;
they had scarcely ever walked out but with each
other. At Tracy's suggestion of a walk with him,
therefore, Jack involuntarily turned her head and cast
at the immovable giant a deprecating, questioning,
even apologetic look, which did not fail to attract
Tracy's notice.

" Oh," said he, with a little sneering, disagreeable
laugh, " so that's the proprietor, is it ? The thing in
the big boots and the black wig ? "

Victred writhed under this speech, in which he saw more offence than Jack did.

"No," she answered simply but rather coldly, "the proprietress is Mrs. de Mowbray. That is—the giant."

"You seemed to think you wanted his permission to go out."

"Oh, that is because it is he who takes me out generally. One mustn't throw over an old friend too abruptly when a new one comes, must one ?"

Her sweetness was irresistible. Tracy bent his head audaciously to look into her face.

"But you'll be a little kind to the new one, won't you ?" he said in a whisper too low for Victred to hear.

"I'll be very grateful to you as long as you give your great talents to the service of The People," answered Jack aloud, with spirit.

And she ran off to change her little page's suit for a dark blue cotton dress and holland sun-bonnet. Victred felt glad when she had gone. He had been so used to associate Jack with a boy's dress, that never once until this evening, when Tracy Fitzalan's critically approving eyes had been unceasingly fixed upon her, had it troubled him that she had to exhibit herself in velvet knickerbockers and a little cavalier cloak. It made her look shorter ; that had always stood as a good and sufficient reason. Now he hated the necessity. Instead of hurrying to remove his "make-up" and change his "props" as usual, he remained sulking in the corner to which he had retreated, on the whole rather willing than not that Tracy should speak to him, and that he should be able to throw off the steam in a furious quarrel. But he was disappointed. As soon as Jack went away, Tracy got down from the stage, and offering a cigarette to Bob, who was much impressed by his manners and appearance, and who described him afterwards as "a real toff and no mistake, a reg'lar out-and-outer," gathered much entertaining lore from that gentleman while he waited for Jack.

Victred contrived to waylay her for a moment

before she joined his cousin. He had nothing in particular to say to her, but he felt uneasy and jealous,
unwilling to let her go out of his sight in the society
of another man, especially such a man as his cousin.
He was frightened by the intensity of his own feeling
when she put her hand into his and said laughing:

"Farewell. Don't forget me during my absence."

He tried to laugh back ; and then, peceiving that
his own hand was trembling, and afraid of alarming
the girl, he nodded and turned away. She paused
just one moment, as if a little puzzled by his behaviour, then, saying below her breath, shyly, "Good-
bye," she went rather slowly to the booth-entrance,
where Tracy was standing.

. Victred, after in vain struggling against the impulse, went down into the tent, and from the darkness within, watched the two figures on their way
up the steep street leading to the castle. He was
enduring unspeakable tortures. Never before had he
known, in the enjoyment of Jack's society, whither he
was drifting. It was, he felt, to a passion of which he
had never thought himself capable, an absorbing passion which would soon make it impossible to be with
her and be silent, and therefore impossible to be with
her at all. He had been patting himself on the back
for his reserve and self-control ; and now, the very
first time that she passed half-an-hour in the society
of another man, he was thrown into a state bordering
on frenzy.

It was not fear for her that troubled him. Victred
knew that there was no danger for her in that walk
at any rate. It was the knowledge that Tracy was
free, while he himself was not : the knowledge that,
even if she were in danger, he had no *right* to pro-
tect her, and that he never could have that right. He
sat there tormenting himself with self-reproach and
with forebodings until he saw the figures of Jack and
Tracy returning down the hill. Ashamed of watching them, he withdrew into the curtained-off corner
where he dressed and made up, and where the " pro-

perties" were kept, divested himself of his make-up, drew out his little stove, and began to get it ready for cooking their supper, which was to consist on this occasion of poached eggs and toast.

Presently he, on the alert, heard steps and voices outside. As they came nearer he could distinguish the tones, Tracy's sentimental, Jack's sympathetic. It maddened him. Then they came into the booth, hidden from Victred's sight by the curtain, and Tracy heaved a great sigh.

"Well, Jack," said he, as if making an effort to be lively in spite of himself, "I must leave you now, I suppose. I think you might have come to supper with me this once, considering what a long time it may be before I see you again. Come, little one, won't you change your mind?"

"No, thank you, Mr. Fitzalan."

"'No, thank you, Mr. Fitzalan!'" echoed Tracy, mimicking her demure tone. "Well, you will give me a kiss, won't you?"

"No."

"Well, you'll let me take one?"

"No."

"Why not? You're not so unkind to the giant, I'm sure. Come, I must have one."

There were sounds of rapid feet, of a struggle, of Jack's panting breath. Victred sprang on the stage, and down to the floor of the booth. It was too dark for either him or his cousin to see one another clearly, so that he trusted still to remain unrecognised.

As soon as Tracy heard Victred spring from the stage to the ground, he relaxed his hold of Jack, who at once escaped through the open doorway. Victred would have followed her, but his cousin, with a couple of rapid steps, barred the way out with his person.

"Hallo, so you've dropped the lion's skin, have you?" said Tracy in a jeering tone.

Victred made no answer, and turned to retreat into his corner. But he was stopped by his cousin's next words, uttered in a low voice.

"May I venture to ask what right you, a married man, have to interfere with the friendships, or amusements, or flirtations—call them what you like, of a young girl?"

Victred hesitated. Tracy went on:

"You see I'm quite ready to respect your incognito, knowing that there are good reasons for it. But it seems odd you should have thought a little Armenian bole and a wig enough disguise for *me* !"

Victred strode up to him menacingly.

"As to that, you infernal scoundrel, there wouldn't be any reason for my being incog. if you'd told the truth like a man at the inquest."

In the dark the faces of the men came closer together; and Tracy, who could bluster, but with whom physical courage was not a strong point, attempted to turn for the doorway. But Victred caught his arm in a paralysing grip.

"I—I—I did tell the truth; I—I—you've misunderstood. I could only say what I saw. And—and —it was true that you and Malpas didn't get on—I had to say it, everybody knew it. And—and—if——"

Victred cut him short with a contemptuous laugh.

"Look here, you needn't waste that stammering on me. I know you pretty well, and I know you'd sell your own soul, or anybody else's body, for a trifling advantage to Tracy Fitzalan. But what are you doing hanging about that girl?"

Tracy, partly relieved at the turn the conversation was taking, but roused to real anger by the mention of Jack, affected a laugh of bitter amusement.

"What am *I* doing? I like that. What are *you* doing is a question more to the point. It's nothing but 'Mr. Watt and I do this,' 'Mr. Watt and I saw that,' all the time one talks to her."

Victred trembled. The words filled him with astonishment, with horror, and yet with a sense of rebellious delight.

"I treat her as a child, and she looks upon me almost as she would upon her father."

"Knows you're a married man, I suppose?" said Tracy, daring, now that Victred had grown humble and apologetic, to put a little sarcasm into his tone.

"I don't know that she does. I'm not particularly fond of talking about my wife."

"You have no objection to her knowing, I suppose?"

At these words, uttered in this tone, Victred became convulsed with passion; it was only by seizing one of the wooden supports of the booth and gripping it tightly that he kept back the blow which he was burning to deliver full in his cousin's smirking face. And the worst of it was that the very repugnance he felt to Tracy's suggestion told him that he must not refuse. The blood surging up into his head made him feel as if his brain would burst. He tried to speak, but his voice was too husky, and he stopped.

"Yes?" said Tracy suavely.

"You can tell her, of course," said Victred.

And mechanically feeling in his pockets for his tobacco and his pipe, he walked unsteadily out of the booth and stood in the open air.

CHAPTER XVII.

" To-morrow we meet the same then, dearest?
May I take your hand in mine?
Mere friends are we,—well, friends the merest
Keep much that I resign."
—BROWNING.

"It will make no difference," Victred kept saying to himself. "Jack looks upon me exactly as she would upon a big brother; and I—well, I've always *treated* her as, well, as brothers never do treat their sisters, but as they might—in Arcadia. It will make no difference."

· But already the mere suggestion had made a difference, already he felt that the serpent had entered their paradise, making evil what was good. There was nothing left to hope now but that Tracy, in communicating the fact of Victred's marriage to Jack, would not succeed in poisoning her mind against her unlucky friend.

While he stood thus on the stones of the market-place, racked by miserable fears, seeing the lights of the town dancing in a mist, a demure voice startled him.

"I'm quite ready for supper, when you've finished studying the stars."

She was close to his elbow, looking up and smiling in his face. But instead of answering in the same tone of playful familiarity, he fell a-trembling and stammered as he spoke to her.

"Yes, yes, I——," he began to mumble and then stopped.

She saw that he was much disturbed, and she waited, turning her eyes away from his face, while he recovered himself.

"Jack," he then said incisively, "Fitzalan in there," and he glanced back into the booth, "has something to tell you, something about me."

She looked surprised.

"Something about you? Is it," she went on, looking steadily into his face, "something you don't want me to know? Because if so, I'd rather not know it."

"It is something I've never told you, because it is a subject so hateful to me that I never mention it unless it's necessary. And I didn't think it was necessary."

"Then don't mention it now," said Jack promptly.

"It has become necessary now," said he quietly.

And at that Tracy, who had been listening inside the tent, came out, laughing a little maliciously.

"It is nothing to make a fuss about, as my cousin very truly says, Miss M'Rena," said he. "It is only that I always think it ought to be a point of honour with a married man not to pass himself off, especially with young girls, as a bachelor."

Jack turned to Victred in the simplest, most matter-of-fact way in the world.

"Oh, are you married?" she said, with just the amount of surprise she would have shown if she had been told that he had a strawberry mark on his arm.

"Yes," said he simply.

There was a pause. Tracy could not conceal his disappointment, and Victred was enjoying it. For the girl did not seem to think the announcement of enough importance to comment upon. Tracy had to break the silence.

"You see," he said, "it was nothing so dreadful after all. And now there can be no misunderstanding —thanks to *me*, remember."

"There never would have been any misunderstanding," interposed Jack tranquilly, before Victred could answer with an angry speech. "Good-evening, Mr. Fitzalan."

And she ran between them, with a child's skipping steps, to the tent, with a nod to Victred to intimate that she expected him to follow her. Tracy ran after her and came up with her when she was only just inside the doorway.

"Won't you have my carnation?" said he, taking the flower out of his buttonhole, and offering it to her.

"No, thank you. I don't like wired flowers."

"But it isn't wired—see."

"I don't want it, thank you."

"Because I told you Victred Speke was married!— told you in your own interest! That is so like a woman!"

"I don't wish to be anything else but a woman, Mr. Fitzalan. And I am glad it is like a woman to resent a man's doing a spiteful action."

"I was not spiteful. I spoke in your interest and his own."

"Oh no, Mr. Fitzalan. If you had only wanted to do what was right you would have advised him to tell me, and he would have done so. *You would not have told me yourself.*"

"I don't seem to have done him much harm with you, at any rate."

Jack smiled.

"You don't understand the sort of friendship there is between us. Why, he might be married, and I might be married, and it wouldn't make any difference."

"Excuse me. This friendship of yours has made a difference. You were never rude to me before."

Jack looked surprised ; then she blushed a little.

"Well, I'm sorry if I've been rude."

"Really sorry? Sorry enough to kiss and be friends ? "

"Not sorry enough to kiss, but sorry enough to be friends."

"You are a hard little thing! Do you know I came here to-night to ask you to marry me ? "

"Oh, Mr. Fitzalan, how absurd ! "

"How is it absurd ? You are the only girl I've ever seen, Jack, whom I've never been able to forget. And I'm going to ask you regularly once a month till you give way."

"Very well. Four weeks hence I may expect to see you again then. Good-bye."

She had caught sight of Victred, who, having gone for a stroll while they were talking, had now started with leisurely steps to return to the booth.

Tracy noted that it was to this circumstance he owed his abrupt dismissal, and he met his cousin with the deathly-white complexion he always acquired when he was strongly agitated. Victred saw it by the light of a lamp under which they met, and his spirits rose. It was evident that Jack had not treated him with any deep sense of gratitude.

"Going to turn in ? " asked Victred cheerfully.

"Yes."

"By-the-bye, where are you staying ? "

"At the Midland. Come and have a drink ? "

"Not now, thanks, I've got to get back."

"Oh, I beg your pardon. I forgot there was a lady

waiting for you," sneered Tracy, showing his teeth in a malicious smile.

As Victred said nothing to this, there was a short pause. Then Tracy went on :

" I know you are very careful of other men's morality, but isn't it a bit 'off' for a married man to keep a girl from receiving offers from men who are not married, eh ? "

" Why, what offers is she likely to get while she's travelling round with this show ? "

" One from *me*, to begin with."

" You *marry* her ! " Victred shook his head. " No, Tracy, *that* won't wash. I know you're in love with her, but——"

" You mean to insinuate——"

" Nothing. But as you've always meant to marry a rich wife, a wife without a cent wouldn't be very likely to make you happy or to be happy with you."

" Where's yours at present ? "

" I don't know. But I've got to find her out—to serve her with a writ."

Tracy's face grew gloomy for a moment.

" Divorce, eh ? " then he brightened. " But you can't come forward."

" It can be managed though, I think. I'm going to consult a lawyer as soon as I get to town."

Tracy looked thoughtful.

" You don't know where she is, you say ? " he repeated. Victred shook his head. " Well, I'll try to find her for you. I'm fond of detective work. But remember, perhaps you won't be able to prove anything ? "

" I'm not afraid of much difficulty there," said Victred bitterly.

" Well, I wish you luck, I'm sure. It would be a great thing to be free from that disgrace, even if you couldn't see your way to clearing yourself of the other." He stopped and held out his hand. " It won't be long before I see you again, and perhaps I may have some news for you. Ta-ta."

Victred returned his farewell, and watched him hurry rapidly out of sight, with a good many misgivings. Tracy had brightened up so wonderfully during the latter part of his talk, that his cousin, knowing him to be clever, revengeful and totally unscrupulous, began sincerely to hope that he would not come across Louisa, who would be an easy tool for mischief in such hands. Like most men in his position, although he had often thought of divorce as a means of relief, shame had kept him from seeking it, until a new and irresistible motive sprang up in the form of another woman. If he were free he could marry Jack. She liked him well enough, he thought, to learn to love him with a little persuasion. And then when the inevitable time came for her eyes to be opened concerning The Cause, there would be something left in the world for her to live for.

With these thoughts in his mind he went inside the booth, rather shyly, dreading a little his reception at Jack's hands under the new conditions.

To his great relief, she made no allusion either to Tracy's visit or to the tidings he had brought. Exactly in the same manner as usual she sat down and waited for her supper, talking about trifles, or silently watching Victred at his cooking. Nothing seemed to be changed between them, unless the fact that she presently began again to talk about the Cause of the People, a subject which had lately been seldom heard of between them, were a result of the evening's disclosures.

Next day, however, Victred thought that he detected a difference in her. It may very well have been only a reflection of the change in himself; at any rate, it was certain that she was more thoughtful, less talkative, and that, whether through his fault or hers he did not quite know, they were less together than before. The little rift grew wider day by day until Saturday came; and when with a palpable effort, as different as possible from his old easy familiarity, he asked after treasury: "Where shall we go to-day, Jack?" he was instantly rendered dumb and shy by her prompt answer that she had some work to do, sent by her father, and that therefore she could not go out that day at all. She said it in her old voice and manner, expressing regret in the most natural manner in the world.

Victred looked across the market-place, nodded, and walked away without a word. Just as he was turning down the first street he came to, however, he, in a glance round which was meant to have a careless air of being directed at nothing in particular, observed that she was following him with her eyes; and although it was too far for him to discern this fact clearly, yet he could not help fancying that those eyes of hers were filled with tears.

He hesitated, then pulled himself together, and walked steadily on. A few doors further he came to a flower-shop. As in all the big factory-towns, the display of cut flowers on a Saturday was brilliant. Victred walked in, recklessly chose a dozen of the most beautiful roses, had them put into a paper bag, paid his three shillings and sixpence and another sixpence for a handful of maidenhair fern to be laid on the top of the flowers. Then he went back to the booth, where he found Jack sitting in the doorway in exactly the position in which he had left her.

He came upon her suddenly. She started, reddened; and he saw by her swollen eyelids that the tears really had been there.

"A few flowers for you if you care to have them," said he, with an assumption of carelessness. And passing in front of her, he just dropped the bag into her lap and went on.

He did not go far though; but waiting round the corner of the booth, just out of her sight, he heard her little squeak of pleasure when she opened the bag. Perhaps her instinct told her that he had not gone far, for the next minute she stood before him, hugging her fragile treasures tenderly and most carefully to her breast, while above the blossoms her own little flower-face, flushed, eager, again almost tearful, looked up at him.

"Oh," she said, "Oh, oh! How could you? You —you must have spent all your guinea! I do wish you hadn't!"

"Throw them away then, or give them to Elaine —if you don't like them."

His tone, recalling the fact that he was suffering from her rebuff of half an hour before, caused Jack's face to fall.

"I do like them," she said quietly. "I only didn't want you to spend your money. I thank you very much for them. I've never had such flowers before."

Her little fingers were twitching about them in an ecstasy of the excitement of possession. She turned to go back. Victred hastened to speak, seeing that he was losing his chance.

"I wanted you to have something—something you would like—as you wouldn't—couldn't go out to-day," he stammered. "It's the last time. I'm going to 'chuck the show' to-night."

Jack turned round slowly, looked up at him and burst into tears.

"Why," cried Victred, much moved himself, with pain which was half pleasure, "I didn't think you'd mind!"

"Not mind!" she sobbed below her breath. "Not mind! Oh, no, of course I shouldn't mind, of course I shouldn't!"

He said nothing to this at first, but stared at the flag waving on the castle at the top of the hill, and listened to her sobbing.

"Well," he said presently, "will you come out with me now, now you know it's the last time?"

"Of co—ourse I will."

"Dry your eyes then. It's absurd to cry. And come along."

But still he neither turned nor looked at her. For the fact was he had quite enough to do in keeping the moisture out of his own eyes.

Ten minutes later, soberly, silently, they were walking through the streets together on their way to the station. As Jack insisted on taking all her roses with her, he bought her a basket and a couple of handfuls of damp moss. She reproached him for his extravagance, and he laughed sadly.

"We're going to get through just half the guinea to-day, Jack," said he; "that will leave me enough to pay my fare to town."

Jack said nothing; but looking down at her, he saw the tears had started to her eyes again.

"Then when I am once in town, I can get what money I want."

The girl looked up quickly.

"I see. Yes. You will go back to your old friends and your old life. You will soon forget us then."

Victred did not at once answer. When he did, all he said was: "Not so soon as you would think, perhaps."

Suddenly she stopped short.

"Your wife;" said she in a low voice, "you will see her?"

"Not if I can help it, certainly."

Jack looked up quickly, read the expression of disgust and annoyance upon his face, and walked on without further remark until they reached the station. But as soon as they were seated in a compartment by themselves, and Victred had presented her with a pear for which, in the refreshment-room, he had parted with twopence at one full swoop, she promptly reopened the disagreeable subject.

"I want you," she said steadily, "to tell me about your wife."

"Don't talk of her," said he shortly. "What is the use? She is only my wife in name. And before long she will not even be that."

"She did something wrong then?"

"We were both to blame, I most at the beginning, she most afterwards perhaps. We were unsuited to each other. I can't talk to you about these things. Why do you ask me about them?"

"Because I want it all to come right with you. And it will never come right until you are reconciled to your wife."

Victred looked at the grave, earnest little face, which now wore its far-away rapt expression, the expression which had filled him with vague pity when he first heard her harangue the factory-hands on Crossley Ridge. He smiled very tenderly upon her as he shook his head.

"You are too good to understand, Jack," said he. "But it is impossible. If I could take her back I should be, well, I should be worthy of her."

But Jack ventured quixotically forward, with the sublime or insane faith which has got missionaries eaten.

"Why are you always, you men, so hard upon the woman? You expect her to be quite ready to forgive you, although you say it was you who were at first the most to blame."

"Don't let us talk any more about this, Jack. I know you are obstinate and will stick to your point, but you don't know what you are talking about."

The orator looked rather surprised at this snub, but she dropped obediently into silence and gazed thoughtfully out of the window. Presently she turned her eyes again to her companion's face and broke into a pretty smile.

"I should so like you to be happy, very happy," she said. "When I heard you were married it gave me a great shock, because I knew you must be married unhappily."

"Gave you a great shock!" repeated Victred incredulously. "You didn't show it."

"That was my cunning," she answered with pride. "I didn't want your cousin to know I was surprised."

Victred was amused and touched.

"You are a good little thing, Jack," said he.

And then they both began to feel that the ground

was giving way a little beneath them, and they started other topics, discussing the scenery and the chances of rain.

All through that day they were a little uncertain as to whether they were very happy or very miserable, being indeed both by turns. But in all their after-lives they never forgot the sound the wind made in the trees that day, or the smell of the earth, damp with the rain of the night before. And Victred never again cared to gather nuts from the hazel-bushes, as he did for Jack that afternoon.

The evening was a tempestuous one, in which all sentiment was drowned in mere worry and noise. For Victred, obeying not only Jack's suggestion but his own better impulses, relinquished the idea of leaving Mrs. de Mowbray, who had treated him well after her fashion, entirely without notice. So there was a melodramatic scene, the manageress and Elaine joining the music of their lamentations and reproaches. But Victred's plea of important business was believed and accepted, it having been decided since Tracy's visit that the "giant was a toff under a cloud." For Tracy's swaggering manners had impressed Mrs. de Mowbray and her satellites more than his cousin's quiet ones. The manageress, much to Victred's annoyance, insisted on herself seeing him off to the station. He was going by the express from Manchester which passed through at eleven o'clock. She kept him in conversation until the last moment, so that he had to wait until she had got into the cab she had ordered to give dignity to the occasion, before he could hurry away in search of Jack.

He found her inside the now darkened booth.

"What, Jack, sitting all alone?" said he.

"Yes, that is how I shall have to pass my time now," she said in a choked voice.

Victred's heart leaped up within him.

"Good-bye, Jack," was all he dared to say.

He held out his hand, bending down, hoping she would let him kiss her. For a moment she seemed to hesitate, and he felt, as she gave him her hand, that she was trembling violently. But the next instant she drew back, panting, frightened, the fingers he still held twitching convulsively.

"Good-bye, good-bye," she whispered huskily.

And while he began incoherently to ask her to let him have if it were only one last look at her little face, she pulled her hand away, and waving it to him as she ran, fled out of his reach, out of his sight.

CHAPTER XVIII.

"But homewards——home—what home? Had be a home?"
—TENNYSON.

A QUARTER past five on a Sunday morning is not the hour at which London looks its best in the eyes of a man who arrives there with little money in his pocket and nowhere to go to. Victred walked out of St. Pancras Station in the rather chilling light of a fine September morning, inclined to wonder whether the events of the past few months, the fatal quarrel with his cousin, the life in the booth, had ever really taken place, and whether he was not returning to town after a fortnight's grouse-shooting. A glance down at his shabby clothes, his brown army boots, at the bag he was carrying himself, broke the illusion. Exiled by his own acts, he was returning to that little world which had already in all probability forgotten him, returning like a thief to the city where his father had a big house of which he himself would some day be master.

For after all, his father was Lord Malpas now; the house in Grosvenor Square would be his before many years were over, and Maleigh Abbey, and such revenues as the late possessor of the title had not been able to squander. The atmosphere of his old haunts, as he made his way, on foot, to Piccadilly, seemed to clear his mind of the cobwebs which had collected in his exile; he saw that neither Tracy nor Lady Rushcliffe would have the courage, even if they still had the inclination, to give evidence against him if he were put on his trial, while the character of the third witness would not stand against cross-examination. Victred thought it most probable that, if he were now to come forward and claim his new position as a matter of course, nothing more would be heard of warrant or persecution, and the evil rumours which his disappearance had encouraged would die out in time.

In the face of these beliefs then, why did he not ring the bell of the house in Grosvenor Square, and boldly announce himself to his father, the new master? Certainly poor old Woodward the butler, who had adored him from a child, and who was probably in charge, would be overjoyed at seeing him, and he knew his own little world well enough to understand that the mere fact of his assuming his place as the next heir would make him one of *nous autres* and would transform antagonists into adherents.

But, for one thing, sentiment stood in the way, the sentiment of repugnance to taking advantage of the unhappy act by which he had cleared his way to the title ; for another, his strait-laced father's welcome would be cold indeed ; for a third, the old life had lost its savour for him.

He found himself, during the long saunter with which he began the day, looking at all the old landmarks—the clubs he had belonged to, the houses he had visited, from a new point of view, the view of the million. He found it quite easy to do this now, and he smiled to himself as he thought how little Jack would rejoice if she could know the change which had come over the "bloated aristocrat." Poor little Jack ! His heart melted within him at the thought of her. Now that he was once away from her, the last fragment of the fiction of his brotherly feeling for her broke down utterly. Already he was hungering for a sight of her, picturing her sitting alone on the steps of the living-carriage where she used to sit waiting for him in the morning, ready to jump down at his approach, and to whisper, " Where to-day? Where shall we go to-day ? " with the eagerness of a child.

As the morning wore towards mid-day he returned into the park, threw himself on one of the back row of seats at the Marble Arch corner, and refreshed himself by an *al fresco* doze like a genuine working-man. He had decided upon a plan of action, which had the one disadvantage that he had to fill up the day as best he could before making his first move.   However, he was not penniless, Mrs. de Mowbray having insisted on his borrowing a sovereign at the last ; neither was he hungry, for the same good fairy had forced into his pockets a huge packet of sandwiches, which had afforded him a pleasant resource during the small hours.   So when he felt the slumber, which had evaded him during his uncomfortable journey in a crowded third-class carriage, gaining upon him in the sunshine, he took up his bag, hailed a hansom, and driving to an hotel where he was not known, engaged a room, threw himself on the bed, and slept until evening.

It was eleven o'clock that night when Victred presented himself at the outer door of Teddy Harrington's chambers, commonly reputed to be the snuggest bachelor diggings in town.   The servant who opened the door was a new one, and did not know him.

" What name shall I say, sir ? "

Victred hesitated.

" Tell Mr. Harrington an old friend wishes to see him."

He stepped inside into the little vestibule or ante-room which, with its blue velvet pile carpet, its damask-hung walls, its silver lamp and banks of flowers, was perhaps a trifle too much like a lady's boudoir, but was undeniably soothing to the eyes after four months of living-vans and canvas walls.   Teddy had had to exist on a mere pittance of six hundred a year in his father's life-time ; so that now that eminent company-promoter's death had brought him the comparatively comfortable income of eight thousand, the poor boy was naturally inclined to overdo it.

Teddy had been, both before and after his accession to fortune, Victred's great chum and devoted admirer. Short of stature, rather delicate, the one brother of many sisters, Teddy was inclined to be effeminate, so that Victred's colossal figure and straightforward simplicity of manner had for him the great attraction of contrast. To him, therefore, Victred had come to find out exactly how he now stood in the eyes of his former friends. It was a good test-case, as Teddy Harrington's old friendship and prejudice in his favour might be said to be balanced by his profound respect for "the world's" opinion. It was not without anxiety that the exile awaited the meeting.

He was not long kept in suspense. He heard a door open behind a heavy silk *portière ;* this was drawn a little way back by a cautious hand, and Teddy's twinkling black eyes and small snub nose appeared. The moment he recognised his visitor, however, he gave a little cry of delight, and ran out, extending both hands in a welcome of unmistakable heartiness.

" Speke, is it really you, old chap ? " cried he. " Why, I can't believe my eyes. Where have you been hiding yourself so long ? "

It was not until the last words escaped his lips that he seemed to remember that they accurately conveyed the facts of the case. Instinctively he lowered his voice.

" Won't you come in ? " said he, trying to pull him towards the door through which he had himself come. " I've only got a few fellows—old friends of yours, most of them, as usual. Baccarat and a little supper. Come along."

But Victred shook his head.

" No," said he, glancing down at his shabby light suit and striking boots. " Not in this get-up. At

present I'm labelled 'Out of it.'   I knew I should
catch you in to-night, and I thought you wouldn't
mind my interrupting you for five minutes just to put
me *au courant* a little, for I'm fresh from the wilds."

"You've not been home yet? That is good of you,
old chap, to come straight to me."

"I'm not going—home.   I'm going to see a solicitor
to-morrow morning."

"Well, perhaps that is best.   Not that there will
be any difficulty.   We all thought, you know, that it
was most awfully silly of you not to come forward at
once.   It looked, you see, as if you'd, well——" He
lowered his voice, "as if you'd bolted."

Victred nodded.

"You don't quite know how I was placed, nor how
very bad things were made to look."

"I know—by that blackguard Fitzalan.   But he
hasn't pluck enough to have stood to his colours in
a criminal trial.   Besides, you could have proved
malice so easily!"

"Proved it?"

"Why, yes.   Come in here."   Teddy raised another
portière, and led Victred into a small dining-room,
the walls of which were panelled in dark oak to a
height of six feet, the space to the ceiling being
covered with embossed leather paper.   The ceiling
was also panelled, and in each panel was a little star
of electric light.   The table, which was laid for
supper for eight or ten people, sparkled with silver
fruit and flower bowls.   "Champagne, or whisky and
soda?" asked Teddy, with his finger on the bell.
Then, making Victred sit on one of the red velvet
three-cornered couches, piled high with cushions, which
filled two of the four corners of the room, Teddy,
having poured out the whisky and water his friend
chose, went on with his remarks.   "There have been
a lot of paragraphs pointing to you lately in all the
little low rags which live by scandal, and I happen to
know that some at least of these could be traced to
Fitzalan.   He does the politics for one of the weeklies

now, and pars for a lot of other papers besides : you know little Mansfield of *The Planet?* He tells me all these things."

"Why, what did they say? Called me a murderer right out?"

"Oh, no, no. Said that you—well, that you were married, for one thing."

"Quite true, unfortunately. That's what I'm going to the solicitor's about."

"To get rid of her? Well——" Teddy hesitated, "These miserable paragraphs say you can't."

Victred felt uneasy. He could not help fearing that Tracy, having made up his mind to hinder his divorce, would find a means of putting difficulties in his way.

"Of course," went on Teddy, "we all know why he is so anxious to prevent your getting free. He's making up to your cousin Lady May, and she still thinks of nobody but you. Wherever she goes, he goes too, and he boasts that he will either tire her out, or compromise her in such a way that she will have to marry him."

"He dares to make such a boast as that!"

"Oh, you know Fitzalan! He's just as proud of being a scoundrel as other men are of being thought the soul of honour."

"And there was nobody to kick him?"

"You can't kick Fitzalan, it pleases him so! He always writes to the papers saying that he was the kicker, not the kicked; whether people believe him or not he gets his little puff and is satisfied. Now we are going to have a big picnic up at Cookham on Tuesday, and because she's going he's got invited, and he is sure to be at his old tricks again."

"Not this time," said Victred, rising quickly. "Tell me what time you meet and where."

Before Teddy could answer, a door in the panelling opened a little way, and an amiable if rather foolish young male face peeped in. On seeing who the visitor was, he threw the door wide open with a shout, and a minute later, Victred found himself dragged into the

12*

drawing-room and surrounded by young men whom he would have described as acquaintances, but who, in the warmth of their greeting, of their welcome, were like old friends. He was, moved, shaken, astonished. It was like coming back from death to find that, instead of being forgotten, he was at least remembered, if not beloved. It is true he had only been absent from their midst four months, but for him that period had contained a lifetime of new experiences.

It is not to be supposed that these young men, the sole object of whose lives was pleasure-seeking, would have retained such a vivid interest in him if it had not been for the startling circumstances connected with his disappearance. As it happened, however, Tracy's ill-natured paragraphs, instead of injuring him, had helped to keep him in remembrance and stimulated pity on his behalf. Thus he found himself a lion, a hero of romance in their eyes; and the recital of his adventures in the show, his descriptions of Mrs. de Mowbray and Madame Elaine, of his baked-potato suppers, and of his make-up as a giant, were received with peals of laughter. One detail only he altogether suppressed—the second dwarf.

It was four o'clock in the morning when the party broke up, and then Teddy insisted on his friend's putting up for the night in a spare room which, after the accommodation he had had for the last few months, seemed like a fairy palace.

"There's just one thing I should like to know, old fellow," said Teddy, pausing a moment after wishing his friend good night. "What made you come back in such a deuce of a hurry?"

Victred hesitated an instant, and then said simply: "A woman."

Teddy nodded sympathetically.

"Ah, I was afraid so. Well, good-night, old chap."

"Good-night. It's awfully good of you to take in a ragged rascal like me. I haven't quite forgotten the use of soap and water, but a dressing-table I haven't seen for months, except in dreams."

Victred hardly slept at all that night; the transition from Bohemia to Philistia was too sudden. He lay through the long hours thinking, yet trying not to think, of Jack.

Next day he set about devising a plan to free his cousin May from Tracy's persecution. For he knew how limp and helpless the girl herself would be under the pursuit of a resolute admirer, however unwelcome; while Mrs. Mostyn-Stanningly, the relation in whose care she now was, he knew to be too flaccid and phlegmatic a person to be of much use in protecting her niece.

In pursuance of his good intentions on May's behalf, Victred, having with the help of Teddy arrayed himself once more in the guise of a civilised Briton, which in this case meant flannels and a straw hat, went up to Maidenhead on the Tuesday, and cruised about by himself in a hired skiff between Boulter's Lock and Bray. The party about which Teddy had told him, after coming down the river from Great Marlow and picnicking somewhere on the banks, were to assemble at Maidenhead Station in time to catch the 8.25 train for Paddington. If, as Teddy thought probable, Tracy should try to get left behind with Lady May, she would find an unexpected friend to help her on her way.

It was a lovely evening; and Boulter's Lock, though perhaps not so crowded as it would have been a little earlier in the season, was the scene of a lively gathering. Victred moored his skiff below the lock, and joined the crowd of onlookers who were watching and criticising each boat as, with its burden of athletic young men and prettily dressed girls, it glided into the lock, or, emptied in an instant of its picturesque burden, was run over the rollers.

It was half-past seven when the first batch of boats belonging to the picnic party passed out of the lock. Victred, who kept in the background, not wanting to be recognised by those members of the party who knew him, was able to pick out their boats by the big blue rosette attached to the rudder of each. A second batch of boats passed through, and a third, the occupants of the last full of fears that they were late.

But neither Lady May nor Tracy Fitzalan had been in the boats that passed. Teddy Harrington, who was in the last batch, singled out Victred from the group on the bank, and made a sign to him that the missing ones were far behind. Victred took the hint, left the lock, and ran along the bank above, keeping a sharp look-out as each boat went down the stream past him.

At last he thought he heard a girl's voice which he recognised calling out in distress. He ran faster, and came in a few minutes upon a pair-oared skiff, moored under a tree, half-hidden by the tall leaves of the water-flags. In it sat a girl dressed in white, alone. As Victred parted the branches, knowing who the girl was, she again cried out plaintively:

" Oh, Mr. Fitzalan, make haste, make haste, or we shall be left behind, we shall indeed ; it takes so long to get through the lock ! "

But the sound of Victred's voice, utterly unexpected, threw poor Lady May into such a paroxysm of delight that she could scarcely command the use of her limbs, and he had to drag her out of the boat and help her along with his arm.

" Don't talk," said he, as she began to babble out, panting, all sorts of incoherent expressions of delight and loving welcome.

" He—will be——so angry—and I'm—afraid—of him ! " she managed to gasp out when Victred had handed her into his skiff and taken up the oars. " But I don't care, oh, I don't care ! I would make everybody, everybody in the world angry for the pleasure of seeing you again ! "

Victred began to find his fair charge rather embarrassing. For though she had so strongly objected to being left behind with Tracy, it was only too clear that she was quite ready to be left behind with his cousin, and she persisted in steering such an erratic course that at last Victred told her to unship the rudder and let him do rowing and steering too.

"Where had Fitzalan gone to?" he asked rather abruptly, to check the torrent of affectionate inquiries which was bubbling up to her lips.

"Oh, he would get out and go back to gather me some water-lilies we had passed some time before. I didn't want them; he knew that. He only wanted to be late, so that I should have to go back to town alone with him. He wants to marry me, you know. And——" Here her voice began to threaten sobs— "And I'm afraid he w-w-will."

"How can he if you don't choose to have him?" asked Victred rather impatiently, assuming a big-brother tone with the silly girl.

"Oh-h, but people can do these things, whatever people say! It isn't every girl who marries that wants to get married—at least to the man they marry her to! You know that, Victred. And don't *you* begin to be unkind, or I shall jump over the boat's side into the river. I—I don't care what I do when I'm with you."

Victred felt himself turn cold with horror. She was just one of those ill-regulated creatures who, when their feelings are deeply stirred, may at any moment break out into horrible eccentricities of conduct. So he soothed her and laughed at her, and meanwhile strained every muscle to reach the bank and be rid of his unmanageable passenger. But when he had landed her and told her to make haste to the station, she persisted in clinging to his arm, and in extracting a promise before she would go.

"Say you will come and see me to-morrow, yes, to-morrow," she implored. "Give me your word, your word of honour."

"All right, all right. Now run. If you lose that train, I'll—I'll let you marry Fitzalan."

Lady May ran off awkwardly, as she did everything; holding up her white dress too high on the one side and letting it trail in the dust on the other.

"Why are some women like that, I wonder!" said Victred to himself as he watched her. "Now little Jack would be graceful if she had to jump in a sack!"

And struck with a sudden thought of the difference it would have made in his life if Lady May had been like Jack and Jack like Lady May, he turned again to the river-bank where he had left his skiff.

Another boat had just swum alongside, and the solitary occupant sprang out, and coming up to Victred, shook his fist in his face.

It was Tracy Fitzalan, livid with rage. He literally snarled, his lips curling away from his teeth, as he spoke to his cousin.

"You think you've done a clever thing for once, you great lout, don't you?" said he.

"Why, so I have, for me," answered Victred imperturbably. "I helped that silly girl to catch her train, which she'd have lost if she had waited while you fooled about getting water-lilies.'"

"Well, it was no business of yours."

"Yes, it was. That I've made a mess of matrimony myself is no reason why I should let another member of my family do the same."

"What do you mean by a mess of matrimony? Why shouldn't I marry your cousin?"

"Why not, indeed, if you can win her like a man? But you've no right to force her into marriage by harming her reputation."

Tracy stepped back as if to take a good look at him, with a sniggering laugh.

"Perhaps you're right," he said. "But you see I must get married—if only to have a chance with Jack."

Victred was not easily moved to the point of personal violence, but the words, the tone, the laugh, the sneer at his idol, were too much for him. Before an interested group of Thames watermen, young

rowing-men, and alas! half a dozen ladies, the
"Giant" let out with his right, and landed Tracy, in
his beautiful white flannels, flat on his back in the
slimy soil of the river-bank.

CHAPTER XIX.

"Give her but a least excuse to love me!"
—BROWNING.

"BUT you will write to me?"

"Yes. But my letters won't be worth reading."

"They will—to me. And if you should go abroad,
you w-won't go without letting me know?"

"No, indeed I won't. I should be very ungrateful
if I did, after all your kindness in remembering me."

"Oh, it's not kindness; I can't help it. I couldn't
forget you if I wanted to, Victred; you know that.
But if you really think you have anything to be
grateful to me for, don't, oh don't leave me all these
months again without even letting me know where
you are. I know why it is; you are afraid I should
find you out and come and tease you, but I wouldn't,
I wouldn't indeed, I only want to know you're safe.
And besides, I could let you know, you know, how
things are going on."

"Thank you, May. You are awfully good, really
you are. I'll let you know what I'm going to do as
soon as I know myself. Good-bye."

He left the room hurriedly, having kept his promise
to call at the house in Bruton Street where Lady
May lived, and being very glad the fearsome ordeal
was over. But quick as he was, his cousin was
quicker still; by the time he reached the bottom of
the staircase, Lady May, having characteristically put
her foot through the ruche of lace which trimmed the
hem of her skirt, and torn off yards and yards of it,
was on the bottom step.

"Kiss me, oh, do kiss me, Victred," said she.

Victred complied with her request, telling her

laughingly that she treated him better than he deserved.

"You should keep your kisses for the man who will have a right to ask for them, May."

"Nobody will ever have that right," she said resignedly.

"Why, you told me you might end by marrying Fitzalan?"

"Might have done, if you hadn't come back again. I owe you a debt for that."

"Yes, and so will he!" said Victred with a rueful laugh. "Do you know, May, I think you're rather silly not to have him? He's not a paragon, but he's got his good points like the rest of us. He is loveable, whatever one may think of his principles. And you are so affectionate, you might get a strong influence over him and make the best of him. There's my advice—for what it is worth."

For answer she did the most embarrassing thing she could do, and burst into tears. Victred looked nervously into the furthest recesses of the hall, where he was certain he caught a glimpse of an interested footman behind a reed curtain.

"Sh-sh! May," he said, patting her on the shoulder. "Don't, don't cry, there's a good girl. When there's nothing to cry about too! You must marry some day, and if you only knew it, it isn't always the best men that make the best husbands. You can't have everything; and a pleasant lively companion who would never be unkind to you might be better than some rigid gentleman with a beautiful moral character and a beastly temper. There, there, I was only in fun. I didn't mean to make you cry."

Lady May began to dry her eyes, but her face was full of melancholy.

"Don't talk about that to me again," she sobbed.

Victred promised readily, anxious to soothe her into quietness, and anxious to get away. An interview with his cousin, with her unconcealed adoration, was always a trying ordeal; but to-day it had been worse than usual, as she persisted in being hysterically grateful for his help on the preceding evening. Besides, he had another visit to pay, even less pleasant than this one. Lady May could not help, through her sobs, becoming aware of his impatience. Spasmodically blinking to keep the tears back, she thrust out a long, limp, moist hand.

"Goo-ood-bye, goo-ood-bye," she sobbed. " I know I'm tiresome, Victred, but I will be a real friend to you, if ever you should want one. There isn't anything, anything, I tell you, I wouldn't do for anyone I cared about. And some day you will find I'm a friend worth having. I'm sure of it. Oh, I'm sure of it! Good-bye."

She wrung his hand, and with one long look out of her blurred, tearful eyes, a dog-like look full of passive devotion, she ran upstairs, stumbling over her torn trimmings, and left him.

Victred was engaged to lunch with Teddy Harrington; as soon as they separated, he made his way, doggedly doing penance in a succession of jolting omnibuses and crawling tram-cars, to Hornsey Rise.

Mrs. Brett, who opened the door to him, seemed not only astonished, but rather alarmed, at his coming. She looked as clean and respectable as ever, but she was thinner, and her face had a worried look. Her first impulse seemed to be to shut the door in his face: when she had conquered this, and had answered civilly but tremulously his inquiries as to her health, she glanced anxiously behind her, and murmured that she was very busy that day, and would be glad if he would call again.

"Well," he said, "this is a long way for me to come. I should like to have a few minutes' talk with you now. How is Louisa?"

Mrs. Brett was naturally such a straightforward woman that it was easy to tell when, for some reason or other, she was not confining herself to the exact truth. Victred saw that she was not telling the exact truth in her answer.

"Oh, sir," she said, "Louisa's that changed you wouldn't know her. Such a quiet girl as she's grown, and different altogether!"

"Indeed," said Victred rather coldly. "And how long is it since this change took place?"

"Ever since she see you last, sir, and you said good-bye to her last autumn at Cheston. She seemed to be touched, sir, by your kindness to her, I think. Anyhow, as I say, sir, I've never had any complaint to make about her since."

Victred looked at her keenly: then a suspicion sprang up in his mind and at once found expression.

"Has a gentleman named Fitzalan been to see you?"

Mrs. Brett grew crimson, but she answered promptly, "No, sir."

He did not believe her, so he shrugged his shoulders, and saying simply: "I want to speak to your daughter," he passed her and entered the narrow entrance passage.

She shut the front-door hastily, and hurried past him to the door of the front room.

"She's not in just now, sir, but if you will tell me when you can look in again, I'm sure she'd be very glad to——"

At this moment there was a noise caused by some one pushing against the folding-doors, and Mrs. Brett, with an abrupt apology, and a murmur about a "lodger," left the room. Victred heard sounds as of whispered remonstrance answered by ill-suppressed laughter, and presently the occupants of the back room went upstairs. When Mrs. Brett came down again, Victred saw that she had been crying.

"I hope you'll excuse me running away so abrupt-like, sir," said she. "But I've got a lodger as gives me a deal of trouble, not being very well. I didn't think you'd care to have her so near, sir, while you was talking of private affairs, so I've got her to go upstairs. And now, if you please, if you'll please to sit down, I shall be happy to hear what you've got to say about Louisa."

But Victred declined to sit down.

"Has she received her allowance regularly?"

"Yes, sir, thank you kindly. The lawyer-gentleman wrote to say as how your father had stopped your allowance, all but what you sent to Louisa, and how he hadn't thought right to stop that."

Victred laughed shortly.

"Well," he said, "what I have to say Louisa must hear, so I will call here again to-morrow, when you will please manage that she is sober enough to see me. You see I know who your lodger is, and what it is she suffers from. You used to speak the truth out like an honest woman, Mrs. Brett: I am sorry that any one should have induced you to treat me differently. Good afternoon."

Mrs. Brett began an incoherent murmur about what a woman, left without her proper protector, would do to console herself, as she accompanied her visitor along the passage to the front door. But she did not care to meet his eyes again, and he stalked out of the house without a glance behind.

The next morning he called upon his lawyer, who confirmed Mrs. Brett's account of the new Lord Malpas's liberality.

"He told me," said the lawyer, with a dry look, "that you should starve before he would let you have a penny. I did not attempt to remonstrate, for, as you had disappeared, there wasn't any means of letting you have the penny. But of course you have now only to claim an allowance, and he is bound to give you one. As you are his only son, and there is hardly anything he can leave away from you, if he refused to give you the money, you could easily raise it; and Lord Malpas is just the sort of man to look upon a *post obit* as an attempt on his life. Between you and me, I don't think he will keep you out of the title very long."

"The longer the better," said Victred. "I shall never claim it. I am going abroad—to the backwoods of North America. I don't want an allowance, but I want a sum of money, a couple of thousand would be enough, paid into my account in —— Bank, that I can draw upon at my own pleasure."

"You will not go away without seeing your father? If you really are going away so far, you will never see him again."

Victred hesitated.

"I suppose it seems a horrible thing to say, but I don't want to see him again. At least, I don't want him to see *me*. I know how he would look at me, and speak to me; and I would rather go away without quite hating him. God knows I have gone near enough to that already many a time, when I was a boy! Look here, Mr. Sheldrake. You are a rising man: you will be in Parliament some day. Get a bill introduced authorising any man left a widower with a young child, if he should not be particularly fond of children, to strangle it at once. It will save a lot of misery, take my word for it."

Mr. Sheldrake knew Lord Malpas, a selfish valetudinarian, refined, studious, unapproachable, well enough not to be much surprised at this outburst. He promised to do his best for Victred, and to let him know the result as early as possible. In the meantime he advanced him twenty pounds, which was all the young man would take. Then he asked if he was to continue the allowance to Victred's wife. His client put his hand up to his moustache, with a frown of anxiety.

"I want," said he shortly, "to get rid of her."

"Well, you will have to employ detectives."

"No," said Victred decidedly, "I won't do that. I don't want any manufactured evidence; and I shouldn't feel justified in using any evidence got in that way."

"What do you intend to do then?"

"To see her, and tell her that I propose to set us both free."

"And supposing she does not care to be set free? I don't see why she should, especially as she is sure to know the position you stand in. Depend upon it, she would make some sacrifices in order not to lose her chance of being Lady Malpas some day." There was a pause, for Victred knew there was reason in what the lawyer said. After a silence, Mr. Sheldrake went on : "You had much better leave it to me. In these cases it is exceedingly dangerous to take any steps except by representatives. Remember that an interview suggests collusion, and it is most important for you to come into court free from all suspicion."

With some reluctance Victred let himself be persuaded to leave the interview with Louisa to Mr. Sheldrake, only stipulating that there was to be no employment of detectives. The lawyer himself was not particularly sanguine of success, and naturally his client was still less so.

"Don't trouble your head any more about this business for a fortnight. Go away somewhere. I will see these people, and when they understand that they can't get at you except through me, they will gradually come round."

These were Mr. Sheldrake's parting words to his client, who judged thereby that he apprehended difficulties serious indeed.

Victred came out of the office dispirited and depressed, feeling his loneliness as he had not done before. He liked the lawyer's advice to go away ; but where was he to go away to ? He had begun to find the society of Teddy Harrington and his feather-brained kind-hearted friends, wearisome in the extreme. Their chatter—for their talk never attained any higher level—which had amused him at first, had begun to bore him. Without being what is called "intellectual," Victred had been forced, by the events and new experiences of the past few months, to consider some aspects of life from a changed standpoint ; and though baccarat did not fill him with the horror with which it inspires the small tradesman, it began to seem to him a ludicrous waste of time and money. This change of sentiment, it will readily be believed, was enough in itself to prove what a gulf now yawned between him and his former chums.

It was in this very dejected mood that he was going along the Strand on his way from Lincoln's Inn to Victoria Street, when just outside the Gaiety bar, he was suddenly greeted by a slap on the back, and "'Ow are yer?" in Mr. Robert de Mowbray's cheery voice. Turning at once, Victred saw that gentleman, in a brand-new suit, a brand-new light overcoat, a brand-new hat, brand-new boots, and brand-new gloves, a radiant and dazzling spectacle. He had a cigar in his mouth, which rather spoiled his appearance by becoming unrolled and suggesting a dried Brussels sprout which has been set on fire. Mr. de Mowbray liked to "cut a dash," but he liked to do it cheaply; and good cigars are expensive.

"Well," said he, "this is a surprise." And then, being chronically at a loss for words, he paused, then thrust his arm through Victred's, and added: "Come and have a drink."

And when Victred refused to have a second, he insisted on his taking a cigar.

Now Victred had seen enough of Mr. Robert de Mowbray to know that this lavishness meant business; therefore he was not surprised when the manager, with a nod of deep meaning, said: "It's a rum thing I should run across you to-day, for it was only last night we was talking of yer, the missus and me."

"Were you? It is very good of Mrs. de Mowbray to think of me at all, when I am afraid I put her to some inconvenience by leaving so suddenly."

"Oh, the missus don't bear malice. Besides, you were quite right. It wasn't good enough—giant at a show!—Not quite! No, the sort of shop you want is something quite different, something refined, artistic —that's *your* line! So I told the missus."

"Well, I'm afraid——" began Victred.

But de Mowbray interrupted him.

"Afraid! Who's afraid? I know what you want

better than you do yourself, I tell yer! You want to go on the reg'lar stage, and show off those props of yours in a good piece."

Victred stared at him doubtfully, but yet with a gleam of hope. If Mr. de Mowbray wanted him to act, why shouldn't he try it? He would be just as safely buried in the "portable" as he had been in the "museum." After witnessing a performance or two by de Mowbray's "crowd," he had acquired a certain modest confidence in his own untried powers. Having once entertained the idea of treating with the manager, Victred thought he would show he knew his value by holding out for terms. So he did not jump at the suggestion, but pulled his moustache and shook his head.

"It's much harder work than being a giant," objected he. "Fifteen parts a week, and sing between!"

To see the look of indignation, pain, and disgust on Mr. de Mowbray's face at these words, you would have thought he was the manager of the handsomest theatre in the metropolis. Having come to the end of the Brussels sprout, he tossed the end into the road with a flourish.

"Fifteen parts a week!" he repeated with ineffable disdain. "Why, what are you thinking of? No. That was good enough for the 'palmy,' but it won't do now. We must go with the times, go with the times. See what I mean?"

"Well, not quite yet," said Victred. "Have you taken a theatre?"

"Theatre! No," replied Mr. de Mowbray with scorn. "What's the good of a theatre? It's the piece, the piece, that's the thing! And I've got a fine piece, a reg'lar stunner—chock full of female interest—situations to make your 'air stand on end— make you laugh till you cry. Never was such a piece!"

"Written by yourself?" said Victred politely.

"No, my boy," answered Robert with a knowing shake of the head and an indulgent wave of the hand,

to imply that he could if he would, but that he spared
the jealous brother-dramatists. "Got one of the big
men to do it; the name's everything, you know.
But I've suggested it all; every blessed situation,
and all the funniest lines—all mine, all mine!" said
he.

"Then why didn't you take the credit of it, and put
your own name to it?" asked Victred with an appearance of verdant innocence.

De Mowbray shook his head astutely.

"Never do, my boy, never do! The critics don't
like it. No, I get the ideas—bit from *Colleen Bawn*,
comic characters out of *The Copper Monarch*, kind-
hearted bobby out of *The Beacons of Brighton*, dying
woman dancing out of *Blind Man's Buff*, a bit from
everything, my boy. That's the way to knock 'em.
You get the best of all the shows in London at one
entertainment, and all at a quarter London prices!
See what I mean?"

"You're going to take it on tour then?" said
Victred.

"Yes. Booked a splendid tour. Going to do the
thing in style. Powerful London Company—carry
all our own scenes—and such posters! None of your
stock stuff! Man in yellow stabbing man in blue,
lady in white fainting O. P., hero in ballet shirt
coming down on tree from cliff above! No, everything special, done for the production. It will be the
biggest thing ever seen on the road. Full company
and no doubles. See what I mean?"

Victred thought there was a little discrepancy
between this glowing account and Mr. de Mowbray's
anxiety to engage himself. This impression gained
upon him when he found that Mr. de Mowbray
proposed to have a part specially written in for him
to show off his clothes.

"Sort of second gentlemanly villain," as the manager explained, "evening dress, and all that, you
know. You've got a dress coat, I dare say?"

Victred admitted that he had. He did not know

how useful that dress coat was going to be to the entire male strength of the company.

With his ambition a little damped by Mr. de Mowbray's evidently higher appreciation of his wardrobe than of his talent, Victred nevertheless made the best bargain he could, and enrolled himself a member of the "Powerful London Company" for the salary of twenty-five shillings a week, which was, in the circumstances, sufficiently handsome remuneration for services which were, however, to be more onerous and more numerous than he expected.

He and his new manager parted mutually satisfied with their bargain, as, indeed, both had reason to be. For Victred had secured the occupation necessary to distract his mind as well as a prospect of safety for his person; and Mr. de Mowbray had retained the services of a servant ten times more active, more intelligent, more sober, more obliging, and more civil than he could have found in the class from which his recruits generally came.

———

CHAPTER XX.

" Only, my Love's away."
—BROWNING.

THIS fresh plunge into Bohemia brought Victred the first sensation of real pleasure which he had known since the transient feeling of relief he had experienced on finding the companions of his old life so ready to welcome him back again into their midst.

That feeling, however, had been quickly followed by a sense on both sides that the old fellowship was gone never to return. In those few short months he had lost touch of Philistia: and now it was with a sigh as for recovered freedom that he returned to the stratum which contained—Jack. That was the secret: he was glad that his body should be where his heart was, among the wanderers of the earth.

To seal his return, he said good-bye to Teddy

13*

Harrington—he did not trouble about the rest—and took lodgings in that part of Hammersmith which does not yet call itself West Kensington. Mr. de Mowbray was rehearsing in London; and the company met daily at "The Oriental," a tavern off the Strand, where they went through their parts in a large upper room smelling strongly of beer and stale tobacco. "The Powerful London Company," as Victred had suspected, proved to be largely made up of such members of the profession as had served Mr. de Mowbray in his less ambitious "portable" days. There were, however, a few newcomers, one in particular, a lady who was reported to have "money," and who gave herself more airs on the strength of this rumoured wealth than she would have been able to do on the score of intelligence, experience, or good breeding. She affected to look down upon all the members of the company, except Victred, who looked down upon her: and she drew upon herself, by her unpunctuality, incompetency, and incivility to everybody, many whispered growls at "amatures." Victred duly found himself cast for "second villain in evening dress and cigarette;" but he also found, in spite of Mr. de Mowbray's assurance that there were to be no "doubles," that it would be considered a favour if he would oblige, "only for a night or two, you know," by coming on as a philosophical casual (*Beacons of Brighton*), a Red Indian (*The Octoroon*), and a Virtuous British Workman out of, for a wonder, no drama in particular.

All this work Victred undertook with the greatest cheerfulness in the world, and he was complimented by the rest of the company to his face on his anxiety to gain experience, and laughed at behind his back for "being such a mug."

The only protest Victred made was embodied in his remark to his manager that the "new and original drama" would be something in the nature of a variety show with himself in the character of a quick-change entertainer. But he was comforted by a slap on the

back, and the oft-repeated assurance that we must go
with the times.

In the meantime Victred was a good deal puzzled
by the fact that, although he had now shown himself
recklessly in all parts of London, in his own proper
person, no attempt had been made to arrest him for
the supposed murder of his cousin. Although the
assurances of his friends had done much to counteract
the effect of Dennis's gloomy foreboding, a charge of
murder hanging over one's head is not a thing which
can be altogether put aside and forgotten ; and the
thought of the danger to which he was hourly exposed served to increase the melancholy to which
absence from Jack and thoughts of Louisa had made
him a prey. The lawyer's words had filled him with
new fears, which his visit to Mrs. Brett had only served
to confirm. What if he were to find it impossible
to free himself from the yoke, which, now that he
loved another woman, had become insupportable?

As soon as the day's rehearsing was over, and he
had left the rest of the company, with the bullying
voice of old Ned Russell, who was stage-managing
the new drama, still in his ears, Victred, therefore,
became a prey to a melancholy from which he found
it impossible to escape. He would walk back from
the Strand to his Hammersmith lodgings, but neither
exertion or fatigue brought him rest. The little
figure of the girl with the pale face and the dark eyes
was always in his mind, the longing to be with her
again was always aching in his breast. How was
she? How were they treating her? Was Tracy
persecuting her? And if so, would her old rogue of
a father interfere? These questions, and a thousand
more like them, tormented Victred almost past
endurance. He tried to keep his thoughts away;
but whether he turned over in his own mind his prospects of getting free from Louisa, or whether he wondered how his father was, and whether that severe
father would receive again his scapegrace son, his
thoughts always came back to the same point ; the

face of little Jack danced before his eyes in the
October mist all the way from Hammersmith to the
Strand, and all the way back again from the Strand
to Hammersmith.

When the day for the production of the piece drew
near, Victred at length found himself possessed of
sufficient courage or sufficient philosophy to risk a
rebuff by writing to his father. It was a difficult
matter considering the relations which had always
existed between them, of natural reticence on the
one side and forced reticence on the other: Victred
tore up a dozen letters before he wrote the one in
which, although it was worded with all the reserve he
thought necessary to satisfy Lord Malpas, there
peeped out the natural longing of the child to be
forgiven and taken back by its father.

To this letter, however, he received no reply.

Then he called at his father's residence, and was
told by the servant that Lord Malpas was not at
home. The man's face was new to Victred; but
something in the interested, startled expression of it
struck his attention.

"Have you been told," he asked, looking straight
into the man's face, "that Lord Malpas is never at
home to me?"

"Ye—yes, sir," said the man, growing red and looking down uneasily.

"Then tell his lordship that I shall not trouble him
again," said Victred, as he turned away with more ease
of manner than lightness of heart.

He felt at that moment such a longing to see his
father again as he had never thought that prim and
bloodless parent could inspire in him. For he knew
the new Earl well enough to understand that this
decision was final, and that any further efforts on his
part to break down the barrier between them would
be thrown away.

This rebuff had one instantaneous bad effect: Victred
was so heart-sore, so reckless at his father's treatment,
that the longing he felt for the sight of a sympathetic

face made him break his wise resolution not to try to see Jack again for the present. Having learnt from Mr. de Mowbray that the "missus," with the "museum," was at a place about twenty miles north of London, Victred took the train one day, as soon as rehearsal was over, and found himself, after a slow and tiresome journey, stopping at each uninviting station, once more in sight of the canvas roof he had so often helped to put up. Victred was nervous; he would not go boldly up to the booth, but prowled about among the swings, shooting-galleries, and roundabouts which showed that the ground was dedicated to "all the fun of the fair." He was hoping to come upon Jack alone, so that his meeting with her should not be spoilt by the coarse "chaff" of the Manageress and her satellites.

A loud cry in a voice which was certainly not Jack's, followed by a slap on the back which all but threw him on his face; and he was in the grasp of Mrs. de M. once more.

"Well, who'd 'a thought o' seein' you!" exclaimed the lady, greeting him with a hearty and open affection which would at one time have disgusted him, but which now, by its evident sincerity, brought the tears to his eyes. "That's why there was a stranger in my tea-cup this morning; I showed it to Ellen. For a stranger you are now, and no mistake; worse luck! Oh, the bother I've had since you went away, you'd never believe! What with the new giant being such a nuisance, and not able to turn his hand to a thing, and puts on such a lot of side, and him only picked up playing a tin whistle at a 'free an' easy,' when all's said and done! But there now, come an' 'ave a drink, and I'll tell you all the news."

And so she did: pouring out her woes into his sympathetic ear, telling of the change for the worse in Ellen's temper, "which was never of the best, as you know!" Of the way the business had fallen off, so that it was really hardly worth while keeping the show open, "not paying the cost of the lighting!"

And last of all, of Dennis having fetched his daughter
away, "just when she was beginning to be of use,
and me having had to board and lodge her all this
time for nothing!"

Victred's heart sank. Jack was gone then. Well,
perhaps it was better. He found it difficult to ask
without a tremor in his voice how she was.

To his horror Mrs. de Mowbray shook her head.

"Not as well as I should like to see her," she said.
" I can't help fancying she's moped a bit since you've
been gone. Do you know I used to fancy you and
her were sweet ǒn-each other! I up and told her so
one night, but she laughed and said how you'd
quarrelled with the woman you were fond of, but
you'd gone back to make it up again. And how she
and you were brother and sister. But brother and
sister's all bosh! Don't tell me!"

Victred did not tell her. He said that Jack was a
dear little thing, and that he was afraid her father
overworked her. To which Mrs. de Mowbray replied
that he would work her harder than ever soon, as he
was going to take her to America with him, and that
of course Jack was to be the "draw."

"Good Heavens! If he does that, he'll never bring
her back alive!" exclaimed Victred.

"So I told him myself," answered Mrs. de Mowbray
with a nod on the same stupendous scale as the rest
of her gestures. "He'd much better let her marry
that swell young cousin of yours, though she doesn't
seem to care much about him. For there's no doubt
he's awfully gone on her; he's been hanging about
the show ever since you went away."

Victred was not surprised to hear this, and he
wished he could come across Dennis, to warn him of
the double game Tracy was playing between Jack and
Lady May. The rest of his late manageress's discourse
was lost upon him, and he took the first opportunity
of making an excuse to get away. Mrs. de Mowbray,
while affecting to deplore his readiness to leave without seeing Madame Elaine, was in reality delighted

at this slight to her favourite parasite, between whom and herself there had existed a certain jealousy as to Victred's perfunctory attentions.

" There, you'd better see her," she advised magnanimously, with a wave of the hand. " Or I'll never hear the last of it. And look 'ere, Fred, there's just one thing I want to let you know, and that is—if you *should* get sick of the crowd Bob's got, I'm always ready to take you back ; and I don't care if I raise your screw, there! "

Victred would have escaped, but Mrs. de Mowbray was inexorable. So he went through the ordeal of an interview with the Fat Lady, who was so much moved at the meeting with Victred, for whom, in spite of his indifference, she still cherished the sacred relics of a tender passion, that she shed copious tears, and was only brought to consider his departure with fortitude by the application of a plentiful supply of hot drinks at the loved one's expense.

Victred went back to town in the gloomiest of moods, ate with resignation the dried - up steak prepared by the landlady, drew a chair to the fire and remained for a long time with his head in his hands, nursing his melancholy thoughts. The news he had of Jack was indeed calculated to fill him with alarm. The girl was not robust, and she had been unduly tried by the hard and wandering existence of the past two winters with her father. And now she was about to start upon an undertaking to which her former journeys were nothing. He knew that Dennis had for a long time projected a trip to America and a tour in that country, and he knew that Dennis was particularly anxious to make what he called " a great splash " there. And that this great splash was to be made at the expense of poor little Jack he could not doubt. The only scrap of comfort he had was in the thought that in America she would at any rate be free from Tracy's doubtful acquaintance.

If he had only been free! If he had only been free! And following the impulse of wild longing,

came a sudden fear lest not only he, but she also, was
suffering from their separation. Mrs. de Mowbray
had said that the girl "moped" since his going away.
There was no selfish comfort to Victred in this intelligence. He had striven loyally and successfully
to hide from her innocent eyes all that was passionate,
all that was selfish in his love; and he would have
had her heart untroubled by the pangs of a passion
which was an echo to his own.

The remains of his unsatisfactory tea-dinner had
been tardily cleared away, and one gas-burner had
been lit by the "slavey"; and still he sat brooding by
the fire. He was presently interrupted by the re-
appearance of Martha, who informed him that a lady
was downstairs, who wished to speak to him.

"A lady!" exclaimed Victred, starting, with a
sudden wild hope that it might be Jack. "Show her
up, please."

Martha disappeared, with the sheepish but interested
grin that a member of her class always bears on such
occasions. Even before she had disappeared, Victred,
with a shrug, told himself that his hopes had deceived
him, and that his visitor must be his cousin May.

Even this revulsion of feeling, however, did not
sufficiently prepare him for the disappointment he
felt when the door again opened, and he found himself
face to face with his wife. There was no mistaking
the change of expression on his face; and, unfortunately, Louisa was not in the mood to pass over the
slight of such a reception.

"Yes, it's me," she said defiantly, as soon as she
had passed the doorway.

"So I see," returned Victred drily, as he passed
her, waited with the door wide open while Martha,
full of baffled curiosity, shuffled downstairs, and then
shut himself in with his unwelcome visitor.

"You wanted to see me a fortnight ago, so you
told mother," she said. "So now I've come. But
perhaps you've changed your mind, and don't want
to see me now!"

"Well, I think on the whole it would have been more pleasant for us both if we had left our intercourse to the lawyers," said he, as he offered her a chair. "But now you're here I'm quite ready to hear anything you have to say."

He had seated himself a few feet from her, and was looking at her curiously. Louisa noticed the closeness of his scrutiny, and resented it.

"What are you staring at?" she asked abruptly.

"You are changed," replied Victred shortly.

She laughed, half uneasily, and looked at him with an expression partly suspicious, partly satisfied.

For she was conscious that the change he noted was for the better. Louisa was still beautiful, though maturity had altered the outlines of her beauty, and her face, while a little thinner than before, seemed to Victred to bear traces of dissipation. But that the manner, the "style," of the woman, had undergone a vast improvement it was impossible to deny. Her dress showed this in a very marked degree. It was not only handsome, but well chosen. The flagrant hat had been exchanged for a dark velvet bonnet, from under which her beautiful hair, properly dressed, escaped less rebelliously than of yore.

"How—changed?"

"Well, you are dressed—differently."

"Better—eh?"

"Well, yes," said Victred dubiously.

Louisa laughed, with an extremely disagreeable sound in her voice.

"Well, you see, as I shall be a Countess some day, I thought I'd better begin to live up to the character."

Victred looked at her with a puzzled frown. The very words she chose denoted that Louisa had received some sort of education since they last met. He got up, and leaned against the mantel-piece, with his face turned from her.

"Haven't you seen Mr. Sheldrake?" he asked abruptly.

"Oh, yes, I've seen him! And I've told him what I thought of him, trying to come between husband and wife, and spoil their chances of happy life together!"

"Oh, oh, you talked to him like that, did you? He must have been surprised."

"Ye-es," said Louisa imperturbably. "I think I did surprise him. I meant to, at any rate. I told him that I was much obliged for his kind interest in me, but that as I'd never done anything wrong, I didn't mean to be treated as if I had. And I just wanted to know, you know, who the woman was that had put it into your head to get a divorce from me."

Victred felt his heart sink. There was something in her manner which betrayed a consciousness of strength in her own cause.

"I know who it *isn't*," she went on. "It isn't the whey-faced girl who came to see me at Cheston."

"Oh, you know that! And pray, who told you?"

Victred had a very good idea who her informant was, and it was strengthened by her answer.

"Never mind. But it comes from a quarter I can trust. And now look here, Vic; I'm much obliged to you for your kind intention of getting rid of me. But I'm not going to be got rid of, my boy. I'm going to be Lady Malpas, and I'm going to be presented at Court with the swells. So there now."

"I'm afraid there will be some little difficulties in the way of that," said Victred, his temper rising at the measure of her insolent assurance. "They are very particular about the character of the ladies received there."

"Well, you're the only person who ever did any harm to my character. But as you married me, I can look over that, and so they will at Court, I expect," she said coolly.

A tempest of strong feeling, of disgust, repulsion, remorse, and of suspicion besides, kept Victred for a few moments silent.

Then he asked, in so quiet a voice that the words sounded almost like a casual remark:

"Where have you learnt—what you have learnt since I saw you last?"

She watched him narrowly as she answered:

"I've been on the stage."

Now this accounted for part of the improvement in her, but not, so Victred thought, for all.

"Well?" said he.

"Well," retorted she defiantly, "that's all." Then, after a pause: "You don't believe me?"

"My lawyers will find out what I am to believe."

She laughed triumphantly.

"Well, let them try. And in the meantime I shan't trouble any lawyers to find out what I want to know about *your* goings on. I shall watch you myself, and so I tell you."

Now this threat showed Tracy's handiwork conclusively, Victred thought. And when she added: "I know where you've been to-day too!" he felt more convinced than ever.

"We need not prolong this interview further," said he suavely, as he crossed the room and took his hat from the sofa; "we seem to understand each other very well, or perhaps I had better say—to mis-understand each other very well. I wish I could make you see that it is no ill-feeling towards you which prompts me to try and get rid of the tie between us. You left me of your own accord, you know. Have I treated you so badly in return that you need want to spoil my life out of vindictiveness? What good would the title be to you, even if I were to live long enough to give it to you? And you have nothing else to gain by opposing the divorce. For you know that I should provide for you always, whatever happened."

"Nothing to gain! With you trying to take away my character!"

Victred crossed the room quickly, and stood in front of her, looking into her face with a stern, penetrating expression.

"Do you think I would try to do that if your

character could be hurt ?   I must speak frankly now.
How can I believe that it would be ?   I know that
it would not ! "

She was watching him, watching him always.

" *Know!* You say you know? *How* do you
know ? "

She said this with the assurance of one sure of her
ground. Victred was rather taken aback by the
question. He knew by a thousand minutest signs,
in the past and in the present, of voice, of gesture, of
manner, that, whatever her conduct might be now, it
had not, in these years that she had been living away
from him, been always unimpeachable. But these
signs, conclusive as they were to him, were not
evidence for a jury. This disquieting thought flashed
into his mind as he prepared to answer her defiant
question.

" How do I know ? " he repeated bitterly. " Why,
I saw it in the looks of the men that night of the
ball at Cheston, men who seemed to know you better
than I did."

" Well," said Louisa sullenly, lowering her eyes for
one brief moment, " that's a long while ago ; and you
wouldn't find it so easy to rake up anything against
me even then ; besides, you took me yourself to the
hotel that night. That would be called in the
lawyers' jargon 'condonation,' wouldn't it ? "

" Very likely," said Victred despondently. " But
why need we go on talking ?   If you have made up
your mind that you will not let me free myself, there
is an end of it. For I have no intention of ' raking
up' anything. I should not feel justified in doing
that. But I had hoped that, as you hated me so
much that you not only ran away from me, but
declined to let me see you, you might be glad, as I
should myself be glad, to be free to lead a respectable
life with a more congenial partner."

" But I don't want to lead a respectable life ! "
burst out Louisa with incautious frankness.

Victred laughed bitterly.

" I thought not," exclaimed he with dry emphasis.
" Unfortunately I do."

Louisa, unabashed, looked at him with a suspicious
frown.

" You're in love with some other woman ! You
want to marry her," exclaimed she, with all that
British horror of any breach of the strictest matri-
monial code which is never more strongly expressed
than by the most flagrant sinners against it.

Victred looked at her indignant face with contemptuous astonishment.

" It is rather shocking, isn't it," said he quietly,
" that your wifely devotion should not satisfy me ? "

But sarcasm was thrown away on Louisa.

" I'm not going to let you get rid of me just so you
can make another woman Lady Malpas," she went on
stubbornly. " Not likely ! No ! I'm your lawful
wife, and I mean to remain so. And as for the other
woman she can——"

He stopped her by seizing her arm in a grip so
forcible that she uttered a little scream of pain. But
with the instinct of her class, she respected him more
for this act of physical violence than for all his
previous generous treatment and forbearance. As
women of a higher type honour a man for strength
combined with skill, women of the low types admire
him for strength manifested in kicks and blows and
rough personal treatment of themselves. So Louisa,
really impressed by this act of which he was ashamed,
listened in passive silence to the short, sharp remonstrance he administered to her before he let her go.

" Don't dare to mention her, to allude to her," he
said with closed teeth ; " I don't deny that I love
another woman. Even you must admit that a wife
who leaves her husband as you left me, has no right
to be astonished at that. But as you will not let me
be free to marry her, she will never even know that I
love her."

" Oh, I dare say ! " commented Louisa faintly.

" For," went on Victred, " she is a woman of a

better sort than you could understand. Now go,
please, and be kind enough not to trouble me again."

And Louisa went, after a pause of bewilderment,
murmuring that this was pretty treatment of a lawful
wife.

Now something in the very last glance cast upon
him by Louisa convinced him that he was to have
more trouble at that lady's hands : and so it proved.
The next day he found her carrying out her threat of
following him. At first the discovery did not trouble
him, as he thought she would soon grow tired of
watching his very innocent and uninteresting journeys
between his lodgings and the Strand. But as the
days went by, and this espionage continued, he passed
from wonder that she should interest herself in his
movements at all to annoyance at her persistency, and
thence to the determination to "lead her a dance."
This, on the very next day, he proceeded to do.

All over the West End, all over the East End, in a
tram-car along the south side of the Thames, in a
train to Hampstead, he went and she followed. He
intended, when they were both worn out, to turn
round suddenly and, becoming pursuer in his turn,
to meet her face to face, and convict her of her folly,
at the same time threatening more serious action
unless she desisted.

But the tiring-out process succeeded a little too
well in the case of Louisa, and resulted in her availing
herself of so many occasions for obtaining alcoholic
refreshment, that, when at last they again reached
Regent Street, and Victred was trying, for about the
fourth time that day, the ruse of crossing the street in
a crowded part, Louisa, still valiant in pursuit, but
less wary than heretofore, slipped and fell down in
the road, almost under the hoofs of the horses of an
omnibus. Having lost her cautiousness of earlier in
the day, she was so close to Victred when the accident
happened, that he was immediately aware of it. In
another moment the horses would have been upon
her. Without the loss of half a moment, however,

Victred sprang in front of them, and dragged her aside, at the cost to himself of a dislocated shoulder.

Louisa herself, though much frightened and entirely sobered, was unhurt.

When he had pulled her across the road to the pavement, where they were instantly surrounded by an interested, pushing crowd, she saw, by the contortions of his pale face, that he was in pain.

"You are hurt! Oh, you are hurt; I'm sure you are!" exclaimed she with real feeling.

"Never mind me," returned he shortly, as he hailed a hansom, and by a gesture invited her to enter it. "Now go straight home, and let this be a lesson to you to leave me alone."

"But you will come too, won't you? Or let me go home with you? When it was saving me—I can't bear to—Oh, do let me come with you!"

"No, thank you," said he very coldly, unmoved except perhaps to disgust by her genuine distress.

She, by this time in the hansom, would have burst into strong language at this rebuff; but he did not give her time. Stepping quickly back, he gave the cabman the address, and raising his hat without looking at her, walked rapidly away.

When he reached his lodging that evening, after having his injured shoulder attended to by a doctor, he found a telegram awaiting him. It was from Mr. Sheldrake, and was as follows:

"Your father died suddenly last night of heart-disease. Must see you at once."

Victred felt a sharp pang of remorseful grief at the news.

"Well," said he to himself at last, after staring with dry eyes at the little flimsy bit of paper which meant so much, "it was his fault, not mine, that we were estranged at the end." And presently there came another thought, one which brought to his lips a bitter, joyless laugh: "So that beauty is Lady Malpas after all!"

And then, having borne a good deal that day in the
way of fatigue, pain, and strong emotion, the new
Earl of Malpas celebrated the occasion and surprised
himself by falling insensible on the hearthrug, just
as a tap came at the door, and a woman's voice said :
" May I come in ? "

CHAPTER XXI.

" I stood slighted,
Forgotten and contemned : my soft embraces,
And those sweet kisses you called Elysium,
As letters writ in sand, no more remember'd."
BEAUMONT AND FLETCHER.

VICTRED came to himself with a consciousness, a
vague and confused consciousness, of being gently
tended and well cared for. Before he opened his
eyes, he felt a hand laid softly on his head ; and remembering dimly the tap at the door which he had
heard as he lost consciousness, he began to nurse the
sweet belief that the hands whose touch he felt were
those of little Jack. And yet this belief was not
strong enough for him to dare to open his eyes in the
assurance that it was a reality.

This phase lasted, of course, only a few seconds.
But before it came to an abrupt end, he felt a kiss
pressed softly on his forehead.

" Jack ? " he cried, as he sprang up and opened his
eyes.

But it was not Jack. Victred, who had been placed
on the sofa, staggered as he reached his feet. For on
her knees beside him, still holding the smelling-bottle
she had been using in her efforts to revive him, was
Louisa.

Victred laughed awkwardly, stammered, began to
explain. Fortunately, the woman was as uneasy as he ;
and it was from her lips that he learnt that his explanation was dangerous and unnecessary.

" The gentleman isn't here," said she with a laugh
which was almost bashful.

And Victred realised with relief that there was safety in the masculine name.

"Are you better now? You are not in pain now, are you?" went on Louisa with a new warmth and feminine gentleness which Victred, not unnaturally perhaps, altogether misinterpreted. For the sight of the telegram, lying on the floor in the corner by the fireplace, suggested at once to his mind that she had read the message, and that her solicitude was a consequence of his changed condition.

"Yes, thank you. I'm all right now," said he shortly, as he stooped to pick up the paper, throwing a suspicious glance at her as he did so. " You've read this, I suppose?"

" No," said Louisa ; adding ingenuously : " I didn't see it."

"There you are then," said he, in a curious tone, with a sort of flippant, hard gaiety which was new to her in him. " It contains a piece of news which you will think very good," and he handed her the paper, which she read slowly, at first not taking in the import of the message. Victred leaned with his back against the mantel-piece, frowning and irritable. He was smarting under the irony of fate, not quite master enough of himself to be able to hide the effects of his bitter disappointment on finding who it was that he had mistaken for Jack. The very sight of this woman standing before him, unintelligently spelling out the words, moved him to impatience.

" Don't you understand, your ladyship, don't you understand?" said he irritably. And taking the paper from her, he smoothed it out upon the table and read the message with jerky emphasis on every word.

" Your—father—died—suddenly—last—night."

Victred's voice broke suddenly upon the last word, and he threw himself into a chair, turning his face away from her. But Louisa said nothing. Very soon it dawned upon him that this was surprising,

14ᵏ

and he raised his head quickly to look at her. She
was standing by the table, leaning upon it, her long
dark velvet cloak slipping off her shoulders, her hair
pushed back under her bonnet. He saw then by her
attitude, and still more by the bewildered expression
of her face, that she had not known, until he told her,
the meaning of the news. As he looked at her, she
recovered herself enough to speak.

"Then you are a lord, a real lord now?" she asked
in a feeble voice.

"Yes, a real lord, and you a real countess—Lady
Malpas of—of the Strand!" cried Victred, with a reckless air more like that of a man in a state of intoxication than of a sober citizen who has received a
startling piece of news. "And I am an earl, a real
live earl, earning twenty-five shillings a week as long
as he can dodge the police, and with a very fair
prospect of picking oakum for the term of his natural
life when he can dodge them no longer."

And he burst into a loud laugh, leaning back in his
armchair, with his eyes on the ceiling.

"Oh, don't, don't!" cried Louisa. "It ain't really
as bad as that, is it now?"

And clasping her hands tightly together, and
bending her head eagerly forward, she came a step
nearer to him, looking eagerly, and with a passionate
fear, into his face. Victred was struck by her tone.
He looked at her, and as he looked there dawned
upon him the surprising conviction that she, the coarse,
loose-lived woman whom he had reason to think
utterly heartless, was showing real emotion, almost
real dignity, under his own mocking and contemptuous words. He uncrossed his knees, and stared
at her incredulously.

"What does it matter to you?" he asked shortly.
"It won't make any difference as far as you are concerned, whether I'm at Portland or in Grosvenor
Square. Nothing your unworthy husband can do will
affect your right to the title, I assure you."

Her emotion, her appearance of womanliness,

annoyed him. He wanted to provoke her to show
the coarse, the cruel side of her nature, the one he
was most used to, the one from which he had suffered.
It irritated him that she should suddenly seem to try
to put him in the wrong by this assumption of warm
and tender feelings on his account. For of course
he considered it as an assumption only. But she
remained provokingly humble, irritatingly con-
siderate.

"I—I didn't mean for that," she said quite gently.
"I—I—Vic, I can't get over this afternoon!   I can't.
It's no good.   I've tried—and I can't!" and she burst
into tears and sobs, and an incoherent whispered
word or two. "Why—why didn't you let me be run
over, Vic?   Then you'd have been rid of me, and
nobody couldn't have blamed you?   Why didn't you?
Tell me, tell me?" and the woman, her face con-
torted by strong passions of curiosity, and gratitude,
and even fear, pressed nearer to his chair, and bent
down lower and lower till she sank upon her knees
beside him. "You hated me ; you as good as told me
so. Well, well, why did you do it?"

Victred, leaning upon the arm of his chair which
was furthest from her, looked at her out of the corners
of his eyes.   He began to be afraid of the mysterious spirit he had unconsciously roused in this
beautiful animal, and the repulsion he felt towards her
increased.

"Why, what would you have had me do?"
asked he coldly.   "Isn't the death of one fellow-
creature enough for a man to have on his conscience?"

"But it wouldn't have mattered, this one!" she
sobbed. "Who'd have missed me?   Who'd have
cared if I was dead, except p'raps mother, and even
she'd have been glad to be done with such a
nuisance as me, when she'd had time to think it
over."

At last the genuineness of the feeling she showed
was gaining upon Victred who, never really hard,
had been stung for a little while into an appearance

of harshness which a woman's tears allayed easily
enough. He moved restlessly in his chair as he spoke
to her, and in a voice which betrayed under its impatience the kindly feeling which went so far to make
him a favourite with men and women too, said :

"Don't be foolish. There isn't anything to cry
about. When you see a person that's going to be run
over, you pull that person out of the way as a matter
of course. It's instinct, and there's an end of it. So
there's nothing to make a scene about. I never
thought you'd think twice about it. I didn't."

But she sobbed on, and continued to be oppres-
sively grateful. At last he rose and said :

"Come, you know, it's no use going on like like
this. How do you get back ? Train or omnibus, or
what ? I must see you off, as I have to go and see
Mr. Sheldrake to-night."

"Not to-night, oh, not to-night, if it's about me ! "
cried Louisa piteously, rising from her knees and
continuing to dry her eyes.

"It's not about you at all. You said it was of no
use consulting him about you, you know."

Louisa began to tremble, and to twist her hand-
kerchief, in one of the old habits of her " Seven
Stars " days, long since forgotten, but which had come
back to her in her excitement. Her face moved convulsively meanwhile ; and her great blue eyes, which
even now retained something of their plaintive, child-
like look, were fixed upon his face, with an expression
in them as of the mute pleading of an animal.

"But listen, listen, Vic," said she in a breathless
voice, after a pause during which he had had his
hand impatiently on the door, while she hung back,
watching him intently with frightened eyes. "Do
listen. You'll be glad after, if you will."

Infected in spite of himself by her earnestness,
Victred shut the door, and leaned against it, waiting
for her to speak. But at first she could not ; she
stood silent before him, her breast heaving, her eyes
cast down.

' No, don't go," she burst out at last, when a slight movement on his part gave her for the moment the erroneous impression that he was going. Then, clasping her hands tightly together, and speaking rapidly, as if the words she uttered were being torn out of her, she said :

" You don't believe what I said—that I am grateful for—for what you did this afternoon. Well, you *shall* believe it ! Look here, haven't you heard that some bad people are not all bad, just as some good people, lots of 'em ! are not all good? Haven't you heard that, eh? I'm bad, as you know ; if I don't know it myself, it's not for want of bein' told, is it ? "

" Well, I don't think I have ever told you that you were so very bad," said Victred gently. "Indeed I know you are a great deal better than you like to make out yourself, or you wouldn't have been so kind to me when you found me this evening. You might have gone away and left me to come round on the floor. For I was on the floor, wasn't I ? "

" Yes, and I carried and dragged you, somehow, to the sofa," answered Louisa with a sudden change to wistful gentleness. " All by myself. Not bad for a little 'un, was it ? "

As if uncertain how her pleasantry would be received, she glanced up with a sidelong look. But when she saw on his face an expression which showed him to be deeply moved, she kindled into new vigour.

" Ah, and I'll do more for you than that, much more, so as you shall know how I feel. Go to your lawyer, Vic, and tell him as what you've got such a case as was never before the Court yet. I'll give him proofs enough to free half-a-dozen husbands."

" For God's sake don't talk like that ! " cried Victred, horror-struck. "Why, woman, estranged as we are, I'd give the world to believe we'd wronged you in thinking any ill of you ! "

" But you haven't, that's the worst of it," retorted she, in a tone of cynical defiance in which, however,

Victred heard a slight tremor which pierced him to
the heart. "There isn't a fast place in town where
they don't know me, I tell you. And if you'd only
done what any other man in your place would have
done, and set a tec to work, he'd have had evidence
enough and to spare in less than no time. There, are
you satisfied now?"

Victred was shaking like a leaf in the wind. His
face was ghastly white even to the lips. She could
see the glistening drops on his forehead as his answer,
in hoarse and quavering tones, came from his dry lips.

"Satisfied! O my God!"

"Why, it was what you wanted, evidence, wasn't
it?" said Louisa in surprise. "And here it is, any
amount. Look!"

She produced from her pocket a bundle of papers,
which she offered to him, and, as he declined to take
them, flung them down pell-mell on the table. Letters,
bills, receipts, a mass of documents which the most
casual glance would have verified as sufficiently in-
criminating, fell in all directions. But Victred would
not look at them.

"Look, look, why don't you look?" cried Louisa
impatiently. "It is what you wanted. You can get
free with these. It hasn't been such a pleasure bringing them that you need take it like that! I don't
feel so proud of the present as you might think. Vic,
Vic, speak to me, say something!" she suddenly
burst out hysterically, covering her face with her
hands. "Say it don't make you think worse of me
than what you did before!"

She wept aloud in such a pitiful way that Victred
was touched to the quick.

"Hush, Lou, hush!" whispered he, in a broken
voice. "Think worse of you! No, of course I don't.
Do you think I'm a brute? But don't you see, girl,
what an awful thing it is you expect me to thank you
for?"

"Well, it can't be helped. Let's get it over. Take
'em, and let's get it over!" sobbed Louisa.

As she was still sobbing bitterly, Victred stooped and laid his hand kindly on her shoulder. In another instant she became as quiet as the dead, and remained perfectly still while he spoke again.

"Did you bring those—those letters and things here this evening—on purpose?"

"I—I don't know exactly," she answered in that curiously childish manner she often fell into when answering a straightly put question. "I—I think I must have had it in my mind, when I was thinking what there was as I could do to show just how I felt. Anyhow I put 'em in my pocket, and there they are. Do thank me, Vic! For I'd rather not have had to do it. I'd rather have let you go on not knowing how bad I was, and been able to put on airs to you as if you was treating me badly, instead of me you. For now you know me for just the creature I am, and I can't put on no airs to you again."

"Get up, Lou, and let me look at you," said Victred suddenly. "You've knocked me over altogether. Don't you know that if I divorce you you can't be Lady Malpas?"

She rose and nodded, drying her eyes.

"Yes, I know that," she said. "And I don't mind. A pretty countess I should make, as you said yourself! All I mind is that—that there'll be another one!"

She had accepted his tacit invitation to be seated, and had taken one of the shabby armchairs by the fireplace. Victred took the other. There was silence for a time, while Victred looked at the red coals, and Louisa looked at him. At last he said:

"Why didn't you show some of this generosity and self-sacrifice in the old days at Oxford, when I first married you, Lou? Was it I who was to blame? Looking back, I don't think it was; and yet—and yet—look here! How is it I never found out the best that was in you? How was it? Do you know?"

He glanced at her, and saw that her great eyes

were staring at him with a puzzled expression in
them.

"Best in me don't amount to much, Vic," she
answered at last, shaking her head. "In the old
days, when we was at Oxford"— she paused, and
seemed to be trying to recollect her old sensations,
"Well, I wasn't happy. I didn't feel at home with
you. And with you always a-looking at me, as if
you thought I ought to be doing something more
than what I could do. And then, what with your
frowning when I spoke wrong, and me not understanding nor p'raps caring much about you, and not
being good enough for you, and knowing it and not
wanting to be better—in fact wanting to be worse!
There, that's how it was!" she finished off recklessly.
"But why trouble your head about it now?"

"Because I can't help thinking that if we had only
been able to drag on a little longer, it might have
come all right, instead of all wrong," said Victred
sadly.

"No, it wouldn't, I'm not the sort. Look here,
Vic: I had to find out what other men were like
before I appreciated you. See? It's what I've gone
through knocking about made me feel I must buy a
kind look and a kind word from you, whatever I did
for it, Vic. And now you've given them to me, and
now I've been able to do something for you, I'm
satisfied, Vic."

And she leaned forward in her chair, as she let her
voice fall to a whisper, seeking with her eyes a return
glance from him. Victred looked long and earnestly,
with a wondering expression, at her face. At last he
said slowly:

"And if I divorce you, what sort of life will you
lead? Do you know some man who would marry
you, and to whom you could feel you would try to be
a good wife?"

For answer she burst into tears again.

"Me a good wife!" she sobbed, laughing hysterically. "What rot you're talking!"

"I don't think so. I was a young fool, and couldn't manage you, couldn't understand you, but some man might."

"And would you advise a man to take a wife like me?" she asked mockingly.

Victred evaded the direct question.

"Some men do," said he. "A man who loved you might."

"There isn't one," she answered half-sullenly, but yet with a touch of defiant sadness. After a moment's pause she broke into a reckless laugh. "Don't you trouble your head about me, I tell you," she went on. "You get free and go your own way and I'll go mine."

She sat up, threw herself back in her chair, put her hands on the arms of it, and crossed her knees, with an assumption of reckless indifference which did not deceive Victred. He looked at her with eyes full of pity, half realising that the wreck that she had made of her life was not his fault, but the result of an inevitable destiny which had been fixed from her birth; yet he was full of remorse too. Then he took up the tongs which were lying in the grate.

"Are you going to dash my brains out?" asked she with a flippant laugh.

"No, that was not my intention," he said quietly, as he got up and went to the table. She watched him with wide-open mouth and staring eyes as he picked up one by one with the tongs the letters and papers which were strewn over the table and the floor; and one by one, without any apparent excitement, he placed them on the fire, until there remained of the evidence which was to purchase his freedom nothing but a few bits of curled black film flying up the chimney. Louisa watched the papers burn without a word. She had risen from her chair, but stood trembling, without daring to interfere. When the last paper was destroyed, Victred assisting the process by stirring the fire with the tongs, she murmured, in a low voice:

"What did you do that for?"

"Because I wanted to destroy the evidence of my wife's shame—and mine."

"Your wife! But I shouldn't have been your wife if you'd used these papers! Don't you understand that they'd have made you free?" she asked wonderingly.

"I understand. But I don't choose to use them. I'm not going to get free, Lou; I'm going to let you be Countess of Malpas——"

"But, but——"

"But you have to do something in return," said Victred gravely, bending down to look sternly into her face. "You'll have to lead a decent woman's, life."

Louisa was taken aback.

"But, but——" she began again.

"You hear what I say. You have to promise me, swear to me now that you will. Mind, I can't force you to do it; I have to trust to your honour." He checked her mocking laugh by a touch on her shoulder. "Your honour, yes. You've shown me to-night qualities that I didn't know of before; you're too good for the life you've been leading, Lou, and you must give it up. Mind, I shall have to trust you to do it, as it will be better that we should not meet again." She began to sob softly at these words. "But you are to remember that I have given up something, that I have given up the hope of ever having a wife by my side to love and to care for. You must remember that, I say, and be worthy of my trust."

"But why, why—?" she sobbed out. "Why don't you get free, when it's so easy?"

"Because, Lou, I think you've got a soul worth saving, and I see no other way of trying to save it except my way."

For a few minutes the woman, who was deeply touched, and who showed it after the emotional, irresponsible manner of her kind, wept so violently that speech on either side was impossible. Suddenly she raised her head, and looked up at him out of blurred, tear-swollen eyes.

"Vic, you're a fool," she cried passionately. "You're throwing away your own life, and you'll do me no good. Why, why," here she broke into sobs again, "you've done me ha—harm already! Yesterday I didn't care for you or anybody, and I could make myself happy my own way. But—but if I do what you want me to, I shall be too good for one set, and too b—b—bad for another, and I shall be neither f—fish, flesh, fowl, nor g—g—good red herring!"

"Well, you try it," said Victred persuasively, as he gave her an encouraging pat on the shoulder.

"All right," said Louisa dismally. "I'll try, because you've been so good to me. But, o—h—h Vic, it's much harder than w—what I wanted to do."

"I know that," said Victred apologetically, "but I want you to try it, all the same."

Louisa seemed still to hesitate, as she looked ruefully at the fire.

"And you—what are you going to do?" she asked at last in a low voice, with some diffidence.

"I? Oh, I'm going to bury myself again, as I did before. One can get something out of life, even in that underground fashion."

Still she was not satisfied. It was again in a low, shame-faced voice that she said:

"You have been very good to me, Vic," she hesitated. "I—I shouldn't like never to see you again, Vic!"

She spoke with diffidence, and yet almost caressingly. But when, on these last words, she ventured to look up, she saw that his face was not only grave but cold, and that he already wore an impatient, absent expression.

"I'm outstaying my welcome, I expect," she said briskly, in quite a different tone.

Victred did not answer. The truth was that his

shoulder was paining him, probably as the result of some incautious movement during the interview he had just gone through ; so that he felt faint and ill. He put out his hand.

" You are going ? Good-bye," said he.

Louisa looked shyly, but rather hopelessly up at him for the last time.

" You are ill, I can see," she said sadly. " I suppose —you won't let me stay—a little while—and—and take care of you ? "

Victred answered all too promptly.

" No, oh, no, thank you. Not on any account. I'm all right, I assure you."

Louisa only replied to this by a short nod. She put her hand in his offered palm, and then, bending suddenly, kissed his hand fervently. Then she raised her head, but not her eyes, with a defiant laugh.

" *That* can't pollute you, can it ? The hand doesn't count."

He laughed good-humouredly, and said :

" Nonsense ! "

But if, in the moment she yet lingered, she had hoped that he would offer to kiss her face, she was disappointed.

And so, with just " Good-bye " and " Good-bye," they parted : he remaining in his room, while she slipped quietly down the stairs and out of the house.

CHAPTER XXII.

" Upon my head they placed a fruitless crown,
And put a barren sceptre in my gripe.'
—SHAKESPEARE.

INSTEAD of enjoying the bliss which ought to follow an act of honourable self-sacrifice, Victred remained overwhelmed by the feeling that he had made a fool of himself. He had been surprised and touched by the unexpected display of qualities in Louisa for which no one seemed previously to have given her credit, any more than he had done. He had been moved, too, by a plaintive look in her eyes, that look as of a dumb animal in pain which, in the eyes of a beautiful woman, can scarcely fail to affect any man who is not made of stone. No doubt the improvement in her appearance and manner had also, by marking an alteration in the pronounced vulgarity of the old days, contributed to this result.

But now that she was gone, the revulsion of feeling came quickly. He recognised the fact that, although she was evidently capable of generous emotion, it was too probable that such emotion was only transient, and that it by no means followed that she was capable of steady persistence in the better mode of life which he had marked out for her. It was more than likely that her good resolutions would but stand the test of a week or two, and that at the end of that time she would relax into her old habits, leaving him to carry out, on his side, the terms of a one-sided bargain.

Yet Victred did not go so far as to repent of the compact he had made with her. He understood to the full, as he had done at the time he married her, the responsibility which a man takes upon himself with a partner for life. Of his own free will he had married this woman, with open eyes and the fullest reason to be conscious of her imperfections, moral and other. While, therefore, there remained a possibility that, by taking advantage of an auspicious moment, he could raise her from the degradation into which, of her own free-will, she had walked, he felt bound to make any sacrifice of himself rather than lose the chance of saving her.

Luckily, he told himself, there was no question of sacrificing any one but himself. Little Jack believed in the amiable fiction of his brotherly regard, knew that he was married, was even anxious in a beautiful child-like way, for his reconciliation with the wife she did not know. She was with her father now, and would soon be in America with him, away from all danger of Tracy's further persecution. Besides, Victred believed that, when Dennis learnt that Fitzalan was wooing Lady May in earnest, the agitator would be roused to proper natural resentment of the young man's conduct towards Jack.

This was what he *thought*, and he told himself that he had acted rightly. But what he *felt* was that little Jack was lost to him for ever; that the hope of having some day a real wife to cherish; the hope of feeling some day Jack's arms round his neck, of hearing her voice in his ear calling him husband! was dead and must be buried for ever. And all for a woman who was nothing to him but a name, a shame, and a responsibility: a woman whom he not only despised, but hated; whom to touch without showing his repulsion required a strong effort of self-control.

Well, it was done, it was over. After all there might still be some pleasure left in a bachelor life; and if the police should lay hands on him after all, and if a jury, assisted by his cousin Tracy, Lady Rushcliffe, and Jerry Coggin, should treat him hardly, it was just as well that there should be no loving woman to leave, whose heart might be broken by his punishment.

And by the time Victred had threshed all this out in his mind, he was in a mood to say that lawyers might hang and must wait; so he went to bed instead of seeking out Mr. Sheldrake.

Next day he sent a messenger to the Oriental with a note to Mr. de Mowbray, asking that gentleman to excuse him from rehearsal, on the score of urgent private affairs. Then he went to the house of his late father, and looked for the last time upon the face which was scarcely colder to him in death than it had been in life.

And when he came out of the death-chamber, he was met by his cousin May.

"I knew you would come here," said she, in a whisper from which she tried to extract her evident joy at the sight of him. "I want you to come home with me, Victred. The brougham is waiting. I want to have a talk to you about your affairs. A serious one, mind. I've seen Mr. Sheldrake."

Victred tried to excuse himself, but unavailingly.

"To tell you the truth," she said, "Mr. Sheldrake suspected you would delay your visit to him, and he engaged me as deputy, to do some of his work for him with you."

"Well, I suppose I can't refuse a lady," said Victred. "I accept the change with gratitude; for you won't be so long-winded as Sheldrake, and you can't be so technical."

So he drove back to Bruton Street with his cousin, had luncheon with her and her apathetic chaperon, and found himself constrained to spend with the ladies an afternoon which was not so tedious as he had expected. Her own good sense or some wise counsellor had persuaded Lady May to try fresh tactics with her adored cousin. Instead of sighs, she gave him smiles. Instead of lamentations over his misfortunes, she gave him sensible advice. Mr. Sheldrake, it seemed, had decided that Victred must now come forward and take his trial, a proceeding which he said was absolutely necessary before he could take his place as Earl of Malpas.

"Well," objected Victred, "but it is pretty certain that I should not be allowed to take that place at all."

"But Mr. Sheldrake says he is not so sure about that. He has got some evidence in your favour, I think; and he says he only wants your help to get more. You know very well, Victred, that I should be the last person in the world to suggest your giving yourself up if I thought any harm would come to you by it," she went on, with a dangerous inclination to relapse into sentimentality apparent in her voice and in her eyes. "But I think you will be very unwise if you do not go to him and hear what he has to say. And you really owe him this courtesy, for I know he worked very hard on your behalf with your father, though he did not succeed in persuading him to be reconciled to you."

This advice was so reasonable that Victred was constrained to promise to follow it. And then he

would have availed himself of this opportunity to go :
but Lady May begged so hard that he would put off
his visit to the lawyer until the following day, and
stay to have tea with her, that he yielded to her kindly
persuasions.

In spite of himself, Victred found himself experi-
encing keen pleasure in his cousin's pretty care and
hospitality. For nearly a year now ladies' drawing-
rooms had been to him a memory only. He had forgotten how very delicious tea could taste when it is
served in egg-shell china, poured out and handed to
you by a lady. He had forgotten the shaded lamps,
the flower-laden vases, the dainty work-baskets full of
ethereal marvels of dainty handiwork which never got
finished. For although Teddy Harrington's flat had
bridged over the gulf between his tenting life and
Lady May's luxurious surroundings, Teddy, with all
his effeminacy, or perhaps because of it, just missed
that last touch of luxurious refinement which seemed
to be attained with ease by Lady May and her
guardian.

He was leaning back very comfortably in a low
armchair by the fire, eating tiny rolls of bread and
butter and making fun of them, telling his cousin that
her ignorance of the measure of a back-woodsman's
appetite was lamentable and that he should really
have to ask for the loaf, when their pleasant *tête-à-tête*,
to which Mrs. Mostyn-Stanningly's counting of the
stitches of her knitting made an unheeded accompaniment, was disturbed by the arrival of a visitor.

Victred jumped up and wanted to go before the new
comer entered. While he was still arguing the point
with Lady May, who implored him to stay, the door
opened, and to the horror of everybody, the footman
announced :

" Lady Rushcliffe."

Lady May turned crimson with anger.

" *That* woman ! How dares she come to my
house ! " cried she, in a voice which trembled with
passion.

As for Victred, he was so petrified with astonishment that he was for the moment both speechless and motionless.

It was at this point that Lady Rushcliffe, sweet and smiling, and with a manner at once dignified and dashing, entered the room, and embraced May before the amazed girl had time to make a movement in her own defence. May uttered an exclamation of indignation; but it was entirely lost upon her effusive visitor. Lady Rushcliffe had by this time passed on to Mrs. Mostyn-Stanningly, and having shaken her by the hand before that lady had gathered her wits sufficiently to remember whether she had or had not been introduced to the visitor, turned to Victred with a cry which, if not one of joy, was an admirable imitation.

"Oh!" she cried as she seized the hand which he had not offered, "how I have longed to see you again! It was about you that I came here this afternoon. I wanted to know where you were, and I thought," she continued archly, glancing at May, "that here would be my best chance of hearing of you, and fate has been even kinder to me than I had hoped."

"Then fate has been kinder to you than you were to me upon a certain occasion, Lady Rushcliffe," said Victred dryly, but with a flash in his eyes, while his cousin May gave him a look which was equivalent to applause.

"Ah, I know what you mean! Don't speak of that," cried Lady Rushcliffe with a beautiful shudder, closing her eyes for a moment as if to shut out some horrible picture suddenly called up before her. "I have thought of it night and day, I have been tormented with remorse. For a long time I did not care to seek you out, to beg your forgiveness. I said to myself: how can I expect him to be just to me? How can I expect him to realise what a woman feels when the man she has loved so much, adored, is suddenly stricken down almost before her eyes? Shall I be able to make him understand that at such

15*

a moment a woman, a passionate, impulsive woman
like myself, can think only of one thing—that he
whom she loved is dead, is gone for ever, and that
upon that thought there comes always a desire for
revenge, insensate, mad revenge upon somebody!
And how can I tell him that there follows a terrible
reaction, when one would give the world to recall
one's mad foolish words: to throw one's self, as it
were, at the feet of the man one has wronged, and
implore his forgiveness! May," continued she, turning with an appearance of spontaneous impulsiveness,
to the still sullen and angry girl, " plead for me! He
will listen to you."

But Lady May remained cold. " Indeed, Lady Rushcliffe," she said, "you are much more eloquent than I !"

Victred was disgusted, and he did not try to hide
his feeling.

"You were even more eloquent," he said, " before
the jury. It is you I have to thank, Lady Rushcliffe,
you and your sorry tool Coggin for the warrant which
still hangs over my head."

But Lady Rushcliffe was unabashed. She clasped
her beautifully gloved hands in a picturesque attitude
of entreaty.

"Oh, don't say that, don't say that, I implore you,"
she cried. And then deftly carrying the war into the
enemy's country, she added : " Nobody would have
considered my wild words as anything but the ravings
of a heartbroken woman, unworthy of attention, if you
had not gone away."

There was just enough substance of truth in this
remark to cause Victred and Lady May to exchange
glances. Lady Rushcliffe pursued her advantage.

" If you had come forward, stood face to face with
me, challenged me to tell exactly what I knew in distinction to what I only imagined, would there, do you
think, have been a single creature in the whole court
to listen to my hysterical words in the face of your
calm statement of fact ? "

Now, of course, the lady's hearers both knew that

the lady had not been hysterical, but calmly and coolly vindictive, in her utterances before the jury. But they saw, especially Lady May, whose love for her cousin rendered her specially keen on any point which concerned his interest, that the best thing to be done was to accept the terms of peace offered by the reformed virago. Victred was still hesitating when May, having already made up her mind to secure this turncoat at any cost, held out her hand, and thanked her for coming.

" And you would come forward and undo the harm you unthinkingly did him, at any time when it should be necessary, wouldn't you?" she continued coaxingly.

Victred frowned; feeling that he would rather be hanged outright and have done with it than owe his escape to this hateful woman. He remained as much as possible in the background, being indeed encouraged therein by the caution of his cousin, while Lady Rushcliffe drank tea and ate bread and butter.

Lady May's wise exertions on her cousin's behalf did not stop here. She took the opportunity, when Lady Rushcliffe was occupied with the other lady to whisper to the still sulky Victred :

" You must go and be civil to her. I insist. I know she is hateful, but her evidence can get you off."

With much reluctance Victred found himself constrained, therefore, not indeed to be civil to Lady Rushcliffe, so much as to allow her to be civil to him. And in the course of these civilities the motive of them peeped out very clearly.

" I was so exceedingly distressed to hear of your father's death," she said in the softest and most caressing of .voices. " And the report that you had not been on good terms with him lately was so terrible at such a time that I cried as if my heart would break when I heard the sad tidings. And that you should bear a title which had been so dear to me at one time! I think that fact softened me towards you more than all the rest. So I said to my *fiancé*—for

I'm engaged to be married again, I have felt so lonely that I felt bound to do so—I said to him : I must find out that poor boy and see if I can do anything to comfort him !" Victred bowed without speaking. "So you will forgive me, won't you? You can't refuse, when you remember how difficult it is for a woman to own herself in the wrong ! And you'll come and see me when I'm married, won't you? I shall depend upon you and May here to come and give a 'tone' to my little 'at-homes.' For Mr. Robinson is only a solicitor, though he is very rich, and I shall have quite hard work at first to keep my own 'set' together, when they hear that I've committed high treason by marrying out of it !"

And Lady Rushcliffe put her head a little on one side against her left shoulder in the most charmingly coquettish way in the world, and gave Victred a smile which was a compound of archness and persuasive sweetness. Victred, although by no means won over by these very transparent blandishments, thought it prudent to be grateful, and gave some vague promises. He began to understand the immense difference that lies between the heir to an earldom and the actual earl.

When Lady Rushcliffe at last took her departure, the innocent Mrs. Mostyn-Stanningly thought that the well-preserved and well-dressed woman and Victred and May were the dearest of friends.

But no sooner was the door closed behind the visitor than Lady May asked Victred to ring the bell.

"Let's have the lamps," said she, "and make the place look different, and forget she's been here !"

"With all my heart," said Victred obeying with alacrity.

He refused to stay to dinner, but Lady May insisted on keeping him until the latest possible moment, exerting all her powers of persuasion to induce him to come back, as she put it, to civilisation. He could not deny now that the possibility was open to him. He did not quite care to tell his cousin, what indeed she would scarcely have understood, how entirely the old life had lost its zest for him. To change the subject, he asked her if Tracy had troubled her further.

She shrugged her shoulders.

"Oh yes," she answered lightly, "that's a perennial trouble now. He sees me as often as possible, and when he does the intercourse between us consists entirely of one long, monotonous proposal on his part, and of one long, monotonous refusal on mine. Don't let's spoil this pleasant time by talking about him!"

"I'm afraid I must spoil it by going away," said Victred, rising. "You forget that Hammersmith is a long way off, and that my present democratic habits compel me to walk."

"But that's silly, isn't it? It's all very well to be democratic when you can't afford to be anything else; but it's only eccentricity in you now, Victred; and an earl ought to keep eccentricities as a resource for his old age."

"It's the earldom I'm going to keep as a resource for my old age, not the eccentricity."

Lady May's face was instantly convulsed with alarm.

"Victred," she cried in a voice full of passion, detaining his hand in a grip the strength of which surprised him, "I will not let you go till you have promised to come back, to come back in a proper manner, I mean, and take your place as Earl of Malpas."

Victred looked down at her eager face with a curious little smile. She had behaved more sensibly to-day than was usual with her where he was concerned, and in consequence he liked her better than usual. The habit of entertaining was giving her more ease of manner too. She was getting more of a personage, to be consulted and spoken with straightforwardly.

So he said, "My dear May, what's the good?" in a

manner which allowed her to understand that he
referred to his unfortunate marriage.

And, reddening deeply, and modestly casting down
her eyes, poor Lady May, without a suspicion of that
third woman about whom she had never heard, answered with modest hesitation :

" Oh, well, you could get free, I suppose, if you
liked ! "

" I shall never get free, May," said Victred gravely.

And poor Lady May, whom he forthwith left to
herself with a warm shake of the hand and a kindly
farewell, was left to lament the backwardness of the
awkward sex.

But if I had been handsome, she reflected, while the
tears welled up to her eyes, he wouldn't have had any
scruples of conscience at all.

CHAPTER XXIII.

" In sadness, cousin, I do love a woman."
— SHAKESPEARE.

EARL OF MALPAS ! Earl of Malpas ! Victred repeated
the words to himself again and again as he walked
along. And " Utility " in Mr de Mowbray's " crowd " !
The oddity of the combination amused him, as he
walked towards Hammersmith through a thick fog.
He was in a state of indecision, being unable to make
up his mind whether he should go on tour with de
Mowbray. Inclination said yes ; the irresponsible
wandering life had charms for him ; the chance of
meeting Dennis and his daughter had more. On the
other hand this was, now that he had bound himself
to remain the nominal husband of Louisa, a temptation to which it was unwise of him to expose himself.
To go back to his old life and his new position seemed
at any moment to become more clearly his obvious
duty, until by the time he had reached his lodging his
show life had assumed the guise of a radiant paradise
from which he felt that he ought to shut himself out.

In this mood it may be judged what his feelings were when, on entering the sitting-room, he found Dennis M'Rena comfortably seated in his most comfortable armchair, with a pile beside him of all the literature the room contained, which he was sampling at his leisure. The agitator sprang up at his entrance, and greeted him as a long-lost brother.

"Why, you're mighty modest in your lodging for a new-made earl!" cried he. "I expected to be told that you'd moved into Grosvenor Square, where I should have had humbly to present myself at the back door."

"To leave a message that I was a doomed man, eh, Dennis?"

"Not at all, not at all," returned the Irishman indulgently. "Every man to his trade. It's not your fault that you're an earl, any more than it's mine that I'm an agitator. I bear you no malice on that account, I assure you."

"And I shan't have to bear you malice either; because as I'm not going to claim the title, I don't deserve the privilege of being preached at."

Dennis looked at him dubiously.

"You mean you're afraid of being had up for murder?"

"No, I begin to think that difficulty could be got over."

There was no mistaking the fact that Dennis's face fell.

"How—got over?"

"I've found out that some of the witnesses would not be so ready to give evidence against Lord Malpas as they were to give it against Victred Speke."

"H'm! I wouldn't count upon that, if I were you. A witness who says one thing one time and another at another is worse than no witness at all. And juries get such radical notions now-a-days, that they're often nastier to a big pot than to a little one."

"Well, it doesn't much matter," returned Victred,

as he produced tobacco and whiskey from the side-board, "as I only want a good excuse for remaining out of it altogether."

Dennis looked at him with absolute consternation.

"You want a good excuse for—for not claiming the title, *really?*"

Victred nodded. "That's it, Dennis."

Having convinced himself, by a penetrating examination of the young man's face, that this surprising confession was genuine, Dennis filled his pipe and remained for a short time lost in mournful speculation. At last, however, he made a brisk gesture as if to drive away dull care, and burst out with "Ah, well, that fit won't last! You're not such a fool, whatever you may think."

"Hallo, are those sentiments becoming a true radical and patriot?"

"Faith, they're becoming to any man who isn't an idiot," answered the Irishman with cynical coolness. "Do you think if I'd been born with a gold spoon in my mouth, I'd be so anxious to snatch them out of the mouths of other people? Me bhoy, it's not in reason!"

"Then you're an agitator from other motives than conviction?"

"No. From the conviction that any state of things in which Dennis M'Rena doesn't get his share of the good things of the world is a state which ought to be altered."

Victred had long believed this, but he had never expected to hear it from the man's own lips.

"Then you agitate merely as a trade?"

"Or profession, whichever ye like to call it. The people who agitate from conviction are just amateurs. We most of us begin like that, but it don't last."

Victred thought of poor little Jack and her religious dreams of her father as a king among men, using heart and brain and muscle in a Cause for which he was ready to die.

"Of course," went on Dennis, leaning back luxuriously, and looking approvingly at his whiskey and water, " I don't say this to everybody. It wouldn't do for the parson to wind up his sermon by an excuse for its badness on the score of his having been hustled into the Church because he wasn't fit for anything else. We're all supposed to work from conviction; the lawyer to run you up six-and-eightpences for your good; the doctor to prescribe for you because he was born with a mission to heal. But parson, lawyer, doctor and agitator have to get a living out of it all the same."

" But come, Dennis," objected Victred, " the other professions you mentioned are not absolutely mischievous, at any rate ! "

" Matter of opinion," remarked Dennis sententiously. " I've heard some men that have had dealings with lawyers express different sentiments, and as to doctors ! why, there isn't a rich man in the kingdom who hasn't suffered more pecuniary damage at his physician's hands than he has ever done at mine ! "

Although he had been little in the mood for laughter when he entered the room, Victred was amused in spite of himself.

" And as you don't find that sedition pays well enough over here, you are going to carry it across the herring pond ? "

" Well, I feel bound to give the New Country a turn, especially as the Old Country has shown her want of appreciation by filing against me a criminal information, on the ground of seditious libel."

" Hallo ! that's serious, isn't it ? "

" Well, it might be if I intended remaining here. But I don't. This day week, aided by a disguise and an alias, I shall be half way to New York."

There was a short pause, during which both men smoked on. At last Dennis said :

" I came here to-night to ask you to come and attend me farewell lecture, which I'll be giving to-morrow night near Stafford. Jack's there waiting for me. You'll come ? "

Victred had a struggle with himself, conquered, and said, " No." Dennis looked unfeignedly disappointed.

" Oh, but ye must now. I've come fifty miles this day to ask ye, and I'll not take a refusal. By what I'd heard, I should have thought ye'd have jumped at the chance of seeing Jack."

Victred had another struggle with himself, not so severe as the last though. Then he said in a voice which sounded dry and hard :

" You wouldn't have had to ask me twice if I'd been a free man, Dennis."

M'Rena said " Ah !" with much interest. " Then it's true then, what your cousin Tracy was telling me, that you've a wife already. But I did the poor lad injustice ; for when he told me who she was, I disbelieved him altogether. Ah, Mr. Speke, I mean your lordship——"

Victred made a gesture of disgust, and Dennis winked. " I understand why you don't care for your title now ! I'm heartily sorry for you, my lad, I am indeed." After a few minutes spent in deep thought, the agitator raised his shrewd blue eyes to the other man's face : " Can't you get rid of her ? "

Victred shook his head, and Dennis followed his example dolefully, and refrained from asking further delicate questions. At last he said, as if awaking from a day-dream :

" Ah, well, it'll have to be the other one then ! "

A horrible inspiration as to his meaning turned Victred cold from head to foot.

" What do you mean ? " he asked with a hoarse and trembling voice.

Dennis answered regretfully : " Why, I've got to find a husband for her before I go away, and——"

Victor started up.

" But she's going with you, isn't she ? You wouldn't leave her behind ? I—I——"

But Dennis checked him sorrowfully enough by a wave of the hand.

"Ah, and so I meant to do, you may be sure. For it's a poor welcome I'll get by myself compared to what I'd have got with my little Jack. And it's a bold stroke enough I've got to make, to go out with a proper splash now I can't take her with me."

"But why—why not?" stammered Victred. "She's not ill?" he exclaimed with sudden terror.

Dennis frowned. "Well no, no, not exactly ill," he answered hastily. "But she's had a nasty cold on her of late, and the doctor says, in fact two of them say she'd never stand the work, the travelling, the one and two night stands, and all that. You see America's such a big place, you have to do a lot of getting about in it, letting alone that, if we made the splash I have in my mind, we might chance to have the authorities at our heels over there too."

Victred was paralysed by anxiety and horror. In a little while he found words in which to give some weak expression to the feelings which raged within him: fear for her, jealousy, and a hunger to shelter the poor little bird that had been lamed so early in its flight.

"Dennis," he said huskily, as he leaned against the mantelpiece, hiding his face with the upraised hand which was tugging at his moustache, "Dennis, you'll not do it. You're too clever not to know my cousin. How could you trust her to him?"

He almost sobbed on the last words. Dennis replied gently enough.

"Well, me bhoy, I'd rather have trusted her with you. It's what I was fishing for just now. But as your tour's booked, as you told me yourself, I have to look out for another vacancy."

"But you don't know that Fitzalan is making up to my cousin, Lady May Speke. I saw her only to-day, and he proposes twice a week!"

"Ah," replied Dennis with the old sly twinkle in his eye, "but I can soon put a stop to that. Mr. Fitzalan has had some dealings with me, and I've learnt how to manage the young gentleman. He's

done some literary work for me, under a *nom de plume*
of course, which would ruin him if it were traced
home to him.   Well, he thinks he's made himself safe
against such a contingency; but he hasn't!" and
Dennis chuckled.   "I've taken unheard-of pains to
secure enough of the original manuscript (which he
thinks he's destroyed) to tar him with the brush of
seditious libel too.   So it stands this way, ye see;
either ruin with no wife or with any other wife; or
prosperity with me daughter for wife.   And as inclination jumps the same way as necessity, it'll be a
match, me bhoy, depend upon it."

"Even if—even if," said Victred in a low voice, "she
has a dislike to him?"

But Dennis waved away such an imaginary objection as this with his hand.

"Why should she object?   If she liked any one
else now, she might object, of course.   But she's seen
no one else much, except you.   And I know you
better than to think," continued he, "that you would
have said anything to her of that nature, seeing you
couldn't marry her."

Dennis said this in a very emphatic and decided
tone; but if Victred had been looking at him, he
might have seen a trace of anxiety in the agitator's
blue eyes.

"I thank you for doing me justice," said Victred
sadly.   "And I hope you don't think what I have
said to you about Fitzalan is only the result of
jealousy.   I think I could get the better of that feeling easily enough if Jack were going to marry a man
who would make her a happy wife."

Dennis got up from his chair, and buttoned his coat
with his usual cheery alacrity of manner.

" I do you justice, me bhoy," he said briskly, " but I
do your cousin justice too.   Depend upon it, I love
my little daughter too well to trust her to any man
who wouldn't appreciate the gift.   And so you won't
come to hear me last speech in England to-morrow
night?"

Victred hesitated, and Dennis already enjoyed a triumph as he looked at him out of the corners of his eyes. The temptation to see Jack when he had believed her to be on the eve of a long journey had been great; now that she might be on the eve of marriage with Tracy it was irresistible.

"I'll come," said he quietly.

"That's right. Six o'clock sharp at a place called Little Clumpton, six miles from Stafford. There's a railway station, and then you walk a mile and a half to Grey Man's Barn on the Knowle road. There'll be a platform erected in the barn, and on it, at six punctually, you'll find me and Jack. Till then goodbye. And try to bring a livelier face with you, or you'll give the bumpkins fits!"

Dennis's departure plunged Victred into even deeper melancholy than he had been a prey to before. His own troubles, his difficulties, his anxieties, seemed nothing compared with those which surrounded Jack. On the one hand, her devotion and obedience to her father were so great that it was possible she might even go so far as to accept at his bidding a husband who was little short of personally distasteful to her. On the other hand, if she did so, Tracy certainly would never take the trouble either to keep up to her his affectation of devotion to the Cause of the People, or to respect her belief in her father. And this belief being a religion to the poor child, Victred dreaded what the result might be of a ruthless destruction of it.

Having tortured himself for hours with these and similar fears, the reaction of what is generally known as common sense came at last; he scoffed at his own folly, and told himself that not only would Jack's own fanatical passion for the people melt in the everyday sunshine of domestic life, but that Tracy, whose passion for her was certainly sincere of its kind, might not only succeed in winning her heart, but might also end by becoming a reformed character, and might make her a kind and affectionate husband.

Nevertheless, it was with many misgivings and with

a heavy heart that, when the rehearsal was over on the following day, he set out for Little Clumpton from Euston Station.

The rehearsal had gone badly. Already the production of the piece had been postponed for a fortnight to suit the convenience of Miss Leonora Hartington, the leading lady, a circumstance which proved quite clearly to the company that Miss Hartington herself had money in the venture. She had been absent from rehearsal for nearly a week on the excuse of illness, but the company had discovered that the time had been passed in Paris. And now, on her return, she had not only forgotten everything which had been carefully drilled into her, but had conceived the idea that the enterprise was "not good enough." So she complained of the piece, of the part, of the company, of the posters, of the towns which were to be visited, of the scenery which was to be used. The dresses she had got were much too good, she said ; and she ended by making herself so unpleasant to everybody, not excepting Mr. Robert de Mowbray himself, that the company all but rose in open revolt, and the manager was heard to remark that he should bring the missus to tackle her the next time. Whereupon there was much chuckling among the older members of the company, who opined that Miss Leonora Hartington's refinement would " peel off like paper from a wall " on the occasion of the encounter. Victred in particular had had to suffer through Miss Hartington's caprices, as in two of the small parts he played he had to meet the leading lady, and in consequence of her having forgotten her part, he had had to "go back " again and again that morning until she was " perfect " in her scene with him, there being some " business " about a stolen jewel which he, in his character of Red Indian, had to restore to her, which was considered to have an important bearing on the plot.

De Mowbray had apologised to Victred, drawing him aside, in a friendly manner, to explain that it shouldn't happen again.

"If she don't choose to do better to-morrow," said that gentleman, "why, she must go. Time's too short to stand any more nonsense. We must open the day after to-morrow. And if she was as bad then as she's been to-day, she'd queer the show!"

So Victred, who was as anxious about the success of the piece and about his own first appearance as if he had been about to play Hamlet at the Lyceum, had a fresh anxiety suddenly thrust upon him further to depress his spirits.

CHAPTER XXIV.

"Might she have loved me? just as well
She might have hated, who can tell!
Where had I been now if the worst befell?
And here we are riding, she and I."

BROWNING.

IT was a cold and foggy evening. Victred, when he got out of the train at Clumpton, was reminded of the evening, now a year ago, on which he first met Jack. Once more the rain beat in his face, as it had done a year ago on the bleak Lancashire moors. Only now the "clatter-a-dat, clatter-a-dat!" of the North country clogs was exchanged for the "clump-clump" of the Midland hob-nails; and now his heart, instead of beating at a normal rate when he impatiently wished that he had not come, was leaping in his breast. For now that he was getting at every step nearer to Jack, a very madness of longing was upon him. He told himself that he would see her only, feast his hungry eyes once more on the little flower face, and creep quietly away again into the mists of the evening. For if he were to speak with her now, to hold her hand in his, to look down into her eyes, no effort that he could make would suffice to hide from her that love which to her must remain a secret.

Grey Man's Barn was easily found; for Dennis had the art of advertising himself so well, albeit so cautiously, that at any meeting over which he pre-

sided there was always a goodly gathering. Victred,
therefore, as on a previous occasion, had only to go
with the stream. On the whole, it seemed to him
that the men around him were riper for Dennis's
seditious teachings than had been the operatives of
the North. Radicals there were among them of such
an advanced type that it occurred to Victred to think
Dennis's utterances would seem quite tame to some
of them. But he did the agitator injustice : Dennis
knew his trade, and suited his oratory to his hearers.

The barn was an enormous building, and by the
time Victred reached it there was already assembled
a goodly audience. The platform, however, was
empty. So intent was he on thoughts of Jack that
he did not much notice his fellow-auditors. They
were a rough lot, but not so rough and not so rugged
as the Northerners ; heavier of feature, more stolid,
and, on the whole, less intelligent-looking. These
impressions had scarcely reached him when there was
a movement and a hum in the big building, and a
lane was made from the door by which the audience
had entered for the speakers. Victred, on fire as he
was, would not press near to the in-comers. He
remained on the spot he had chosen, in the midst of
the crowd, some yards away from the platform, and
waited for a sight of Jack until she and her father had
made their way through the audience and climbed on
to the platform.

But at the first sight of her, his feelings underwent
such a sudden revulsion that he seemed to leap right
out of himself and to forget his own personality altogether; his self-consciousness, everything lost, overwhelmed in a feeling of pity so strong that the whole
heart of the man seemed to go out to her in one low
sigh.

For Jack was changed, terribly changed. The
little face, in which he had seen the rosy tint of health
by slow degrees begin to steal, seemed to him to have
grown whiter than ever, the eyes to have grown larger,
until in the whole face a stranger would have noticed

no other feature. Above all, the expression was altered. She no longer wore the rapt look of the dreamy fanatic, nor the tired look of the worn-out speaker, nor the happy child-like countenance, over which a tender half-smile seemed to be always hovering, which he had known during their life in the booth. She wore instead an expression in which fear mingled with sadness: and as she glanced up at her father before he began to speak, it flashed through Victred's mind that she had felt her first doubt of the Cause and its prophet. The next moment her glance wandered to the audience, and her eyes travelled steadily along line after line of the mass. She was in search of her old comrade: and he knew it.

A faint pink flush rising in her face was the only intimation she gave when she had succeeded. This pained Victred: he would have had her face light up in the old straightforward way, as it used to light up at his coming in the "museum" days. As this thought passed through his mind, the powerful voice of the agitator rang through the building; Dennis had begun his address.

Victred soon discovered how deeply he had wronged the clever Irishman in thinking he would be found wanting by even the most ferociously Radical of audiences. If he had been seditious in his speeches in the North Country, what was he now? Treason, rank treason now fell from his lips! fiery and inflated language rang in the rafters, all uttered with a dash and a spirit which carried his willing hearers along with him, and awoke cheer after cheer. Even Victred, although he felt no conviction, listened with interest. Dennis had been at the pains to prepare a list of the crimes of Capital against Labour, of the Upper against the Lower Classes, the recital of which was received with acclamation, only tempered by the scoffing question shouted at him from the furthest end of the barn:

"Well, sir, but that's all talk, that is. What have yer ever *done ?* that's what we want to 'ear about!

16*

'Ave yer ever proved yer sentiments agin the big pots
'cepting by talk, eh?"

Dennis was ready; so ready, in fact, that it occurred
to Victred to suspect that the scoffing voice was that
of a confederate posted by Dennis among the audience
with the express object of creating an effect for the
orator. And the answer to the challenge was of a
nature to take one hearer's breath away.

"Yes, sir, I have proved them, proved them at the
risk of my liberty, nay, of my life," thundered the
orator with passion. " I have proved my love for the
People as opposed to the Classes who make them
their prey, in a manner you little think of. No one
until to-night has heard the story; but you shall hear
it now. No one has known it for the very good reason
that if they had, I might never again have been able
to address you, never again have had the privilege
of stirring up your courage, of hearing the shout
of welcome from your friendly voices, as I do now.
But I am on the eve of leaving you : such work as I
had to do among you I have done; such blessings
as I have deserved at your hands I have already
earned. I go to a new country, among new faces,
and I hope new friends. What better occasion
could I find to make my confession? For a confession it is that you are going to hear, a confession
which will put it in the power of any one here to
deliver me up to the police on a grave charge, in
fact, the gravest of all possible charges—the charge
of murder!"

There was a movement and a murmur from end to
end of the long building. Victred felt hot and cold,
divining as he did what the so-called "confession"
would be. And then the name of his dead cousin, the
name he himself now bore, fell upon his ears. Dennis
was giving an appalling list of the vices, follies, and
misdeeds of Eugene, Lord Malpas; and Victred
learnt for the first time how widespread had been the
scandal caused by Eugene's acts, when down here, a
hundred miles from any part of his estates, the men-

tion of his name provoked a murmur of assent with the speaker's opinions.

"You may all remember," went on Dennis in an earnest voice, raising his hand as if to impose upon the assembly a silence which was already profound, "how a year ago, on an evening just such as this, while his tenants were shivering and his work-people were starving, and he himself had just come home from enjoying himself at a ball, with wine and dancing and a supper of the best, as you may be sure, that this Eugene, Lord Malpas, was found lying on the ground before the steps of his own mansion, dead. It was said he had been murdered : and so many were there who had cause to wish his death that the rumour was easily believed. He was *not* murdered, my friends : he was righteously slain, in the cause of the suffering People, by this hand."

And amid the louder murmurs of the assembly, murmurs of hearty approval for the most part, so it seemed to Victred, the agitator raised towards the roof with an emphatic gesture of triumph his own right hand.

Victred was rather shocked. But even at that exciting moment he observed that poor little Jack was far more shocked than he. That her father should slightly pervert the truth was an experience not unknown to her. But that he should lie boldly and openly to the People, the sacred People, and that too by appropriating to himself the credit of what she considered the righteous action of another man, was to the poor little misguided creature a revelation terrible indeed.

Meanwhile Dennis went on :

"It was no murder, I repeat. I had been pleading with him the cause of some of his outcast tenants, creatures who, for non-payment of the rents which his rapacity had made too exorbitant for them to pay, had been thrust out of their homes as ruthlessly as the Irish tenants he had evicted by hundreds the year before. He would not hear me, and indignant at my holding my ground, he attempted to thrust me aside, and enter the house to shut out my unwelcome voice. But I would not be thrust aside; I held my ground until he struck me, struck me full in the face. And then, my friends, in the Cause of Liberty and the People, I struck him back. He fell on the stone steps as you have heard ; fell, mind, as he would have had me fall. Was it, my friends, I ask you, by my fault or by the vengeance of the Almighty, that when they found him, just as he had fallen, he lay dead ? "

Victred, amazed and bewildered by the man's audacity, wondered how this declaration would be received. The event proved that Dennis knew his audience. For thunders of applause shook the rafters of the old building, and Dennis finished his address amid the cheers and acclamations of his hearers.

The proceedings terminated with a short speech from a working man, who got on the platform to express the wishes of those assembled for Dennis's success in the New World, and by the ceremony of handshaking between Dennis on the one side and as many of his admirers as could get near the platform on the other.

Before this began, Jack had disappeared.

Victred had been singled out by Dennis, who gave him a nod and a jerk of the head to signify that he wished the young man to wait for him outside. So Victred went out with the rest of the audience into the lane. A few feet away was a covered cart, and as he was pushed close against the wheels of it by the crowd, he felt a soft touch on his shoulder, a touch which thrilled him from head to foot.

Even before he turned, his heart throbbed with excitement which intoxicated him.

Yet it was in the very quietest of quiet voices that he said, as he looked under the hood of the cart :

" Hallo, Jack ! "

" O Fred ! "

" Well ? ".

She had never called him Fred before.

"I'm glad to see you."

That was all she had to say. But it was enough for Victred, who was holding her hand, his face on a level with hers.

"That's all right," said he.

But his voice was rather unsteady.

"You've got a cold," said she. "I can hear it in your voice."

Victred admitted that he had a cold, which was not true. He cleared his throat in a vain attempt to get rid of the huskiness she had noticed, and said :

"It's not so bad as yours, though. I heard you coughing all the while your father was speaking. You've been neglecting yourself again, Jack."

She shook her head. He could scarcely see her face now, for there was only an old lantern hung at the side of the cart to give them light; so that she seemed now more like the old Jack as she had sat inside the tent so often, watching him prepare the supper. Even as she spoke to him, too, her cheerfulness seemed to be returning.

"I don't think I have. But I got my feet wet one day, and then had to sit in damp boots for four or five hours. You see you've spoilt me by always carrying me over the wet places."

There was a silence, during which Victred heartily cursed Dennis for his want of care for his fragile little daughter. Then she spoke, in a very melancholy voice, which trembled with unshed tears.

"I'm not going to America with my father. Did you know that ? "

Victred nodded. There was silence between them again. The audience had by this time all dispersed, and the sound of their voices came faintly over fields and hedges, through the thick, moist air. The old worn-out horse attached to the cart was so quiet that they might have thought that the canvas cover of the cart was the roof of the booth. There were lights still in the barn, and voices. Victred drew himself up, letting his hands slide off the back of the cart.

" Yes, I know that," said he. " Are you very sorry? "

He stole a glance at her, and saw in the weak light how her face clouded over.

" I'm not so sorry as I should have been a year ago," she said with a sigh, in a weary voice. " At least, I shouldn't feel if—— Do you know that my father wants me to marry—your cousin ? "

Victred nodded. But for a few moments he said nothing.

" Well ? " said she.

Victred pulled himself together, and said briskly :

" Don't you want to then ? "

" How can you ask ? " she answered impatiently. " You *know* I don't."

Both were suddenly startled by a cheery voice a little way behind.

" Tell her, Fred, that it's for her good, or her father wouldn't wish it," cried Dennis, as he came through the soft mud towards them.

But Victred was not sure enough of that to give more than a qualified opinion on this point.   Still, he felt that he had no right to object, so he said, turning to Dennis : " Indeed, I hope it may be for her good—if it comes to pass."

" If! If! If ! " cried Dennis cheerily.   " There is no if about it, me bhoy.   I saw Mr. Fitzalan last night," he continued in a lower voice, drawing Victred out of Jack's hearing, " told him that I had a father's anxieties for me daughter, and asked him point-blank ʼif he wanted to marry her.   He thanked me with tears in his eyes, tears in his eyes, me bhoy," continued Dennis triumphantly.   " He said it had been the wish of his heart for months and months, but that he had never dared to hope that Jack cared for him enough to accept him for her husband."

" And what if she doesn't ? " said Victred drily.

" She must, me bhoy, she must.   What is there else for her to do ?   I can't take her with me ; the doctors say it would kill her.   I can't leave her unprotected here."

"But couldn't you find her a better protector?"

"——Than a member of your family? I think not, sir," replied Dennis with a grand air.

Victred saw that persuasion and argument were useless, and that they did not come well from himself. So, reluctantly enough, he changed the subject. "And pray what made you give out that you killed my cousin Eugene?" he said drily.

"Well, sure I thought ye wouldn't grudge me the honour!" returned Dennis good-humouredly. "And ye see it'll give me a good send-off over there. It doesn't matter what you do over yonder as long as it makes you talked about. The rule applies in most cases, but more particularly over there. Ye see I depended on Jack to help me to make a splash; so I'm thrown on my beam ends, don't you see? And then this idea came to me as a happy thought. Why, what objection can you have? Ye ought to be grateful to me!"

"I'm not so sure about that. And was this what you had in your mind when you persuaded me to run away from Maleigh and hide myself?"

"There ye are again! Always suspicious! No, I hadn't that in my mind. I helped ye because, for one thing, I make it a rule never to miss the chance of doing a fellow creature a good turn. Once out of every hundred times the fellow creature is grateful; and once out of every thousand times, gratitude makes a fellow creature useful."

Then Victred, putting one thing and another rapidly together in his mind, came to something very near the truth when he remembered that Dennis had taken him to Mrs. de Mowbray, and that it was to the same refuge that she had sent Jack. Dennis had not known that he had a wife, and he might have reckoned on Jack's influencing him as she had influenced Tracy. Not thinking any the better of Dennis, Victred then suggested that that gentleman would find himself in an awkward position if, on his arrival in New York, the first thing he read in the papers should be that Victred, Lord Malpas, had surrendered himself to take his trial for the alleged murder of his cousin. But Dennis only begged him, if he had any such idea, to put off the execution of it for a little while, " until I have got a fair start," urged he.

" Ye see it won't matter when I've once got a hearing. After that, if the truth should come out, even if it were believed it would do me no harm. Rather the other way, in fact : it might pass for a noble act of self-sacrifice. If ye'll only remember not to give me away for six weeks from now at least."

Victred was so much amused by Dennis's shamelessly cynical confidences that, though he would not give the required promise, he let the Irishman see that his wish would be respected. Dennis then led him back to the cart in great good humour.

" Ye'll come back to the inn where we're staying, and have supper with us ? " said he.

Victred would have refused, but Jack just looked at him with eyes which said " Come," and he gave way.

So they all jogged along in the cart, through the mist, to an inn in a town a few miles off, an inn chosen by Dennis because it was old-fashioned, comfortable, and close to the railway station. The drive was a joy both to Victred and to Jack, to be remembered for ever. But the supper which followed was, as far as they were concerned, a failure. For while in the cart they sat side by side, allowing Dennis to talk to them, but replying and commenting as briefly as possible, less conscious of his eloquence than of their proximity to each other, in the bright light of the supper-table everything was changed. For it now occurred to Victred that Dennis had invited him only that he might study the attitude towards each other of his daughter and himself. The idea made Victred self-conscious, and this self-consciousness seemed to communicate itself to Jack who, once more in her boy's dress, already lost something to Victred, by reminding him less in this costume of the old days of their wanderings.

So the merriment of the meal was kept up chiefly by Dennis, who toasted Jack and Tracy together as bride and bridegroom. Victred drank the toast in silence, with a sidelong look at Jack. She looked whiter and more wan than ever, but she made no protest.

Then Victred, unable any longer to bear the pain of this thought, pretended that there was a train back to town which he could catch, and sprang up to go.

Jack fixed her great eyes upon him sadly, without inquiry or surprise. Before Dennis could protest against this hurried departure she had held out her hand.

"Good-bye," said she.

"Good-bye, Jack. I hope you will be happy, whatever you do. There is nothing I wish so much."

She shook her head, with a faint flicker of a smile.

"I have still the Cause," she said. But she spoke without the old girlish fervour. Then, as, after a moment's hesitation, he was about to go, she said: "But there are many things I wanted to ask you—about yourself. Are you happy now, among your old friends?"

"I am not with my old friends, at least my oldest. I'm going on tour with de Mowbray."

She had not known this, and her face flushed with interest.

"And are you"— she went on in a lower voice, "are you reconciled to your wife?"

"Reconciled! No. But I have forgiven her."

"That is right," said Jack softly.

They were under the observant eyes of Dennis, and each felt in the circumstances that this was all the farewell they cared for.

So Victred turned to Dennis, with a great air of hearty cheerfulness, shook hands with him, and wished him all good fortune on his travels. Then he ran downstairs, as if in a great hurry for that phantom train.

But Jack knew that it was a phantom; and he had not stood many moments outside the inn door, wondering what he should do with his time until the mail came through in an hour's time, when Jack's hand was put softly through his arm. She gave no explanation of her coming, but plunged into the matter which brought her.

"If I should be ill, Fred, very ill I mean, would your wife let you come and see me?"

Victred shook from head to foot.

"Ill! Oh, my God, Jack, don't talk like that! And that woman— How dare you call her my wife? Do you think I should ask her for permission to do anything? That too! Why, Jack, I'd come to you, come to you from the end of the world. Oh, Jack, my dear, I'm broken-hearted about you."

Jack came round so that she could face him in the light from the inn window. She put her arms on his arms, and looked, laughing the ghost of her own laugh, into his face.

"Silly Fred! You who are so big are sillier than I who am so little, ever so much sillier! I'm not ill, not a bit. But I only thought—if I ever should be, I might like to see you again. But perhaps I mightn't, you know! Good-bye."

She held out her hand again, with an affectation of brightness. But Victred's trembled.

"Shall I never see you again, I wonder?"

"Yes, you will. Oh, I can promise that. Good-bye."

Victred was sobbing like a child. He gave a low cry: "Jack!" and put out his arms. But he was blind for the moment, and he encircled only thin air. Then he dashed away the tears from his eyes.

But Jack was gone.

CHAPTER XXV.

" For I was true at least—Oh, true enough !
And, Dear, truth is not as good as it seems !
Commend me to conscience ! Idle stuff !
Much help is in mine, as I mope and pine,
And skulk through day, and scowl in my dreams
At my Swan's obtaining the crow's rebuff."

—BROWNING.

AND so Victred had to go back to town more
miserable than he left it. He found a letter from
Mr. Sheldrake waiting for him ; but he did not even
open it. He knew very well it was only to upbraid
him for his neglect of his affairs, and just now he
was in a mood to neglect them more than ever.

He had forgotten the time of the "call" for the
rehearsal next day, so he turned up at the "Oriental"
half an hour too soon, and found only Mr. de Mowbray there. The manager was in a jubilant mood,
and insisted on taking Victred to have a drink, in
spite of the protest of the latter that it was too early.

"I've done the best day's work I've done for a
long time," said the manager, as he drew out his
moustache with the extra care of a man who feels
that he has reason to be proud of himself.

And then, with his habitual caution, he fell into
sudden silence as if fearing that he had betrayed too
much. He looked quite suspiciously at Victred,
when the latter, as in duty bound, affected interest
in these tidings. But at length, allowing his exultation to triumph over his wariness, he said :

"I've given Hartington the chuck."

Victred was unfeignedly glad to hear this. There
was no doubt that, whoever was to replace her, the
piece would gain by the change. He was pretty
certain in his own mind that de Mowbray had made
a slight misstatement, and that instead of his having
given "Hartington the chuck," which he had not the
courage to do, it was the lady who had applied that

process to him. However, the result was good, so the details didn't matter.

"Indeed, I'm awfully glad to hear it," said Victred heartily. "Do you know, I was afraid she would spoil the piece?"

"So she would have done, my boy, not a doubt of it!" cried Robert, with as much heartiness as if he had not told Victred a dozen times that Miss Hartington's fine appearance and magnificent wardrobe would pull her through right enough. "I saw that all along, and at last I says to myself that she must be got rid of. And the missus said so too."

With what infinite force and variety the "missus" had said so, and with what delightful freedom from restraint she had applied not only her remarks but her hands to the incompetent leading lady, Victred had yet to learn.

"And she was just nobody at all, for all the airs she gave herself; and 'ad no money worth speaking about," continued de Mowbray with contempt.

"And who have you got instead of her?" asked Victred.

Robert's face lighted up with enthusiasm.

"Ah, ah, the real thing this time, my boy, and no mistake! Picked up all in a minute too. Such a chance! I ran into Blackmore's yesterday afternoon —just after the row, you know!" Here de Mowbray pulled himself up short, finding that he had been betrayed into an indiscretion. "And he says to me: 'Look here, I've got the very woman you want waiting in the other room.' And my word, my boy, she's a ripper! Such style! Dresses so well. Has had experience too—play anything and everything. No airs nor nothing! Like all your real swells, as obliging as anything."

"But can she get a long part like that by to-morrow night?" said Victred doubtfully.

He thought the prospect seemed just a little too good, and inclined to the suspicion that there must be something wrong about the lady.

"Well, I've had to postpone the opening two nights more, so we don't open till Saturday. You see this is only a trial trip, as it were, to get the piece in working order by Christmas, so a day or two sooner or later don't matter much."

"What's the lady's name?"

"Burleigh, Miss Burleigh. She's one of the right sort, heart in her work, see what I mean? Liked the part immensely, said she'd sit up all night to study it. Says it's a lovely piece, and she feels it's an honour to play in it."

Victred became more and more curious to see the lady with such an odd literary and dramatic taste, and felt more convinced at every word that poor Robert had been "had." Indeed, Victred thought it likely that the "ripper" would never turn up at all.

Great, then, was his interest, his delight, when on arrival at the "Oriental" for rehearsal, Tom Fenton, who was carpenter, baggage-man, and actor of small parts, greeted the manager with the announcement that "the new lady" had arrived.

"What is she like, Tom?" asked Victred, as the manager hurried in.

Victred thought it would be amusing to hear a less prejudiced opinion than de Mowbray's. And Tom Fenton was a shrewd fellow, not so easily deceived as his manager.

Tom shrugged his shoulders.

"Guv'nor thinks a lot of her," he said with reticence. "She's dressed up to the nines. That's all I know at present. But Churchill says he's seen her about town for a long while."

Victred went upstairs, hoping that poor de Mowbray had not gone from bad to worse, "from the frying-pan into the fire," as Tom suggested with a knowing nod.

At the top of the stairs, just inside the room, de Mowbray was talking to a lady. She had her back to Victred as he came up, and the manager, on seeing him, said, with all the ceremony due to an important introduction :

"Oh, Mr. Watt, let me introduce you to Miss Louise Burleigh."

The lady turned round quickly, and Victred fell back a step.

For in Miss Burleigh he recognised his wife Louisa.

His first impulse was to turn and run downstairs, never to appear again in Mr. de Mowbray's company. But Louisa saw his intention, and was too quick for him.

"I'm very pleased to know Mr. Watt, I'm sure," she said, bowing exactly as if he had been a stranger.

Bewildered, miserable, but yet grateful to her for this act of grace, Victred bowed in return, and murmured a most insincere expression on his side. Then an influx of the other members of the company caused him to be pushed up the stairs into the room, to the furthest corner of which he retreated, affecting to be studying his part, or rather parts, for that of a signalman had now been added.

What was the meaning of this new move of hers? Did she intend to play the spy on him? The idea, considering their relative positions, was absurd, but it seemed none the less likely on that account. He was furious. Conscious that he had treated this woman very well, it certainly seemed as if she in return was treating him very badly. He decided that the best thing he could do now that she had had the decency not to recognise him, was to let the rehearsal pass, and then meet her and either insist on her leaving the company or avow his intention of doing so himself.

In the meantime the rehearsal, to his surprise, was going on smoothly enough. Louisa had kept her word to the manager, and knew as much of her part as could be expected at such short notice. She was moreover teachable, civil, and smiling, and was hailed as a boon and a blessing to men after the impracticable Miss Hartington. In fact, as Victred said to himself, she was on her best behaviour all round. Two out of the three other ladies of the company "took to her," as they said, at once. These were Daisy Lisle, the fat and vulgar wife of Tom Fenton, who said that her "line was chambermaids," but who was somehow always cast for old women: and Lily Mannering, *née* Eliza Moger, a tall and beautiful fair woman, with the silky light hair, and round soft face of a cherub, and the mind, manners, voice and boots of a washerwoman. The remaining female member of the cast, Miss Kate Green, a quiet, lady-like girl with a plain face, who was an excellent dancer, was not so much attracted. Old Ned Russell shook his head, and looked at her askance, having strong opinions as to the type of ladies who "only do harm to the profession, boy, and cause people to talk ill of the real hard-working actresses."

Harry Churchill and William Waters foregathered in corners to discuss her, with side-long looks which, as they were cast at the woman who legally bore his name, turned Victred sick with shame. Churchill was the juvenile man of the company, and considered himself to be possessed of good looks, good manners, and great genius. He was supposed to "mash 'em" with the greatest ease, and this process he performed by fixing upon the lady upon whom for the time his fickle fancy chose to fall, two uninteresting ferret's eyes in a gimlet stare, which was believed (by himself) to possess irresistible fascination for the fair sex. He was an indifferent actor; but his energy and lung power made him useful to de Mowbray, who thought highly of him. William Waters was the low comedian, the very low comedian; and being a typical representative of his class, it is hardly necessary to say more of him than that his great ambition was to become proprietor of a public house, and that he had the reputation, in pantomime, of "collaring everybody else's wheezes." But at bottom he was not a bad-hearted man.

Victred, as he gathered some words of the conversation of these two, admiring comments in their way, saw that Churchill did indeed know something about

17

Louisa, not altogether to her credit.   On the other
hand, as he had evidently not the least suspicion of
the relationship in which she stood to " Fred Watt,"
or of the fact that she was married to a gentleman,
Victred perceived that the woman had always been
prevented by some sense of perhaps honest shame
from boasting that she was the wife of a man of
good family.

Tom's voice behind him broke in upon his unpleasant reflections.

" You should 'ave been 'ere yesterday when the
row was on ! It was when re'earsal was over, soon
after you left, that Mrs. de M. turned up.   I think
she had a notion what was going to happen, for when
Hartington said something about re'earsing interfering with her social duties, Mrs. de M. was up in a
moment. Well, then they began. Language ? Why,
it would have made a respectable coalheaver turn
blue.   And the best of it was that high-toned Miss
Hartington was quite a match for our champion.
Well, at last there was muffs a-flying about. We
began to think it would end in scratching faces.
And there was the poor guv'nor, behind a table,
piping out ' Ladies ! Ladies ! Business, *please !* '   But
perhaps you won't be surprised to hear that neither
of them answered to the name.   I don't know how
we managed to get 'em apart.   Somebody called
' Fire ! ' but that was no good, and somebody else
said the landlord was coming up.   Anyhow it ended
by both of 'em saying they wouldn't stay in the room
with ' that low woman.'   And when they had been
got out, Hartington sent up a man who had been
waiting for her, who she said was her solicitor.   But
he only winked, and said she shouldn't trouble us
again.   What do you think of the new one ? "

" It's rather early to tell yet," said Victred, moving
away to avoid continuing the conversation.

Victred got away as soon as rehearsal was over,
feeling sure that he need not seek out Louisa, as she
would be sure to seek him out.   He was right.   He

went homewards by way of the embankment, and had not got far when his steps were arrested by the sound of someone hurrying after him. It was Louisa, as he had expected.

"O Vic, I must speak to you," she said, in a pleading voice. "Don't be angry with me. You see I never let them know, and I never will if you let me stay."

"You can stay if you like," answered Victred gloomily. "I shan't stand in the way of your earning an honest living. But you can't expect me to remain in the company, can you?"

Louisa grew red, and looked down. She spoke with some agitation.

"I had hoped you might. You needn't think I wouldn't behave myself properly. And I'd never let out I'd so much as met you before. You said you wanted me to lead a straight life, Vic, and if I start under your own eyes like, you'll know if I'm in earnest, won't you? And—and if you don't let me," her voice shook a little, "I shall think you don't care."

Victred was filled with horror. He hated the woman; the continual sight of her, however faithfully she might keep the secret of their relationship, would irritate and torture him beyond endurance. On the other hand he had put into her hands, in all honest purpose, a weapon which he could not consistently forbid her to use. He had said to her, "Lead an honest life," and she practically replied, "I will, under your own eye." If he retorted that this was not in the bond, what more likely than that she should repudiate her share in the bargain altogether? While he hesitated to answer, she pressed her point.

"You see, Vic, you can always get away at a minute's notice, if you find it won't do," she urged, with such deep earnestness that it was impossible to break away, or even to remain quite unmoved. "And why need you be afraid? Who'd believe me if I was to tell I was your wife? Just try me, Vic, only just

17*

try me, and see if I'm quite the bad creature you thought I was, after all!"

"Haven't I proved that I don't think anything of the sort?"

"Well, prove it this way too. Look here," she went on, with a change of tone, "I'm not asking so much after all. I'm still your wife, for you wouldn't take the chance I offered you of getting rid of me. Well then, what am I asking? Not to be acknowledged, mind, and not to worry you. Only for you and me not to be miles apart. I know you don't care to see my face, Vic; but I feel, after what you've done, and what you've said—your kindness and all, that I can't live without seeing yours."

During this speech her voice had become more and more broken, until, as she ended, she burst into violent weeping. Victred was so much scandalised that he felt little pity.

"For goodness' sake don't," he cried hastily, as he looked wildly about to see whether any one was noticing them. But on a foggy November afternoon the foot-passengers on the embankment were few. With relief he saw a crawling hansom approaching, and he hailed it. But seeing that their *tête-à-tête* was coming to an abrupt end, Louisa became more persistent.

"You must answer me, Vic, you must!" cried she hysterically, clinging to his arm.

She was not menacing or angry, only pleading, despairing. "If you will only consent, you will find me easy enough to manage, I tell you. For remember, I shall be entirely at your mercy."

Now this was not exactly true, although perhaps she believed it. She uttered the words as if she did; and Victred, who was tender-hearted, and who had, as he had told her, never shirked his responsibility towards the woman he had married, gave way.

"All right," he said rather suddenly, as the hansom stopped before them. "But mind, the first word to anybody, and the bargain's at an end."

Louisa's gratitude was boundless. She wept more violently than ever. There on the embankment, in the fog, under the cabman's eyes, she seized his hands and would, but for his violent exertions, have covered them with kisses.

"You've saved me, Vic, you've saved me," she cried in a hoarse hysterical whisper. "I'll never forget your kindness, never! I'll be your slave! And some day—and some day——"

Victred cut her short by lifting her off her feet and thrusting her into the hansom. All this, on the embankment, was more than human flesh could bear. He paid the fare, at least gave the man half-a-sovereign, and walked quickly away, and swore to himself as far as Charing Cross. He did wish now, most emphatically, that he had not allowed an impulse of strained generosity to carry him so far as it had done on the evening of her visit to him at his Hammersmith lodgings. He saw, as he put it to himself, that he was "in for a rough time." For in Louisa's eyes he had perceived an expression, which told him he had not now to do with a frivolous and fickle girl, but with a passionate and violent woman, whose love and whose hate were to be feared in the same degree, and that a high one.

CHAPTER XXVI.

" Madam, methinks, if you did love him dearly,
You do not hold the method to enforce
The like from him."

—SHAKESPEARE.

THE time was so short before the production of the new piece, which was to be played for seven nights at one of the out-lying London theatres, that Louisa had enough to do in studying her part, and had no leisure to trouble Victred. But Victred felt that this was a respite only, and although even that was something to be thankful for, he was not lulled into a vain belief that his anxieties on her account were over. He had at present absolutely nothing to complain about in her manners and conduct. She appeared at rehearsal every morning punctually to time, well and quietly dressed, took the greatest pains with her work, and allowed Ned Russell, who was one of the old-fashioned bullying stage-managers, to drill her and drive her until she was mechanically perfect in every word, every inflection, every movement, every gesture.

The result was that "Miss Burleigh" speedily became popular with everybody, except Harry Churchill, who exercised the fascination of his gimlet-like eyes upon her in vain. For, in the endeavour to please Victred by the reserve of her conduct, she was much more prudish than an innocent woman would have been. Robert de Mowbray thought that he had got a prize indeed in his new leading lady, and even "the missus" was satisfied. Both had heard injurious rumours concerning Miss Burleigh's previous life ; but as, among theatrical folk, such reports are always held "not proven" as long as the subject of them makes no scandal by obvious misconduct, Louisa profited by the unwritten law of mercy which is one of the noblest traditions of the stage, and made her first essays in respectability under the most favourable circumstances imaginable.

On the night of the production of the play, Victred's nervousness was so great that he ran terrible risks of mixing all his parts, and of giving the words of the Red Indian to the Honest British Workman. He got through, however, better than he expected, finding that his experience as giant had done more to break him in than he had ventured to hope.

The piece was called *By Aid of the Law*, a title which had been selected for no particular relation which it bore to the drama, but because it was supposed to "look well on the bills." Of its kind, and considering the class of patrons it was designed to attract, it was a good play : that is to say, the story, which was the usual stupid old story of a man wrongfully accused of a crime which one would have liked him the better if he had committed, never stood still.

Something was always happening; generally the last thing that would have happened under the circumstances, but that did not matter. Whether it was an earthquake which suddenly reduced to ruins the house in which the heroine had taken refuge in the Old Kent Road, or the discovery by the unprincipled lady of noble birth that the burglar who enters at the dead of night to carry off her obviously artificial diamond necklace is her long-lost husband, the spectator never had to sigh for fresh incident. Scarcely had you gaped at one improbability, when quick upon its heels followed another more daring still. " Incident, my boy, incident, that's what the public want ! " de Mowbray would say. And they saw that they got it.

The piece went so well that the manager and his wife were bemoaning, throughout the last act, that the closeness of the " dramatic ring " had prevented its production at Drury Lane.

" There'd have been a fortune, there'd have been a fortune in it, my boy ! " moaned Robert, when he had come round from the front to congratulate the performers generally, and at the same time to exhort them to "speak up "and "let 'em have it."

And Robert went back to the " missus," grumbling because the theatre was not twice the size it was, and expressing his conviction that the smallness of the building (which, as a matter of fact, was by no means unduly crowded) was " pounds out of his pocket."

Miss Burleigh, whose type of beauty was well suited to the stage, came in for much congratulation. Indeed, as she had a strong voice, and bawled her part through from end to end without a sign of fatigue, and struggled with the villain with an uncompromising realism which threatened to throw that gentleman into the orchestra, de Mowbray pronounced her an actress of much power. And the audience seemed to agree with him.

Victred felt a little easier when the first night was over. For one thing, the manager was satisfied with his first appearance, or rather first appearances, and

for another, the rehearsals being now over, he saw
nothing of Louisa except at night, and then only for
the few moments during which they were on the
stage at the same time. On the fourth night, while
Victred was standing waiting for his cue, de Mowbray, looking particularly satisfied and jubilant, spoke
to him with a triumphant nod.

" Told you this piece would go," he began defiantly,
as if Victred had vehemently opposed the possibility
of such a thing. " Wish I'd been booked here for
another week! We should have had West End
audiences in full dress and all next week. See that
private box ? "

Victred followed the direction of the manager's
glance, and saw, to his confusion, his cousin May,
accompanied by a middle-aged lady and gentleman,
in one of the stage boxes.

De Mowbray went on proudly. " Reg'lar swells,
ain't they? Drove up in a carriage and pair, flunkey
and all. Never saw such a turn-out. Only give 'em
a good piece, and you're sure to bring 'em out!
They'll tell their friends what a piece it is—none of
your watered-down rubbish like what they're playing
at the West End shows ; and, mark my words, by
Friday we shall have a Haymarket audience."

Victred did not echo these sentiments as heartily as
the manager could have wished. Indeed he ventured
to hint that one swallow in the boxes did not make a
summer in the pit-stalls. He hoped for de Mowbray's
sake as well as his own that Lady May would go
quietly home again without attempting to communicate with him. This was especially desirable, as
Louisa had recognised her, and was glaring angrily at
the woman whose interest in Victred she guessed to
be as great as her own.

But the sight of Louisa, whom Lady May recognised on her side, filled the girl with curiosity which
she was anxious to satisfy at once. So she got one of
the attendants to show her to the stage door, and sent
in a message to Mr. Watt, to the effect that she would

like to speak to him. The attendant had offered to take her right in, but she was too shy to accept the invitation, until Mr. de Mowbray, hearing of the matter, came to the door and invited her on to the stage.

De Mowbray recognised one of the ladies from the much observed box, and was enormously impressed by the magnificence of her furs ; for Lady May, who had of late begun to bestow much attention upon her dress, wore a long seal-skin cloak with a border of Russian sable tails, which, as she was tall and thin, became her better than any garment she had ever worn before.

"You want to see Mr. Watt, madam ? " said de Mowbray, while his utility man rose by enormous degrees in his opinion.

"Oh yes, if you please. Say that it is his cousin."

Unfortunately, Victred's reception of her was not as cordial as that of his manager. De Mowbray was surprised and shocked to note the ungracious manner in which Fred came forward, and coldly said : "What on earth made you come here ? And come behind too ? "

"I knew you wouldn't come and see me again before you went away," she answered humbly. "So I came to see you. You might have known I should be anxious to know how you got on, and I think you played beautifully."

Victred was somewhat mollified.

"Well, you needn't have come round."

Lady May made answer in a whisper.

"It was seeing who it was that played the heroine," she answered with emotion which she tried in vain to hide. "Have you—have you forgiven her, and been reconciled to her, Victred ? "

Victred moved impatiently. In spite of himself, and although he knew how ignorant May was concerning Louisa's real character, he answered in a very cold tone :

"I have forgiven her, yes, certainly. But reconciled to her ! No, of course I'm not, and I never shall be."

Lady May tried to hide her satisfaction, but did not altogether succeed.

" Indeed ? I—I am sorry," she murmured, as in duty bound, although her looks belied her words. " But it was natural for me to think you were, seeing you together, wasn't it ? "

" That was her doing, not mine."

At that moment Victred heard a sort of sigh coming from someone who was hidden from their sight behind a piece of scenery. He looked behind it, and saw Louisa. The expression of her face, the stormy blue eyes, the compressed mouth, told him that she had heard the conversation between himself and his cousin. He stepped back, and, very much afraid lest Louisa should come forth from her hiding place and allow her anger to get the better of her, he hurried May out by the stage door as quickly as he could.

But this was not the end of the incident. For Mr. de Mowbray, who took care to be in the front after the performance when the much-discussed party from the box were on their way to Lady May's carriage, heard the footman reply to a question from his mistress : " Yes, my lady."

The news flew like wildfire through the company, until everybody, from Robert and the "missus" downwards, was discussing the discovery that Mr. Watt had a cousin who was " a lady in her own right." This mysterious rank, the precise place of which in the peerage they would have found it hard to define, naturally threw its glamour over the person of the unassuming " utility gent," and several members of the company expressed their new-born belief that they had always known that he was a real swell. As a matter of fact, they had done nothing of the kind. Recruits now reach the stage from every class ; the lowest, the obscurest company contains frequently one member at least, male or female, from the ranks of the educated and refined ; so that Victred, being by no means the only gentleman the rest of the company had ever met on the boards, had excited little special comment.

Harry Churchill, always on the watch for an opportunity of breaking down Miss Burleigh's reserve towards him, sought her out, just as she was leaving the theatre, to communicate the news. Every member of the company knew that Miss Burleigh cast more looks in Victred's direction than was compatible with entire indifference ; and he had expected at least a start and an expression of interested amazement. But Miss Burleigh looked down as he told her, and said quietly, when he had finished :

" I knew that."

" Knew that—Fred Watt had a cousin—who was a lady of title ? "

" Yes."

Harry Churchill looked annoyed. He drew back a step, that she might feel the full force of his eyes, and that she might wince under the intense sarcasm which he threw into their glance.

" Oh, I see ! You've known something of him before then ? "

She looked up quickly, blushing red, and began stammeringly to deny this. But Churchill went on unheeding.

" Of course, since you knew he was such a swell, that was why none of the rest of us could get a look in," he sneered. " But perhaps you didn't know the *ladies* of the family ? "

" I knew that one, Lady May Sp——," began Louisa. And she stopped herself.

There was such a straightforward sincerity about this reply, and this abrupt self-interruption, that Churchill was impressed and withdrew rather crestfallen, wondering whether Miss Burleigh herself was a degenerate scion of the same noble race.

Of course the sensation caused by the discovery of Fred Watt's grand connections soon passed away, but its effect upon the ladies of the company remained. As a consequence of the high esteem in which he was held by them, poor Louisa had the greatest difficulty in restraining her inclination to proclaim herself the lawful wife of this high-born and handsome gentleman. Nothing but the well-grounded fear that he would instantly take himself off if she betrayed the secret, enabled her to resist the temptation. As it was, the furtive watch which she kept upon Victred could not fail to excite remarks. She did not deny the imputation of being in love with him, in fact she was rather proud of it; and she could not conceal the fact that she was jealous. Victred soon found himself harassed by her furtive but constant watchfulness. No openly acknowledged wife, however jealous, would ever have dogged his movements so persistently; nor would an overt shadowing have been half so irritating. She would call at his lodging upon some excuse, not to attempt to see him, but to find out whether there was an attractive girl about the place either in the shape of a servant or of a landlady's daughter. He could not exchange half-a-dozen words with one of the other women of the company, without discovering that Louisa's great eyes were watching them with gloomy suspicion from some corner. Naturally this course of action in the attractive leading lady excited remark. Both Victred and she were subjected to a good deal of "chaff"; with this difference: that whereas Victred found it difficult to conceal his annoyance, Louisa was openly delighted to be teased on the subject.

Victred was in constant terror lest some word dropped by Mrs. de Mowbray about Jack should be heard by Louisa. The company was to remain in the neighbourhood of London for some weeks, making a round of the suburban theatres. And then a week at one of the watering-places on the Kentish coast was to bring this short trial tour to an end. Mrs. de Mowbray, naturally as much interested in this fresh venture as her husband, had made arrangements to keep her show within easy reach of the same neighbourhood, more especially as Robert's opinion of the missus's business capacity was so great, that he felt more comfortable in starting this speculation under her eye. From Mrs. de Mowbray, therefore, Victred could easily, without exciting any suspicion of undue interest in her charge, receive tidings of Jack.

Dennis had by this time left England, and Jack had gone back to the " museum."

"Not to work, though, poor dear!" went on Mrs. de Mowbray with some feeling. "She's offered to be dwarf again times out of mind. And such a nice-looking little thing as she is, I'd be glad enough, I'm sure. But let alone that it don't seem the right thing for a girl that's just going to marry a gentleman to be showing herself about like that (not but what Mr. Fitzalan don't seem to mind what she does so long as she'll be his wife), she don't seem up to it somehow. I tell you, Fred, I don't half like the look of the girl, and I sometimes say to Ellen I shouldn't wonder if she was to go off quite sudden or fall into a decline, or something————"

"Don't, don't say that," said Victred, turning white.

"Well, you may be sure I wouldn't say it if I thought different, liking the girl as much as I do," returned Mrs. de Mowbray, shaking her head. "I suppose it's feeling so delicate-like makes her keep putting off the marriage, and saying it'll be time enough in the spring. But it's not fair to the young man, and him so devoted as he is too, and ready to marry her any day if she could only bring herself to say the word. However, she's promised her father she'll have him, and she'll keep her word. So I think it best not to press the matter too much. For my part, I shall be sorry to see her go away; she makes the place quite home-like again, as I say to Ellen, who don't much relish it; for I don't think there was ever much love lost between them two, 'specially on your account, eh, Fred?" and she gave him a wink.

" You're a rare favourite with the ladies, ain't you ?
Why, there's Miss Burleigh here——————"

Victred frowned, with an exclamation of disgust.
Mrs. de Mowbray laughed good-humouredly.

" Well, I know she ain't one of your sort ; but my !
You seem to be one of hers · by the way she looks at
you.   They all say so, and the other men don't half
like it.   And mark my words, Fred, they'll be playing
some trick on you and her one of these days, see if
they don't."

And with a variety of rapid gestures to signify
suspicion and caution against treachery, Mrs. de
Mowbray went off to join the " boss."

There were three things suggested by this talk
of Mrs. de Mowbray's to cause Victred fresh uneasiness.   The one was the state of Jack's health : the
second the suspicion that Tracy, ignoring how com-
pletely he was in Dennis's power, had not the slightest
intention of marrying Jack : the third was the
suggestion of some trick which was to be played upon
Louisa and himself.   It seemed to him highly probable that some plot had already been concocted, and
that Mrs. de Mowbray was good-naturedly putting
him on his guard.

This in fact was the truth of the matter, as he soon
found to his cost.

CHAPTER XXVII.

" For where love reigns, disturbing jealousy
    Doth call himself affection's sentinel ;
    Gives false alarms, suggesteth mutiny,
    And in a peaceful hour doth cry ' Kill, kill.' "
                                —SHAKESPEARE.

It was in December, and near the end of the tour,
when the mischief which had been brewing among
the other men of the company at Victred's expense
took effect.   It was on a bitterly cold Sunday morning that the company assembled at Numboro' Junc-
tian to go by the quick Sunday train to Eastgate-on-
Sea.   Mr. de Mowbray was pulling his long moustache
dolefully, not anticipating that business out of the

season would be very brisk at that popular watering-place. For Moses, whose rings had flashed so brilliantly on Eastgate pier in August, was back in Houndsditch now, gathering skekels for next year's "outing": 'Arry, his brilliant "blazer" carefully put by, was smiling behind the counter in many a London shop: the place, save for that rusty-looking and gone-to-seed population which popular but unfashionable seaside resorts produce in winter, would be empty. The railway company was not one of those which have a high reputation for the accommodation they give to travellers, and instead of the half-dozen compartments which the "heavy lines" give to theatrical companies, had placed at Mr. de Mowbray's disposal only two third-class compartments.

The theatrical custom is for the men and the women to travel in separate compartments; but on an occasion like this, when the accommodation is too limited for comfort, the rule is generally relaxed, as the numerical strength of the company is always greater on the male than on the female side. Victred, therefore, found himself in a compartment with Churchill, Waters, a new man named Peters, who played the heavy lead, Fenton and his wife, and Louisa. The door had been locked, and the guard was stepping back to give the starting signal, when Churchill, who sat near the door, opened it with his railway-key and jumped out. As if by magic, and evidently by preconcerted arrangement, the rest of the people in the carriage, with the exception of the two victims of the plot, jumped out upon the platform. Churchill re-locked the door with his railway-key, and the next moment all the laughing confederates were received into the adjoining compartment.

Victred jumped up in hot anger, brushed past Louisa, whom for the first moment he unjustly took for one of the confederates, and reached the door as the train was starting. But there was no help to be had. A couple of porters grinned and shook their heads as he in vain turned the handle of the door. The guard, scandalised at the breach of the regulations committed by Victred's fellows, turned the vials of his wrath upon Victred, and with a scowl shouted to him to keep his seat.

Victred sat down by the window with an angry frown, and without once glancing at his companion.

Louisa, on her side, was quite as much taken by surprise as he was. Afraid of drawing down upon herself an open expression of his displeasure, she sat, motionless and mute in the middle of the opposite seat, hardly daring to cast from time to time in his direction a frightened glance. They could still hear explosions of loud laughter from the next compartment, from the perpetrators of this trick.

At last she said in a hissing whisper : "It wasn't my doing, Vic, I knew nothing about it. Not a word."

He looked at her, and saw that she was speaking the truth, and that he must not visit the sins of others on her head.

"Well," said he, "it's rather awkward, isn't it?"

"Not for me," she answered promptly. "Since I can't get your company of your own free will, I'm glad to have it against it."

Victred detected the trembling seriousness under her composure, and knew that there would soon be an outburst of emotion on her part.

"You're very kind," said he, as nearly as possible in the tone of deference combined with indifference, which he would have used to a casual acquaintance. "But I'm afraid you'll find me a dull companion."

"Never too dull for me, Vic," she answered with rising passion. "I've got beyond caring what you say, as long as I can hear you talk. Only it's a pleasure you don't often give me ; never if you can help it."

Victred began to suffer unutterable terrors, as he foresaw that the meekness with which Louisa had started the conversation, would not last long, and that probably the perpetrators of the practical joke upon them would have the pleasure of breaking in upon as tempestuous a scene as they could have desired. The thought was not likely to render him more amenable to her influence. His one hope lay in keeping her to common-places, which was just what she wished to avoid.

"I thought we had covered that ground in our compact," said he, as coldly as he dared, blaming himself for his folly in thinking for a moment she would keep to her bargain. "You said, all you wished was to start leading a respectable life under my eye, to prove to me that you were capable of better things. Now is that true, or is it not?"

He asked the question in a dogged, stolid, will-have-an-answer sort of manner, which forced her to reply at once and straightforwardly.

"Y—yes, of course it is. Well, aren't you satisfied? Haven't I done it?"

"Yes. You've carried out that part of the bargain faithfully enough; as I could have trusted you to do, mind, away from me."

"Oh, yes, you'd have been very glad, I've no doubt!" cried Louisa, working herself suddenly to the point of scornful indignation. "All *you* wanted was for me not to be a disgrace to you, and as long as you managed that, little you cared what became of me."

"Now is that true? Just ask yourself if that isn't a ridiculous thing to say to a man who has given up all his hopes of happiness on your account?"

Louisa did not immediately answer. She was evidently agitated by strong and fierce emotion, emotion which was rapidly getting beyond her unaccustomed powers of control.

She sighed, she trembled, she glanced askance at him with luminous, passionate eyes. Then, still panting, she came inch by inch along the seat of the carriage, and when she was opposite to him, slid suddenly down upon her knees.

"Given up—your hopes of happiness! O Vic, can't you forgive me? Really forgive me? Can't you be happy again—with me?"

18

Her voice sank to the lowest, most passionate whisper, as she put her arms round him. The instinctive shudder which passed through him as he felt her touch gave her a more direct and more cruel answer than any words could have done. Still she persisted, clinging to him, caressing him.

"O Vic, you are not cruel, you are not heartless! You shan't repulse me, you shan't chill me with your coldness. Say you will forgive me, really forgive me, and take me back. For I love you, I love you, I worship you, I would die for you. You won't break my heart, you won't, you can't, for you loved me once, Vic, you loved me once."

But all the time that she cried, that she clung to him, there was a note of despair in her passion, and a look of terror in the great yearning blue eyes which were close under his. He felt her breath upon his face, and heard distinctly the sobbing sound with which she drew her breath. But although he was troubled, moved by her entreaties, it was not to acquiescence; and she knew it. He put his own hands up, and taking hers firmly, disengaged himself from her clasp. Then holding one of her wrists in each of his hands, he looked steadily in her face, not unkindly, but with a calmness which she had had experience enough to understand. The power she had had over him in her girlish days was gone, and even she felt how small was the prospect that it would ever return.

"You loved me once, Vic," she wailed again. "And—and it wasn't for my goodness even then, remember! I'm not really so much worse than I was then!"

Dimly Victred knew that this was true. Having no natural chastity, her loss had not been that of a nature essentially pure: she had not felt it with any sense of pain.

"And I couldn't have loved you then, Vic, as I could now, as I do now," she went on in a piteous voice. "There's no woman on earth, whatever you may think," and her face darkened with sudden jealousy, "as could feel for you what I do, as could love you like your poor wife! Why can't you forget what's gone, and love me again? If you were a woman you could."

"Ah, yes, a woman! That's different."

"No, it isn't, and you know it!" burst out Louisa. "A man can forgive just as easy as a woman, when he's in love. Only you're not in love—at least not with *me*." And she gave him another dark look.

"You don't understand," said Victred gloomily. "When a man marries, unless he just marries to get a housekeeper, he doesn't only believe in his wife, but he likes to imagine a lot of things about her which he doesn't exactly believe; and then by taking them all for granted in her, and by letting her know that he does, he gets her to believe them herself. And as he takes care to keep her out of harm's way, they can both go on believing to the end of the chapter. That's the foundation of happy married life. So don't you see that for us it's out of the question?"

Louisa flushed angrily, and with a sudden wrench freed her wrists from his grasp.

"It's all bosh, your talk!" she exclaimed, as she got up and flung herself on the opposite seat, near enough to him to be able to watch his face. "When I know that there's another woman who you don't treat to all this palaver!"

Victred saw the fierce jealousy in her eyes, and wished that he had not been so honest with her, as to mention the fact of the existence of another. He began to understand that he might have to learn a great deal more than he wished of the nature of the woman in front of him. There were depths of passion in her, of recklessness, of cruelty, of which in her girlhood he had never dreamed.

"Indeed I do not," he assented promptly. "As I told you before, on the only occasion when I mentioned the girl to you, I have never given her the least idea that I cared about her, and I never shall!"

18*

"Well, it'll be better for her as well as you, if you keep your word," cried Louisa, who had plunged straight from entreaties to menaces with a violence which was suggestive of much future trouble. " I offered to let you divorce me and have done with it. But as you wouldn't let go your prize, your prize means to look after you and keep you up to the mark, I can tell you."

For a little while there was silence between them, while Victred listened to the whirr of the wheels and to the sounds of merry voices and laughter in the adjoining compartment, and wondered what they would be saying there, if they knew what sort of a *tête-à-tête* it was which they had brought down upon him. He was not left long to his reflections, however, for with lightning speed Louisa's mood changed again. He felt a hand upon his arm, and saw a tearful face presented close to his.

" I didn't mean it, I didn't mean what I said, Vic," she said coaxingly. " I'll go on behaving well, like I'm doing, so it will please you, and so you won't go away. Look, I've given up the drink and everything for your sake, just to be near to you, now haven't I?"

"Well, and don't you feel better, happier?"

" I don't know as I do."

This was honest, but disconcerting.

"But you will, you will," Victred assured her hastily.

But Louisa was occupied still with a matter which she considered more important.

" I s'pose it ain't really that cousin of yours that's always coming after you, the one Fitzalan put me up to, eh?"

Victred started.

" Fitzalan! My cousin?"

Louisa nodded. " It was him sent me down to Maleigh. I've got the paper now. Often enough he's tried to get it away from me, but I've been too smart for him. I'll show it you some day."

But Victred was struck dumb. Inch by inch he had contested the ground as the knowledge of Tracy's treacherous behaviour in every relation of life had forced itself upon him. This last discovery made his heart leap up as he thought of Jack, and on the instant resolved to take active steps to prevent the girl's getting into his cousin's power. Louisa, not guessing what the thoughts and feelings were which filled her companion's breast and throbbed in his brain, watched him intently and curiously. Her voice startled him when she said :

"Didn't you know it was him then, that brought me after you ? "

" I—I— No, I didn't ! " stammered Victred.

" Well," she went on, still eyeing him narrowly and bringing him back to the point, " it wasn't your lady-ship cousin, I suppose ? "

Victred felt bound to divert her wrath from poor May, so he laughed at the notion.

" But he didn't know I was married ! " began Victred, pausing, however, to look at her inter-rogatively.

Louisa flushed again, and looked down.

" I don't know as he believed it," she said sullenly, angry at having betrayed herself : " but I'd met him about, and I did tell him once when he was cheeky, how I was the lawful wife of as good as him. That was long before, but he remembered it, I suppose. He's a smart chap, your cousin."

Victred made no reply. The train was by this time slackening at the first stopping place, and both he and Louisa assumed as much as possible the air of being bored with a long and trifling *tête-à-tête ;* so that the other men of the company, who jumped out of the next compartment and looked mischievously in at the window as soon as the train stopped, were successfully put off the scent of the stormy interview which had really taken place.

By this time, too, the rest of the company were tired of being crammed so tightly as they had been, and some of them got into their victims' compart-ment, while Victred exchanged into the other.

CHAPTER XXVIII.

" He looked at her, as a lover can :
  She looked at him, as one who awakes :
  The past was a sleep, and her life began."
                                    —BROWNING.

SOON after the train left Numboro' Junction snow
had begun to fall ; and it had snowed with steady
persistency ever since. As they neared the coast,
they discovered that the fall had begun earlier there,
and before long the train was delayed here and there
by the drifts which had accumulated on the line.
Robert de Mowbray all but moaned aloud at the
sight. What would business be if this went on ? It
was already difficult enough to get the people to
come out so near Christmas ; but if the weather were
to continue like this it would be impossible.

Instead of arriving at the advertised time, ten
minutes to one, it was not until nearly two o'clock
that the train slowly steamed into Eastgate station.
Mrs. de Mowbray, in her best hat, wearing long gold
earrings and a quantity of fur of a bright yellow tint,
was standing on the platform to welcome them with
becoming *éclat*. She looked very cold, but was not
ill-humoured, considering the circumstances. After
exchanging a kiss with the "boss," she discovered
Victred, and beckoned him to her with one of her
expansive gestures.

"Come round and have a bit of dinner with the
boss and I, two-thirty sharp, 15 Sea View Terrace.
I've got a bit of news for you."

Divining from her manner that the news concerned
Jack, he accepted the invitation readily enough,
saying that he would come round as soon as he had
settled his lodgings.

The agent-in-advance, who had been busily distributing to the various members of the company the
cards of those obliging landladies who "took theatri-

cals," now advanced to him with an address. Victred was staying by himself this week, so it took him very little time to go to the lodging, to leave his travelling bag and rug, and to rejoin the manager and his wife at the appointed time.

Mrs. de Mowbray was alone in the little sitting-room when he entered; and although the table was laid, dinner was not yet served.

She looked at him with a kindly expression, holding her head a little on one side, as if to observe him better.

"Well, I don't 'alf like telling you, I declare," she began. "I don't know how you'll take it."

Victred turned white.

"Go on, go on. Jack?" said he hoarsely.

"Oh yes, it's about Jack sure enough."

"Not ill—dead?"

He did not utter the last word, though his trembling lips formed it.

"Oh no, no. Good gracious, man, it's not so bad as that!" cried Mrs. de Mowbray, first shaking him by the shoulder and then slapping him on the back. "No. Pluck up your spirits. She's not dead; she's only married."

Now although she suspected the depth of Victred's interest in his fellow "freak," she was not prepared for the way in which he received the news. Instead of being horror-struck, or shocked, he seemed to be only anxious to ascertain the truth of this statement. Bending down eagerly towards her, and speaking in a voice which trembled with eagerness, he repeated:

"Married? Are you *sure*?"

Mrs. de Mowbray started and stared at him. Then she brought her large hand down with a thump on the table.

"Bless the man!" she exclaimed. "It's just what I've been wondering myself!"

"My God!" cried Victred.

And utterly unnerved, and rendered for the moment as weak as a child, he sank, trembling from head to foot, on to the hard little lodging-house sofa.

All the womanliness in Mrs. de Mowbray's nature rose to the surface at once. She planted herself on the sofa beside him, pulled him roughly but kindly round to face her, and comforted him alternately with vigorous slaps and warm-hearted words.

"Look here, Fred, my boy, you mustn't take on so! We've no reason, either you or me, to think such things, and I ought to be shot for having let such words pass my lips. And so ought you, Fred, and so ought you."

Shaking and stammering, helpless and in agony, Victred tried to reply.

"But we have reason, we have reason. Don't we know it, both of us? Where did they go? When did he take her?"

And as he uttered these words, Victred sprang up from the sofa and seized his hat. Mrs. de Mowbray rose too, detaining him with a strong hand.

"Wait a bit," said she. "No time's been lost. Keep your 'ead, Fred, and the girl's all right. She's got some gumption in her, has that little Miss Meek; and if she found out he didn't mean to do the right thing by her, she'd just be off then and there like a sky-rocket. I've seen a deal of my lady, and I know her spirit."

"When did she go?"

"Only this morning. Deal's our pitch this week, as you know, and Mr. Fitzalan wrote to say he'd got the licence, and they'd be married at Dover, and go straight off to the Continent for their wedding-trip. Well, he wrote to say he'd got some friends staying at Dover, and she could go and stay with them a day or two and be married from their house. She was to go from Deal to Dover this morning, and he'd meet her at the station at ten minutes past eleven. As we only got to Deal last night, I never thought it odd he should choose a Sunday for her to come; till it flashed into my head as I came on here in the train after seeing her off. Of course it may be all right; he was the man Dennis chose for her and all and——"

Victred interrupted her.

"You won't mind if I go off at once, will you? I can't keep still. You know what the trains are on Sundays. I must go to the station at once." He held out his hand. ."I'm not ungrateful, you know."

"Bless the boy! Ungrateful! Rubbish. Here, wait a second."

She hurried out of the room, and returned almost immediately with a hastily made paper parcel.

"Something to eat in the train as you go along," said she.

And, full of sympathy and nearly as anxious as he, Mrs. de Mowbray pushed him towards the door.

Victred found that he had an hour to wait for his train, but he would not lose sight of the station. The journey was a slow one, and it was very cold. The snow continued to fall heavily, and already deep drifts were forming. At Deal he had to change trains. He was late in arriving there, and on making inquiries, he was told that the snow had already done so much to disorganise traffic that it was very doubtful whether the train which he had proposed to enter would reach Dover that night. They had already received telegrams to say that the weather was even worse at Dover than at Deal. This decided Victred. He gave up the idea of going by train, and set out on foot.

Now he was not actuated solely by the fear of being snowed up in the train. Knowing Jack and her ways, he thought it likely that, if things had gone wrong she, thinking nothing of a long walk, would have started on foot for Deal.

Although it was very heavy going, Victred found relief in the active exertion. The wind was at his back, and although it was much pleasanter for himself on that account, it troubled him to think how hard it would be for little Jack, coming in the opposite direction, to have the snow driving in her face. For he began to lose all doubt on this point. With no better guide to the events of the morning than the

few words he had heard from Mrs. de Mowbray and
his own knowledge of Tracy's character, Victred felt
sure that Jack was coming along this snow-covered
road to meet him. It was growing so dark that he
feared to pass her ; and every few minutes he would
stop and call aloud : " Jack, Jack ! "

But he got no answer. He was on high ground,
and the wind blew strong. Very dimly he could see
the wide white plain on either side of him. He had
struck too far inland for the grey sea to be any longer
in sight. It was difficult enough to keep to the road,
and clever as he knew little Jack to be, and used to
cross-country journeyings with her father, he was in
terror lest she should lose her way, having, as she
would have, if she were on this road, the snow beating
ceaselessly in her face. The distance, if he could
only manage to keep to the road, was only some
eight miles ; but impatient as he was, and difficult as
was the walking, before he had got half-way the
distance seemed sixteen miles at least. There was
not a cart-track to guide him, not a foot-passenger
with whom to exchange a word. The desolation was
complete. At last, when the early-coming night had
closed in, and the snow was so deep that he could
scarcely get along, the fear began to gain upon him
that he had lost his way. Surely a high road could
not be so long deserted as was the road he was with
so much difficulty following, He stopped and looked
around him. Nothing but black night in any direction, with the white flakes falling thickly, and no sign
as yet of the lights of the town. But on the right he
thought he discerned a speck of light. It might, he
thought, show where a dwelling of some sort, cottage,
farm, or inn, stood a little way back from the road.
The longing for a human face, a human voice, after
the cheerless struggle with the snow and the darkness,
was great ; the practical need of a guide was greater.
But Victred did not dare to step aside, so overwhelming was his belief that Jack was on the road, and so
great his fear that he might miss her.

A few steps further he dragged himself through a drift which blocked the way; and then, being by this time sure that the speck he had discerned was a light indeed, he put his hands together and shouted. Then he listened, and heard the echo of his own voice die away. He took one more plunge forward, and all but lost his footing in the deep snow. Then he shouted again. Help was a necessity now. Again he listened, and this time, struggling with the echo of his own voice, he heard a faint little cry, which might have been the bleat of a lamb. But Victred's heart leapt within him: it was no lamb.

"Jack! Jack!" he cried, and the echo quavered like his own voice. "Where are you, Jack?"

One more plunge he made, and yet one more, as he fancied he discerned tracks of footsteps in the snow. And even as the little cry came to his ears again, he perceived that the track which he stooped to examine, and which the falling snow had partially obliterated, was that of feet much smaller than his own. It came towards him, and at this point turned in the direction of the speck of light.

He followed at once, still calling her name, but softly now; for she was near, he knew, and the little footsteps were guide enough. He was now, judging from the uneven bank of snow which covered a hedge on either side of him, in a lane. And he had little doubt that it led to a farmhouse. It was not far from the high road either, but the special circumstances made the way seem miles and miles. And long before Victred reached it he had come upon the object of his journey, a little figure, in the dress of a boy, and as white as the ground itself, staggering to meet him.

Jack fell into his arms.

"Oh!" It was not a cry; it was a sob. "I knew —knew you would find me. But—I began to think —I should be dead first!"

The words gave Victred a stab through the heart, but his joy at finding her swallowed all other feelings a moment after.

"Come along, little one, come along," said he. "We can get shelter here."

And he put his arm round her, and they staggered on together to the farmhouse door.

Victred was right : they found shelter indeed. Jack's disguise would have remained undetected for a month as far as the farmer was concerned ; but his shrewd wife, forming her judgment on face and voice, rather than on the accident of clothes, penetrated it in a moment, and said, as she took off Jack's overcoat, and sent it to be shaken free of the snow :

"Why, bless us, Michael, it's a girl ! "

And then she nodded and looked shrewdly at Victred.

Jack herself was scarcely capable of understanding what the good woman said. She was benumbed with cold, half dead with fatigue, and in her eyes Victred saw the traces of great sorrow. She scarcely spoke, but lay back quietly in the deep armchair in which they had placed her, and kept her eyes fixed upon Victred with a plaintive confidence which to him was inexpressibly touching.

The farmer's wife looked from the young man to the girl, and her rugged face grew soft with pity.

"Dear heart ! " she exclaimed in a low voice to Victred, " she's very ill, I'm fearing ! "

" So am I," answered he despairingly.

The kind-hearted woman glanced at him again, and understood all that this meant to him.

" Well, well, we must hope for the best," she went on, trying to speak more cheerfully. " But my ! " And she turned horror-struck towards the girl, " Where did you get that cough ? "

Jack was shaken, racked, with a fit of coughing, which seemed to threaten to strangle her. When it was over, she lay back in her chair, looking apologetically at her hostess, and murmured that she had caught cold.

" Yes, dear, and we must see about getting you to bed," returned the good woman, making a sign to her husband to follow her out of the room. "There's nothing like a warm bed for taking the cold out of one. And you, sir," she went on to Victred, "I dare say you won't be too particular to make shift for the night on the sofy. It'll be better than a snowdrift, anyhow."

Victred was thanking her, with tears in his eyes, brought there by her kindness to Jack. But the girl herself, catching tardily the sense of the words, sprang up, although she tottered as she did so.

"No, no," she cried, in a voice hoarse with coughing, but with a resoluteness almost fierce, "we must get back, get back to the booth to-night, at once, oh, we must, we must!"

And clinging to the arm of the big chair for support, she cast an imploring look at Victred. He came to her, put her gently back in her chair, and said: "My dear child, do you know what the road is like by this time? How could we get along in the dark, when it was as much as we could do to find our way while the daylight lasted? Since we have had the luck to find such kind friends, what can we do but accept their kindness?"

Jack listened with a piteously puckered little face. Accepting his words as a reproof, she bowed her head and whispered humbly:

"Yes, I know—I am ungrateful. And yet no, it isn't that," and she turned deprecatingly to the farmer and his wife, "it is—that I want—that I am afraid that if we don't make haste, I shall never see the booth—with him again." Her voice failed her for a moment, and Victred would have silenced her, as the farmer and his wife, with great delicacy, opened the door to leave the room. But Jack stopped them with a gesture. "We were so happy together—he taught me to be happy. So that I want to be in the booth with him where we were so happy—once more, for a little while."

"And so you shall, my dear, so you shall," said the good woman reassuringly, while in spite of his own

native kindliness, her husband's stolid, Kentish face
had grown severe at the mention of the booth.
" Only wait till the morning comes, and we'll see if
we can't find some conveyance to take you both on.
Where is it you want to get to ? "

" Deal," answered Victred, to whom this question
was addressed.

" Well, that's only a matter o' six miles from here.
We'll get you over there easy enough in the morning,
eh, Michael ? "

" Ay," said Michael, who would have been willing
to send the strangers on their way without waiting
for morning now that he knew them for little better
than gipsies.

Fearful that he might say something to hurt the
feelings of her *protégés*, his wife now succeeded in
coaxing him out of the kitchen, and Jack and Victred
were left together.

As soon as they were alone, Jack sat up in her
big chair, and, looking round the kitchen with a
searching gaze which penetrated into every corner,
said : " Fred, come here. I've got something to say
to you."

He knelt by her side, and she seized his shoulder
with one hand and took both his hands in the other.

" You knew that I should come along that road.
How did you know ? "

Victred hesitated, avoiding her eyes.

" It was, I suppose, that you knew your cousin
better than I did ! "

" Perhaps I did, Jack," replied Victred, clenching
his teeth.

Then, with a face full of anxiety, of pity, he looked
into her eyes ! " Well, Jack, you had the wit to
escape, thank God ! It didn't take you long to find
him out."

She shook her head slowly.

" You see, I never liked him ; that was what made
it so easy," answered she. There was a short pause
before she went on : " When he met me at Dover

station this morning, I noticed a difference in his manner directly. He wasn't so polite as usual. If I had cared about him I dare say I shouldn't have noticed it, because I should have been so glad to see him. He took me in a cab to a big hotel, and when I was going up the stairs, and he was a long way behind me, I heard him say something to one of the servants, or the manager or somebody, which he thought I was too far off to hear. So we were shown into a sitting-room, and I turned and said : ' Where are the friends I was to stay with ? ' Then he said that they found they couldn't come after all. And he tried to put his arm round me, and asked if I was afraid to be alone with him. And I said : ' No. But why did you call me your wife when you were speaking to that man downstairs ? ' Then he got very pink (you know how he gets pink), and said so I was his wife, his darling wife. And he was going on saying a lot of silly things, when I said that I was not his wife yet. Then he saw in my face that I was not pleased, and he said quickly that he had made arrangements to marry me at the English Embassy in Paris next day, and that we were to cross by the boat that started at one o'clock. Then I refused to go, telling him I would stay at Dover if he liked until to-morrow, but that he must go away and not see me again until we met at the church. He was very angry, but he pretended to be only hurt that I didn't trust him. And when he found he couldn't persuade me, he lost his temper, and said I gave myself absurd airs for the daughter of—of—of—Oh ! I can't tell you what he called my father ! "

And for the first time the pain in Jack's face became acute.

" I said nothing. So at last in a passion because I wouldn't answer, he left the room, saying he would come back when I was in a less sulky humour. And I slipped out of the hotel, and started off on the Deal road."

" But of course you didn't take any notice of what

he said," put in Victred hastily, dreading more than
anything that she should conceive a doubt of her
adored father.

Alas! for answer Jack laid her head upon his
shoulder and sobbed as if her heart would break.
Victred caressed the little head with trembling
fingers.

"You were not so silly as to believe anything
against your father, Jack, or so wicked, I'm sure," he
went on earnestly. "Men like Fitzalan can't understand noble motives, and don't believe in self-
sacrifice in a great cause. They judge everybody by
themselves, and can't conceive that a man may give
himself up, heart and body and soul, to work for the
oppressed People, and to make them happier."

In his anxiety to counteract the cruel effect of
Tracy's brutal frankness, Victred had unconsciously
imitated the pious tones in which Jack used to talk of
her father in the old booth days. To his surprise
and distress, she looked up suddenly in his face, with
a dreary little smile.

"You used not to talk like that, Fred: you used to
say the Cause of the People was stuff and nonsense!"

"Ah, but——" said Victred hastily, reddening
under her gaze, "but you see I've learnt better——"

"No," she broke in sadly, "it is I who have learnt
better, Fred. I know now that there's no Cause;
that it's all a sham! And it was not from your
cousin I learnt it: I knew it before. And it was
that, Fred, not Mr. Fitzalan's conduct, that broke my
heart."

She began to sob again; and Victred, who knew
no remedy for broken ideals, could say nothing to
comfort her.

"I—I shouldn't worry about it, Jack," he said at
last. "After all, there are other ways of doing good
in the world, besides going about making people discontented. And when you are better you'll find
them out, dear."

Jack dried her eyes and shook her head.

"I don't feel as if I should, Fred," said she. But she spoke a little more hopefully. "I don't seem to have spirit enough left to make discoveries. The world seems to have crumbled away. Instead of being the servant of a mighty Cause, as I thought I was," and she smiled half sadly, half contemptuously at herself, "I see that I was only a parrot, repeating what I'd been taught. Only I was sillier than the parrot, for I believed it all."

"And now you can just forget it and be happy again, as we used to be, Jack."

Her face lighted up, and her eyes sparkled.

"In the booth!" she said eagerly. Then her face clouded over at once. "We can't. That is all over. You are with Mr. de Mowbray now. And—and there is your wife!"

"So there was always," returned Victred imperturbably. "As for Robert, he'll let me off; he'll have to. I say we'll go back to the booth. Mrs. de Mowbray said she'd take me back any time I wanted to come, and I do want to come."

He spoke in a dogged tone, and she listened eagerly, with a luminous look in her eyes, as if a new life was springing up in her instead of the old.

"And you'll be giant again, and I'll be dwarf?" she asked breathlessly, like a child.

"Yes, of course we will," answered he almost boisterously. "And we'll have grander times than we had before, Jack, for Mrs. de Mowbray is going to raise my salary and—well, I've got an old stocking now, that I can take half-crowns from without having to do an ironmonger's accounts. Do you remember those two half-crowns, Jack, and how angry you were because you thought I'd cheated the old skinflint, and how you enjoyed the sweetbread for supper all the same? Do you remember, Jack?"

Of course she remembered. Her fingers closed tightly upon his hand as she laughed at the recollection. And they went on recalling incident after incident of the pleasant summer days, laughing

19

heartily sometimes, and looking always for sympathy each into the other's eyes. But they saw there something they had not seen before, an expression of sadness under their surface gaiety, a piteous hungering for the old happiness, and the knowledge underlying all that it was gone never to return.

When the farmer's wife came back to carry Jack off to bed, she found two creatures apparently in the highest spirits, and she marvelled at the change.

But when Jack had gone to bed, and she found Victred sitting on one side of the big kitchen fireplace, talking to her husband on the other, the good woman saw that the Bohemian's gaiety was gone, and that the truth about Jack was no more hidden from him than from herself.

CHAPTER XXIX.

" And love, in life's extremity,
Can lend an hour of cheering."

—SCOTT.

NEXT morning. the outlook was far more cheering than could have been expected from the night. The snow had ceased to fall soon after the arrival of the wanderers at the farm ; and although it lay many inches thick on road and field, it was just possible for a well-horsed and not too heavily-laden vehicle to make its way along the highway between Dover and Deal.

So, before dinner time, Victred had the sad pleasure of bringing the shadow of little Jack back to the "museum." Mrs. de Mowbray welcomed them with a loud cry and an embrace apiece. Madame Elaine was quite ready to bestow, in her turn, an embrace upon Victred, who avoided the attention with difficulty : but even Jack's delicate appearance did not much soften her towards the girl. Jack was "an interloper," and would again, no doubt, "come between her and her rights." But Jack cared little. She was back in the place where she had learnt the meaning of happiness, and by her side was he who had taught her the lesson. Mrs. de Mowbray had had a little hesitation about granting the girl's request that she might be dwarf again. The girl looked so fragile, that she was afraid. But Jack, with a flush in her face and a manner full of animation, entreated, insisted. Behind the girl's back Victred, in answer to Mrs. de Mowbray's inquiring glance, nodded an emphatic assent. They must not thwart her, for a refusal would have broken her heart.

Mrs. de Mowbray, still dubious, then put a direct question to Victred.

"And you, you're going back to Bob's crowd for to-night, eh?"

"No," said he shortly, in answer not only to Mrs. de Mowbray's question, but to Jack's quick look of anxiety. "I want you to do two things for me : first, to get me off with the governor, and secondly, to take me back again as giant." Jack clapped her hands. "You know you said you would at any time I liked to come. *And*, Mrs. de Mowbray," he continued gaily, "and don't forget you promised to raise my salary."

"Lor', I won't forget," said she good-humouredly. "I rather tumbled to how it would be last night, and I gave the boss a hint that he might have to do without you, and he was wild, I can tell you. But there, I'll get round him. And we'll give 'em a real good show to-night. Pity," continued the astute manageress thoughtfully, "we haven't time to get down a new poster, but we might have a few bills. Would you mind, Fred, going down to the printer's and getting a few hand-bills done? Sharp's the word, mind."

And the energetic lady produced from her pocket the stump of a pencil and an envelope that had been through the post, and hastily composed an eloquent advertisement of the museum's unparalleled attractions, murmuring as she did so that "that ought to fetch 'em!" This done, she prepared to return to

Eastgate, to help "the boss" out of his difficulty with
the cast. Just before the train started, Victred, returning from the printer's, rushed breathless to the
window of the compartment in which she had taken
her seat.

"I think I ought to deduct my fares for all this
railway travelling on your account out of your screw
on Saturday, young man," she remarked only half in
jest, as he came panting up.

Victred nodded.

"All right!" said he. "Only do one thing more
for me. Promise not to let Mr. de Mowbray, or any
of them, any of them," he repeated emphatically,
"know where I am, or why I've left. Tell them
anything you like; but let them think I've gone back
to town."

Mrs. de Mowbray nodded reassuringly, and told
him that would be all right.

And so no doubt it would have been if she had not
let her husband partly into the secret of Victred's
abrupt departure the day before.

Meanwhile Victred and Jack were playing at the
old times. Not without success either, in that they
certainly were happy together, as she sat knitting by
the fire in the booth, and he smoked his pipe beside
her. But it was happiness with a difference. Their
emotions were keener now ; the ripples had become
waves ; they had to dam up their thoughts, to restrain
them from flowing into the future. And yet Jack
seemed so much better, there was such a pretty pink
flush in her cheeks, such a brightness in her eyes,
that Victred began almost to cheat himself into hope
that the fulfilment of her wish to be back in the
booth had given her a new lease of life and happiness.
For that she was happy, feverishly happy, there could
be no question. The sorrows of her father's unmask-
ing, of Tracy's treachery, seemed to-day to have fallen
away from her soul, and left it capable of nothing but
pure enjoyment. He, with his fears bubbling up
perpetually among his hopes, and with despair under

both at the thought that there was a barrier between them for ever, wondered at her lightness of heart.

"Why, Jack," he said to her in astonishment, as he leaned forward with his arms on his knees, and his pipe in his mouth, and gazed with tender admiration on her bright little face, "I never knew you so lively! I shall have to rub up all my old jokes to be even with you, or get somebody to make me some new ones."

"The old ones are good enough for me, Fred," she answered gently. "I used to like them, even when they were made at the expense of the—the Cause, you know!"

Looking away from each other, they both gave a little half-hearted laugh at the ghost of the poor old Cause about which they had so often argued, so often nearly quarrelled. Then Jack's face grew very solemn.

"Ah, we can laugh about it now, but I was very much in earnest then."

"Well, you seem to get on just as well without it," said Victred mischievously. "You do better without an idol, Jack."

"I don't do without one," said Jack softly. "I've got a new one, that's all."

There was a pause. Victred puffed at his pipe, and heard the click-click of her knitting-needles.

"And what's the new one?"

"Never mind," said she.

And she knitted, and he smoked; and the winter sun went down: and they, sitting by the booth fire and saying little, were happy.

Mrs. de Mowbray was back in time for the evening shows. Jack was not so well, however, as she had supposed, and fainted while she was dressing for the dwarf. But nothing would dissuade her from playing her little part, and the shows were got through safely, though with a good deal of anxiety on the part of Victred and Mrs. de Mowbray.

Next day Mrs. de Mowbray tried to persuade her

to remain in bed in the living-wagon in which she had passed the night. Jack would not hear of this; but becoming quickly tired, she allowed Victred to make her a couch with a mattress and pillows on the little stage, screened off from the draughts by an improvised wall of canvas on the arrangement of which Victred prided himself. On this she alternately sat and reclined, quite contented but for one thing: Victred had conceived the idea that the pipe made her cough, and declared that he was not in the humour for smoking.

They were more silent to-day, and they looked at each other more often. Towards the afternoon Jack grew too restless to sit or lie comfortably on her couch.

"Lie on my arm," said Victred.

And he sat close to the stage, with his arm upon it; and she, resting upon her pillow, lay quietly on his arm until she fell asleep. And the tears fell on her closed eyelids from Victred's eyes. When the time for opening the show drew near, he woke her with a kiss. She started into immediate and full wakefulness, like a child, sat up, and flung her arms round his neck.

"I've been asleep!" she exclaimed, not realising at first the deep affection her impulsive action betrayed. Then remembrance came back, and she grew red and stammered: "Oh, and your arm! You must be stiff! Oh dear, I'm so sorry!"

"There's nothing to be sorry about, my darling," said Victred in a suffocating voice. And all the passion, and all the tenderness which, with his will or against it, he had cherished for her so long, shone in his eyes and thrilled in his voice, as he folded round her the arms from which she hardly tried to escape. "O Jack, if I could hold you in my arms for ever!"

She only sighed, and let her head rest where it had fallen, against his breast.

"But—you can't, you know!" she whispered at last. "For—for it's time to dress."

"You can't dress to-night!" said Victred imperatively.

"Yes, yes, I can, I will!" she cried imperiously. Then, her tone suddenly changing to entreaty, she whispered into his ear, "Don't you see—when I once give up—it will be all over?"

Victred lifted her up in his arms and carried her to the living-carriage without a word.

She got through the evening better than before; her sleep had done her good, she told Victred.

On the following morning, when Victred was trembling lest she should not have strength even to lie on the couch he had made, she surprised him by running into the booth, looking as well and as strong as he had ever seen her. She herself, with the hopefulness of the consumptive, thought she was cured: Victred, though he knew better, allowed himself to be cajoled into cheerfulness. She felt so much stronger that she even went out with him a little way, and they walked as far as the pebbly beach over the hard white snow. And all the time she was as gay as a squirrel, and tried her hardest to persuade Victred to take her for a row out to sea. But he was inexorable.

"It's too cold," said he. "I'll take you when it's warmer."

"Ah!" she exclaimed, as her face changed suddenly. "I—I mean we, we shan't be here then, you know. I should like to go out to sea with you now, right away from anybody else. Only you—and I—and the sea-gulls: just for once." Then she caught a look of agony on his face, and going up to him quickly, clung to his arm. "No, no, I won't tease you to go. Never mind. Don't spoil the time by looking like that."

"Come along. It's time for you to go in," said Victred severely. "It's getting quite dark already."

And as it was getting dark, he lifted her up, for fear she should slip, as he said; and carried her in his arms back to the booth.

"You've been overtiring her," cried Mrs. de Mowbray with a frown, as she met them.

But to everybody's surprise, Jack sprang to the
ground and gave a little dance to show them that she
was not tired.   And there was no question to-night
about her dressing for the dwarf : it would have been
manifestly absurd to treat her as an invalid.

Now Victred's sudden secession from the company
had not been passed over so quietly as he had hoped.
Louisa, on learning that he was gone, at once made
up her mind, as Victred had anticipated, that he had
gone back to town to escape her ; and she had been
on the point of starting herself for London without
the formality of asking her manager's leave, when a
hint unconsciously given by Fenton made her pause.
The baggage-man had been at the station superin-
tending the unloading of the truck which contained
the scenery and the company's luggage, when he saw
Victred arrive ; and being unaware of any reason for
secrecy, he had mentioned to some other member of
the company the fact that Mr. Watt had been waiting
on the "down" platform.   This piece of information
had circulated until it had come to Louisa's ears, and
it had awakened not only her curiosity, but her suspicion.   Where was he going to, if not to town?   She
determined to stay with the company until she had
succeeded in learning more.

Now Robert de Mowbray not only intended to
obey his wife's injunction to keep the secret of
Victred's whereabouts, but prided himself upon his
"closeness."   Unfortunately, however, he did himself
more than justice in this respect, and he was by no
means proof against the wiles of a handsome and
determined woman.   When, therefore, Louisa bent all
her energies to the task of fascinating poor Robert to
the point of confidence, she found it ridiculously easy
to get out of him all the information she wanted.

It was on the Tuesday that she began the process
of charming the susceptible manager, and it was on
Wednesday that she brought it to a satisfactory end ;
for on the evening of that day, when he and she were
on the stage, conversing between the first and second

acts, he confided to her his belief that " Fred Watt
had gone off on the mash." And Mr. de Mowbray
was quite delighted to have this piece of news to give,
as Miss Burleigh had had eyes for no one else as long
as the " utility gent " was in the company.

Anxious to learn more, Louisa concealed the feelings with which she heard these tidings.

" On the mash, eh ? " said she. " Dear me, I
thought ' mashing ' was quite out of the gentleman's
line, I'm sure. And who's the charmer ? "

" Why, you'd never believe ! " went on simple
Robert, pleased at the opportunity of casting a slur
on the taste of the favoured one, " a little slip of a
girl that plays the dwarf in the missus's show ! He's
that gone on her he can't bear her out of his sight.
She was going off with a swell, a Mr. Fitzalan, who'd
promised to marry her, when our friend Watt steps
in and stops her. Mind, I don't know as I've exactly
got the rights of it, but anyhow she's back again with
the missus at the museum, and so's he."

Miss Burleigh listened without comment until she
heard her cue to go on. But when she was called for
the second act Miss Burleigh had left the theatre.

At Mrs. de Mowbray's " museum," the evening was
passing well, as far as Jack was concerned. The
spirit and energy with which she began the day lasted
throughout the performances of the night. Victred
was delighted, but Mrs. de Mowbray looked grave.

" It's all very well while it lasts," she said to him,
when he remarked upon the change in her, " but she's
not really strong, and she'll pay for the extra exertion
by and by, I'm afraid."

As soon as the last show was over, the manageress
seized Jack with a strong hand, and carried her off,
in spite of her protests that she was going to have
supper with " Fred."

" Nonsense ! 'e can have supper with me," said
Mrs. de Mowbray imperiously, giving Victred a wink
over the girl's shoulder to let him know that he was
to support her view.

Jack pleaded, coaxed, caressed, all to no purpose.
She tried to get Victred to add his entreaties to hers,
but he trusted Mrs. de Mowbray's judgment too well,
and was half-hearted. This scene was typical of the
change which had come over the relations of these
three persons. Victred and Jack had penetrated
under the vulgarity and coarseness of the manageress
to some true grit underneath. They had begun in a
way to love her. Nevertheless, Jack, who was much
more excited than was good for her, fretted under
Mrs. de Mowbray's wise restraint.

" You might have let me, just this once more," she
complained, as Mrs. de Mowbray led her away to the
living-carriage.

" No, my dear, you've been doing too much as it is,
and we don't want to have you ill again. But if you
go to bed like a good girl, you shall sit up and eat
your supper with me, and as a great favour I'll let
Fred bring his too."

This satisfied her, and Victred, who was heart-
broken at having to resist her entreaties. He went
slowly back to his little stove, and began his cooking
alone, sorrowfully enough. Half-an-hour ago everything had been so jolly ; the old times seemed to
have come back indeed. And now he could not help
thinking that she would never have supper with him
by the stove again. However, it was something that
he might be allowed to see her again, and he began
his preparations with extra care. The invalid's
appetite must be tempted. He was rather proud of
his success, and flattered himself that he should receive a good many compliments upon his skill. Jack
was fond of sweetbread, and it would remind her of
that never-to-be-forgotten night when he had earned
the two half-crowns. But that supper was destined
never to be eaten.

Victred was opening the oysters which were to
form the first course of a most luxurious repast, when
he was startled by a cry. He stopped in his work,
and listened with terror in his face. It was not that

the cry was so loud or so piercing, but that this was a time when it might mean so much. For a minute he heard nothing more. Then a door opened, the door of the living-carriage, and Mrs. de Mowbray's voice called out in a terrible whisper:

"Ellen! Ellen! Quick!"

And he heard the fat lady's laboured breathing as she hurried up in obedience to the summons.

For a few seconds he remained quite still, paralysed by his misery. For he had no need to ask; he knew what was at hand. Then the women inside the living-carriage heard a voice outside which they did not know:

"Is she ill?" It was not a question: it was a dreary hopeless assertion. He added, without waiting for a reply or a confirmation: "Shall I go for a doctor?"

The door opened, and Madame Elaine came out sobbing violently. She was carrying a towel in her hand, which was saturated with blood.

"I know, oh, I know," moaned Victred. "She's broken a blood-vessel!"

Through her sobs Madame Elaine confessed that this was so. Mrs. de Mowbray looked out.

"It's no good going for a doctor now," she whispered, as she put her hand heavily upon his shoulder. "He can do nothing. She's going."

Victred looked up into her face without uttering a word; but his eyes, haggard and wild, asked a question which she answered at once.

"Yes, you may come in. She's been asking for you."

Victred staggered up the wooden steps and knelt beside Jack's cot. All the bright colour had left her face, which was a grey, ashy white, even to the lips. Her eyes were closed, and at first Victred thought they would never look upon him again. He bent his head, so that his lips touched her ear, and just whispered: "Jack! look at me, Jack!"

Then he saw a flickering smile on her lips, and she

opened her eyes, turning her head slowly and as if with difficulty towards him.

"I feel—so weak. But I'm better, much better."

"That's right. Don't talk."

He took her hands in his, and presently felt a faint pressure from the little fingers. He longed to press his lips against hers, but was afraid to disturb her; she looked so fragile that he feared the effect of even the tenderest touch. In a few minutes, however, a faint colour came again into her face and the clasp of her hands grew firmer. Fixing her eyes, which had for the time lost the dull and filmy look he had first seen, upon his face, she whispered eagerly:

"Oh, we've been lucky, very, very lucky. Think, Fred, if we'd missed these four days!"

"O Jack, Jack, can't you stay with me? Just a little while, Jack? A few days more? Oh, my darling!"

Jack shook her head.

"If it could have lasted, it wouldn't have been the same," she whispered wisely. "It was only knowing it wouldn't be for long made us so happy. For those few days we could think only of ourselves; while if——" She paused expressively. Then with sudden passion, she drew down his face to hers. "But now, while I live, you're mine; for I shan't live long enough for any one to take you away."

Then his lips met hers, and the fire and the passion in the fragile body flickered up for a few brief moments in one long kiss. At last her head slipped on to his shoulder.

"I feel so tired," she said. "I want to go to sleep again, as I did yesterday, on your arm. But perhaps it is selfish, it makes your arm ache, doesn't it?"

Victred shook his head. He could make no other answer; his throat and lips were dry. So he put her pillow on his arm, and she placed her head upon it, and her eyes, after lingering long upon his face, gradually closed. Then he saw by the slight move-ment of her breast that she was quietly sleeping.

The women had left them together.   Mrs. de Mowbray knew that there was nothing to be done for the
girl but to let her be happy as long as she could with
the creature she loved best.   So she had gone out,
leaving the door ajar, and peeping in noiselessly from
time to time.

It seemed to Victred, who watched Jack's breathing,
counting the very moments that she was left to him,
that she had been asleep a long time, when a sudden
commotion and outbreak of disturbing noise outside
startled him.   He listened   intently   as the   noise
became louder ; and with a sick horror, recognised the
voice of Louisa.   By her indistinct utterance, and by
her boisterous incoherency, he knew that she must be
intoxicated.   Kneeling there, with Jack's head on his
arm, he could not move : he could only hope, pray
that they would be able to keep this drunken virago
from intruding upon Jack in her last moments.
Listening so intently that he held his breath, he heard
every sound outside, and dreaded lest Jack should
wake and hear it too.   Louisa's insulting demands
to see the woman who had taken away her lawful
husband ; her coarse, terrible epithets ; the energetic
protests of Mrs. de Mowbray ; the hysterical ejaculations of Madame Elaine ; the rough expostulations of
the men belonging to the show ; a scuffle ; cries of
indignation, of triumph.

Then the living-carriage shook violently, and he
knew that Louisa was coming up the wooden steps.

The next moment she staggered, flushed, dis-
hevelled, angry, boisterous, into the living-carriage.
There was a lamp hanging on the wall, and Victred
and the pale girl on his arm were in full view of
Louisa even before she entered.   A torrent of coarse
vituperation was rushing from her lips ; she was
advancing with a lurching gait and an uplifted right
arm, when Victred sharply turned his head, and
arrested her with a look only, but a look so savage, so
threatening that words would have said less.

" I'm your lawful wife, your lawful wife, and you

know it. And here I find you carrying on with
a——"

But Victred did not hear her. Turning his head
back again to the face on his arm, he thought he
noticed a change. He bent his head and listened
and he touched the girl, feeling for the heart. All the
time, the woman behind him was pouring out, in a
half-angry, half-grumbling tone an incoherent statement of her wrongs.

Suddenly she was interrupted by a cry, a heart-
broken cry from Victred. He no longer knew,
actively knew at least, that his hateful wife was present.
The merely disagreeable and disgusting fact was
overwhelmed in the tragedy which had fallen upon
him.

For, perhaps hurried out of her lingering life by the
shock of the woman's entrance, or perhaps only
because the last fire had burnt out in her, Jack had
ceased to breathe, and lay, just a little still white body,
in Victred's yearning arms.

Stupefied as she was, Louisa saw what had happened, and as the violent sobs burst from her lawful
husband, she lurched, still grumbling, towards the
door, and left him alone.

"O Jack, Jack, my darling, has she frightened you
away?" he sobbed, pressing the little form to his own
breast, as if the warm loving touch would reanimate
the lifeless frame. "Come back, come back one
moment: she's gone, Jack! She's gone, my darling!
She won't come to disturb you again."

No, never again. Coarse words could not shock
her now, neither could loving touch move her. But
this truth only came gradually to Victred. He felt at
first that she could not have gone far enough, in that
short moment since he had watched her breathing, to
be out of hearing of his heart-broken cry. He believed,
he ached with the belief, that she would come back, if
only for one second, warmed again into momentary
life by the clasp of his arms, for one more look, one
more word. She could not leave him like this,

without warning, without farewell, when he loved her
so !

So he sat there until the lamp died down and went
out, waiting, hoping against hope, like a weak woman.
And with the flickering out of the light the truth came
to him, and he knew that the body in his arms was
growing cold, and that he was alone.

CHAPTER XXX.

" The wine of life is drawn, and the mere lee
Is left this vault to brag of."
—SHAKESPEARE.

IT was Mrs. de Mowbray who played good angel to
Victred in his despair. Her sympathy, being genuine,
moved him even then. She had learnt from Louisa
the real relationship in which that person stood to
Victred, and to Louisa herself the manageress, who
was not deficient in courage, openly expressed her
regret for the circumstance.

" You'd better take yourself off before he comes to
himself enough to remember you're here," she said to
Louisa coldly. " If he finds you about, and the state
you're in too, he'll give you what for, and serve you
right."

Louisa herself, although she still attempted to
assert her dignity, could not help seeing that the
advice was good. Her rival was dead, for one thing ;
and it did not appear that she would get any good to
herself by remaining in the neighbourhood. She had
had time to grow a little more sober too, and as it was
too late to get anything more to drink that night,
she was sinking into low spirits, and becoming less
·aggressive in consequence.

When, therefore, Victred presently came out, and
passed her without even seeing her or hearing her,
although she tried to attract his attention by putting
out imploring hands and by uttering a faltering and
feeble apology, she stood stupefied and dazed for a
few moments, and then slunk away to find some

lodging in the town for the night. She left Deal the next day, thoroughly ashamed of herself, without even attempting to see Victred again.

As for him, he seemed to have forgotten her visit, her very existence, absorbed in the fact of Jack's death. He remained at the booth until they buried her, and then it was Mrs. de Mowbray who roused him sufficiently from the stupor in which he seemed to have fallen to make up his mind what to do with himself.

" I'll go back to town," said Victred meekly.

" You understand, now, don't you, that it ain't because I want to get rid of you?" said Mrs. de Mowbray with genuine feeling. "You might stay here as long as you liked and welcome. But let alone that that woman can always find out where you are as long as you are with me, and which you don't want to be bothered with the creature just now, wife or no wife, it'll be better for you, Fred, to go back among your own friends. It'll help you to forget what you've gone through."

" You are very good to me, and you're quite right," said Victred quietly. "You're a good woman, and I'm very grateful to you."

He pressed her hand; and his face, which had been blank and lifeless ever since the night of Jack's death, softened at last with strong feeling.

The same afternoon he went back to town.

If Mrs. de Mowbray had known the calamity which hung over him, she would not have sent him away. He had made up his mind to give himself up to take his trial for his cousin's death; but when he arrived at the shut-up house in Grosvenor Square, which he had never yet inhabited since he came into his position, he felt so ill that he thought it better to pass the night there before carrying out his intention. The old butler, who was in charge of the house, and with whom he had always been a great favourite, was so struck by his appearance that, without saying anything to his master, he sent for the family physician.

And by the following morning Victred was declared to be suffering from brain fever.

In the meantime Louisa, who was by this time heartily tired of the orderly life she had been leading of late, and to whom the occurrences of the last few days had given the excuse for a relapse, had left Mr. de Mowbray in the lurch, and returned to her old haunts and her old habits. But she had neither forgotten Victred nor forgiven him. Nevertheless the perverse passion which she had conceived for him remained unextinguished ; and, excited by habitual potations, it presently took the form of a desire for revenge, not upon Victred, but upon the person whom she conceived to be not only his worst enemy, but the originator of all her own misfortunes on his account —Tracy Fitzalan. But for Tracy, she told herself, she would never have gone down to Maleigh Abbey at all, but would have lived her own life without ever troubling her head about her nominal husband ; and but for Tracy's misconduct in not marrying the girl whom they called Jack, Jack would not have passed her last hours in Victred's society. So, with a fiery recklessness, born of brandy, Louisa, having found out Tracy's address, presented herself there one afternoon and asked to see Mr. Fitzalan.

Her application could scarcely have been more ill-timed. Tracy had at last got within measurable distance of the goal of his hopes, by obtaining the post of private secretary to a politician in a high position. This gentleman had been struck with the young Irishman's ability, and knowing nothing of his dealings with Dennis, was disposed to look upon him with the highest favour as a rising man to whom his patronage would do credit.

In the study of this gentleman's mansion, from the windows of which the clock-tower of Westminster could be clearly seen, Tracy Fitzalan was consulting with his patron concerning a political crisis which had just been reported from Germany, and the manner in which effective use might be made of the

20

news in a speech which the politician was to deliver
on the following evening to his constituents, when,
without any other warning than a cry of "Stop,
Stop" on the staircase outside, the door burst open,
and Louisa rushed in, slamming it behind her.

The patron, a neat, narrow-headed, dapper man,
with a pervading tone of iron grey, was petrified.
What did this atrocious person, of doubtful sobriety,
and more than doubtful respectability, do here? He
was not long left in doubt.

Springing upon the unfortunate Tracy with a shout
of triumph, Louisa shook him to and fro until, instead
of getting only pink, as he usually did, he became a
livid purple. And while she shook him she declared
her grievances against him in energetic bursts.

"I've found you, my gentleman—I've found you,
and I mean to give you beans before I've done.
What! You tried to swear your cousin's life away,
did you? And to make mischief between him and
his wife, did you? And to carry off a girl who was
too sharp for you, eh? You beauty you!"

Tracy stammered, struggled, in vain. His scandalised patron commanded the servants who now
appeared upon the scene to "take the woman away."

But the two men, having both already suffered
personal damage at the hands of the virago, hesitated
a moment. And that moment Louisa used to fatal
advantage. Taking out of her pocket a small medicine
bottle, and quickly uncorking it, she flung the contents
over Fitzalan, who shrieked and writhed with pain as
the vitriol burned his face, his hands, and soaking
through his clothing, reached his shoulders. Instinctively the servants drew back again, in spite of their
master's more vehement commands and even suppli-
cations.

Louisa swung herself round in a jaunty and defiant
manner, and with a threatening motion of the hand
which still held the bottle.

"You dare to touch me, any of you!" she shouted.
"I'm a Countess, I am! And I'll have the law of

anybody that don't respect my rank. And as for you," she went on, turning to the eminent politician, who made a precipitate retreat behind an armchair, "I wish I'd kept a little of this for you, and given you something to cry for. Ta ta, my dears," and she made a comprehensive curtsey to both the gentlemen, "I shan't trouble your flunkeys to show me down the stairs, thank you."

And while the servants made a feint of attempting to detain her, she marched out of the room, and down the stairs, leaving them to explain as best they could how it was that they had not only let her evade them at the front-door, but find her way to the sacred study.

Her exploit, however, was too serious a one to be passed over, and on the following evening the unfortunate Countess, who was dining with some friends at a restaurant, and entertaining them with a triumphant account of her adventures of the previous morning, found herself suddenly confronted by a detective, who apologised for intruding upon the party, and produced a warrant for Glynn Dorien.

The unfortunate woman started up, crazy with terror. The affair had been to her only a cause of savage exultation tempered with amusement. She fell at once from hysterical pleasure into hysterical despair, and throwing open the window of the room, which was on the first-floor, she jumped out, in a frenzy of fright and intoxication, on to the pavement below. She was picked up still living, but before she could be carried to the hospital, she was dead.

So Victred was freed from the tie which had been the curse of his life. But he could not know it yet.

Victred would have been astonished to find how large the circle was of those who called themselves his friends. To judge by the stream of callers who came or sent day after day during his illness to inquire whether Lord Malpas was better, one would have thought that half London was anxious on his account. The truth was that enough was known of the romantic passages in the young Earl's career to extend the interest taken in him far beyond even that large circle of people who, while they would have called themselves acquaintances of Mr. Victred Speke, were anxious to be known as friends of Victred, Earl of Malpas.

In the midst of this crowd of courteous inquirers was one who, if she could not be called disinterested, was at least absolutely sincere. Lady May hung upon the words of hope the old butler gave her, shivered with agony when she heard of the slightest change for the worse. She called upon the physician in attendance upon Victred to implore him to let her know when he might safely see a visitor ; and as soon as he gave the required permission, she took her docile chaperon to the house in Grosvenor Square. She was burning to be the first to tell him of his freedom, and she was in a flutter of hope as to the result. For there was one passage, and that the all-important one, of Victred's life in Bohemia, of which she knew nothing.

"Yes, he has been down once before already, my lady," said the butler in answer to an inquiry from Lady May, as he led the two ladies into the drawing-room. "He was down here yesterday afternoon, sitting by the fire, and turning over this book, though I don't think he was well enough to read much."

The butler indicated a little volume on a side table near the fire as that which had engaged his master's attention. Lady May took it up with the interest she felt in everything which concerned her adored cousin. It was a novel, a tale of the Wessex country by the greatest of living English novelists. She turned over the leaves quite tenderly, and suddenly uttered a low cry, a cry of such heart-felt delight, that her placid chaperon looked at her with astonishment.

"My dear, what is it ?"

For answer Lady May rushed at her, fell on her neck and burst into sobbing.

"Oh, aunt, oh, aunt, I'm so happy that I don't know

what to do with myself. And mind, mind, when Victred comes in, you are to go into the conservatory, or, or anywhere. Do—o—n't forget!"

"But, my dear," said Mrs. Mostyn-Stanningly, who was not without discreet fears that Lady May was making the running too fast, and too openly, "are you sure? Hadn't you better wait a little, till—till he's stronger?"

But Lady May would scarcely hear her to the end.

"Look, look," cried she, "what I have found in the book he is reading."

And she produced triumphantly the book-marker which she had worked for his birthday years before. On the card-board was scribbled in pencil, so faintly that only Lady May's eyes, sharpened by her interest, could read it, this line:

"A relic of my darling."

And of course poor Lady May could not know that its sacredness lay in the fact that on the day of her death Jack's little fingers had played with it.

Mrs. Mostyn-Stanningly had just taken in what Lady May supposed to be the sense of this discovery, when Victred entered.

Both the ladies were utterly startled by the change in his appearance. Expecting to see a man pulled down by illness merely, they were not prepared for the misery, the hopelessness which were plainly to be seen in his haggard face. The hangings of the room, which were pale blue, enhanced the look of pallor on his face, so that the elder lady believed that notwithstanding the physician's opinion, the young man must be dying. After a decent interval occupied in inquiries and condolences, the elder lady found an opportunity of obeying her instructions, and feigned to be drawn into the conservatory, which opened into the room, by her overwhelming admiration for the palms there. But all the while she was hoping that Lady May would show some mercy and not harry the poor young man too unmercifully. For stolid as she was, Mrs. Mostyn-Stanningly had a very distinct impression that the expression on the face of Lord Malpas as he came in was not that of a man about to rush into the arms of his beloved.

"It is kind of you to come and see me, May," said Victred.

She put her arm tenderly in his and led him to a sofa.

"Sit down," said she. "I am sure you are not strong enough to stand much yet."

"Oh yes, I am. I'm going to give myself up this week to take my trial."

He spoke in a dry tone, the tone, in truth, of a man who finds no further interest in life, and to whom it matters little what course events may take.

Lady May, on the other hand, was much excited by the news, and it gave her the excuse for bursting afresh into sobs, which irritated him.

"Oh, oh," she whimpered, "of course I know it will be all right, but I shall be so, so nervous, and so anxious! And when it's all over, I'll give a ball, or something, I must, I shall feel so crazy with happiness."

"Shall you? It's very kind of you," said Victred indifferently.

"Indeed, indeed I shall. For you will be free, free in *every* sense, Victred. Oh!" she went on, drawing nearer to him and looking up into his face, "I have something to tell you, something which ought to make you look a little brighter. Although, of course, it's very sad," she ended, with a return to conventional propriety. "Victred, I must tell you—prepare yourself! Your wife is dead."

But Victred, although he understood, and although he asked and obtained details of the event, showed no emotion. Indeed he felt none.

"So that now, Victred," continued Lady May bashfully, "you are free to find a wife who would treat you better."

Of course Victred understood what was expected

of him, and the understanding filled him with consternation. He had never cared for May ; and to
think that now he was free it was she and not Jack
whom he had to take for his wife, filled him with repugnance. For that she would marry him he knew.
The triumph of her dogged irritating devotion was
inevitable now. He knew he was ungrateful, told
himself that he was entirely unworthy of her persistent affection ; but it would not do.

And to add to the poignancy of his feeling, she,
with the ill-luck which attends such tactless persons
as she, produced the book-marker, and expressed her
delight at the words she had read on it. He shot at
her one glance, and turned away. And she never
knew the secret.

Although he put off the evil day, and made her no
proposal, Lady May left the house quite happy. And
when Victred had taken his trial, and got off lightly,
as his friends had expected, with a verdict of
manslaughter and a nominal term of imprison-
ment, Lady May became accepted as her cousin's
fiancée by common consent, and without any
active step or definite word on the part of Victred.
She knew, as she told everybody, that he was not
rapturously in love with her ; and she did not care.
She had loved him doggedly and long ; doggedly she
had made up her mind to have him for her husband
some day : and as is usually the case with an adorer of
this persistently " staying " kind, of either sex, she got
what she wanted. And in common with those other
persistent and fortunate admirers of either sex, she
made neither a better nor a worse help-meet than the
average, not by any means sustaining during matrimony the high pitch of devotion which she had attained to before, and yet not falling below it to the
point of outward scandal. And she was a happy
wife as she deserved to be.

But Victred was not a happy husband. He became
morose, unpopular and rather intolerant. He had
lived too full and vivid a life during the months of

his passage through Bohemia, to reconcile himself to the grey tones of the conventional existence to which he now returned. Not strong enough to carve a path for himself, and broken in spirit by the great sorrow of his life, he lived on a colourless life, without acute pain as without joy.

Once, soon after his marriage, the old feelings were recalled vividly by the appearance of Tracy, a disfigured, miserable object, who came to him by night to beg abjectly for the money to take him out of the country. His career had been ruined indeed. The scandal of Louisa's outrage upon him had lost him the protection of his patron; and this misfortune had been followed up by his complete exposure at the hands of Dennis, who had been beside himself with rage on learning from Mrs. De Mowbray of Tracy's treatment of his daughter. Victred gave him what he asked, and let him go with as few words as he could. He could not forgive this man, and yet the very fact that Tracy had cared for Jack, if only in his own base fashion, was enough to secure better treatment from Victred than he deserved.

Lord Malpas and his wife have been married eight years. He spends most of his time in Ireland; she most of hers in London. They have two children, a boy whom his father does not particularly care for, and a tiny girl whom he worships.

For in little Lady Henrietta's great grey eyes her father fancies he sees a look of a pair of eyes he can never see again. And when they are alone together he calls her " Jack."

THE END.

20 HIGHEST AWARDS.

The **Modern "Judgment of Paris,"**

[Paris Exhibition, 1889.]

ONLY GOLD MEDAL.

Pears' Soap

The only Gold Medal ever awarded

SOLELY FOR TOILET SOAP

at any INTERNATIONAL EXHIBITION in the world

Representing the consensus of opinion of more than

100 **Analysts or Soapmakers,**

the chief Experts of the world.

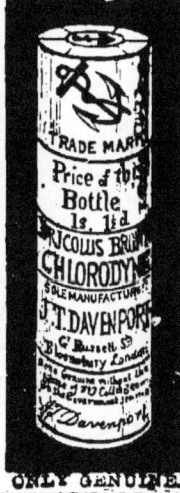